A Beginner's Guide to the End

PRACTICAL ADVICE FOR LIVING LIFE AND FACING DEATH

BJ Miller, MD, and
Shoshana Berger

Illustrations by Marina Luz

SIMON & SCHUSTER

NEW YORK LONDON TORONTO SYDNEY NEW DELHI

Simon & Schuster
1230 Avenue of the Americas
New York, NY 10020

First Simon & Schuster hardcover edition July 2019

SIMON & SCHUSTER and colophon are registered trademarks of Simon & Schuster, Inc.

For information about special discounts for bulk purchases,
please contact Simon & Schuster Special Sales
at 1-866-506-1949 or business@simonandschuster.com.

The Simon & Schuster Speakers Bureau can bring authors to your live event.
For more information or to book an event contact the
Simon & Schuster Speakers Bureau at 1-866-248-3049 or visit
our website at www.simonspeakers.com.

Interior design by Lindsey Turner

Manufactured in the United States of America

1   3   5   7   9   10   8   6   4   2

Library of Congress Cataloging-in-Publication Data

Names: Miller, Bruce L., 1971- author. | Berger, Shoshana, author.
Title: A beginner's guide to the end : practical advice for living life and
facing death / Bruce L Miller, Shoshana Berger.
Description: New York : Simon & Schuster, 2019. | Includes bibliographical
references and index.
Identifiers: LCCN 2018045252 (print) | LCCN 2019003657 (ebook) |
ISBN 9781501157226 (Ebook) | ISBN 9781501157165 (hardback)
Subjects: LCSH: Death—Planning. | Terminal care. | BISAC: SELF–HELP / Death,
Grief, Bereavement. | FAMILY & RELATIONSHIPS / Death, Grief, Bereavement.
| HOUSE & HOME / Cleaning & Caretaking.
Classification: LCC HQ1073 (ebook) | LCC HQ1073 .M53 2019 (print) |
DDC 306.9—dc23

LC record available at https://lccn.loc.gov/2018045252

ISBN 978-1-5011-5716-5
ISBN 978-1-5011-5722-6 (ebook)

For

Stanley

Starrett

Lisa

CONTENTS

I'm killing time while I wait for life
to shower me with meaning and happiness.
—Bill Watterson, *Calvin and Hobbes*

This Is Not Life Interrupted. This Is Life

There is nothing wrong with you for dying.

But you'd never know it from the way we talk about death. We actually call it a failure: *Her health is failing. He failed treatment.* If you believe what you read, the entire enterprise of aging is optional. Eat kale, drink red wine, walk 10,000 steps every day. If we can't beat death, then clearly our character or will or faith isn't strong enough.

And what about all those fighting words? *Beating death, defying aging, the war on cancer*: all battles we're sure to lose.

Next to birth, death is one of our most profound experiences—shouldn't we talk about it, prepare for it, use what it can teach us about how to live?

We wrote this book to help make dying something we can get to know a little better.

We don't mean to suggest that you—or anyone—can take the reins and control how all of it is going to go; part of the challenge is tempering that need for control.

Holding on. Letting go. There will be lots of *boths*. Not one feeling or another but a combination. Death, as a subject, is not easy, and dying is not painless. We make no promises to the contrary, and we encourage you to run from anyone who does. But we do believe this book will help dying be *less* painful and *more* meaningful.

——

Your Goals of Care

ONLY A SMALL FRACTION OF US, 10 TO 20 PERCENT, WILL DIE WITHOUT warning. The rest of us will have time to get to know what's going to end our lives. As discomfiting as that can be, it does afford us time to live with this knowledge, get used to it, and respond. We do have some choice about how we orient ourselves toward the inevitable. Where we'll die, maybe. Around whom. And, most important, how to spend time meanwhile. To make those choices manifest, you'll need to be clear about your "goals of care," a phrase borrowed from the field of palliative care that's becoming increasingly common. By thinking through how you want the end of your life to look, you'll find a useful way to face decisions that need to be made along the way. Identifying your goals is more than simply making a list of priorities; it's a process that helps you figure out what your priorities are while traversing aging or infirmity. That means listening to yourself as well as to others and communicating with those around you about how you feel and what you think. It's a sure way to land on decisions you (and those around you) can live with.

Your goals of care will follow from your answers to questions such as: What's most important to you now? What can you live without? How much treatment do you want and what kind? Where do you want to be when you die? How do you hope to be remembered? Your wishes also need to square with the practical realities of your situation, including logistics and costs. We are not suggesting that your goals are fixed—they will change over time, as your life does. But if you can articulate them, they will become a compass.

In this book, we move chronologically through the steps toward the end of life, but you may be on a different schedule, and that's fine, too. We are not here to load you up with work. We're here to help you navigate the work that's coming. Use this material in whatever way fits for you.

The vast majority of you will bump up against the health care system at some point, and it will likely have a significant impact on how you experience life with illness and your own dying process. Our system has profound weaknesses, along with its astonishing strengths, and moving through it can be a counterintuitive and vexing experience. There are many reasons for this, but one way or another they all spring from the fact that the health care system was designed with diseases, not people, at its core. That may change in the years to come, but this book is meant to help you manage the system we have now, not the one we wish we had.

That's another reason why the *care* part of health care must always return to you, the human at the center: *You need to stake that claim and protect it.*

Though it's impossible to throw a footbridge over every trench, we set out to explain plainly what you're getting into, with practical advice for how to approach it all: feelings, thoughts, logistics, costs. We must acknowledge that culture, religion, and other belief systems play crucial roles in how we experience life and death. We can't do justice here to the power of those perspectives, but we can make space for you to consider the specific challenges laid out in these pages. It is *you* who will provide the depth to this book through the texture and color of your situation and who you are.

It's natural to arrive at this subject with some trepidation. We all do. In fact, we should caution you that reading through this book, or even just picking it up, might trigger difficult emotions. It certainly did for us while writing it. No one is asking that you give up the fear of death, but with the guidance of those you meet in this book, you might find that it fades or softens. Our ultimate purpose here isn't so much to help you die as it is to free up as much life as possible until you do.

———

Defining Terms

WE WILL INTERCHANGEABLY ASSUME THE FIRST PERSON. SOMETIMES "I" refers to Shoshana, while other times it refers to BJ. We wrote this book together, so it feels right for us (and less cumbersome for you) not to have to distinguish between us.

Though we refer to the "patient" throughout, please know that it's not to reduce you to someone who passively receives a doctor's orders. At its root, *patient* means *one who bears*, and you should reclaim the word—and with it your role as a participant in the care you receive.

Likewise, "For Caregivers" boxes throughout address those of you who have, or anticipate taking on, the role of caregiver. Other words we'll use include *family*, *friend*, and *loved one*. We trust that you can readily find yourself somewhere in this mix. Whether you come to this voluntarily or kicking and screaming, and whatever term rings truest to you, we salute you—it's a hard job, even when you love it.

——

ABOUT US

BJ's Story

PART OF THE REASON I WOUND UP BECOMING A DOCTOR IS THAT I came close to death in my own life, earlier than expected and in a dramatic enough way that I had little choice but to sit up and take notice.

One night when I was a sophomore in college, a couple of friends and I headed out for an hour or two on the town and then made our way to the Wawa for hoagies. On the way, we crossed the old rail line. There sat the Dinky, a two-car commuter train that ran from Princeton to Princeton Junction, with a ladder up the back. We were exuberant kids spotting a perfectly climbable tree.

I jumped on first, and when I stood up the electric current arced to my metal wristwatch, blowing 11,000 volts up my arm and down and out my feet.

For the lark, I lost half of an arm and both legs below the knee. I was taken to St. Barnabas Hospital in Livingston, New Jersey's one burn unit. I was intubated but awake, and could hear the trauma team taking bets on my survival, some saying "This guy's a goner"; others betting "We got this." The nurse, Joi, who would become a guiding light for me, must have seen my eyes widening, so she told them to shut up and came to my side. She showed me I was safe there, even amidst danger. Together with close friends, family, and the staff of the burn unit, I would begin to learn what it felt like to be cared for. The terror and grace of depending on others for life.

That place would be home for the next four months. One night, it began to snow outside. I remember the nurses chatting about the drive in. There was no window in my room, but it was all lovely and frustrating to imagine. The next day, my friend Pete smuggled in a snowball for me. Drip by drip, that little shrinking thing unpacked a rapture. Snow, time, water. Now, knowing that creation held room for both ends, it mattered less whether *I* lived or died. For a moment death was in its place: obvious, common, benign.

So began my formal relationship with death.

I returned to college in the fall. I was trying to be a normal college student, but things were not normal yet. I'd ditched the wheelchair for a used golf cart, but I had a giant right arm from pushing myself around for months. The rest of me was rail thin. I wore a brown prescription compression vest over my scar tissue so it wouldn't ball up. My skin was sallow. I had a hook at the end of my arm stump that I rarely used and just hung there instead.

Really, I was pretty disgusting, always drenched in sweat, squishing around in my legs that had their own odor, leaving puddles wherever I sat. I'd go into the dorm showers on my knees, sitting down amid the hair balls and athlete's foot flakes, so I was never sure if showering actually made me cleaner. But that didn't matter; water running over my skin didn't hurt anymore. It felt downright glorious.

My leg prostheses were sheathed in flesh-colored nylons and fitted into style-free orthopedic shoes that took me about twenty minutes per shoe to lace up with one hand and a hook, so I never took them off and they soon molded when the rains came. When you start out on prostheses, you're constantly building up your tolerance, walking just a few steps more at a time, turning your skin from thin to callused. Making the unnatural natural. Learning and changing, as a newborn does.

I had a service dog named Vermont who saved me again and again. Five minutes playing fetch with him pulled me out of just about every psychological spiral I might spin down. Watching him run and leap never failed to yank me past bitterness: it might as well have been me running around the field. I watched him always be present, never burning time wondering why his life wasn't different than it was. I aspired to be more like him. Plus, he needed *me*, and I loved him with every cell I had left, which was plenty.

Tantrums came and went less and less often. I shrunk my needs and got much more specific about *couldn't*s versus *wouldn't*s. Could I really not get onto an escalator now, or did I need not worry so much about leaning into someone? Could I really not go shopping, or was I too proud to use my wheelchair? Could I really not dance, or was I afraid of embarrassing myself? The practice was tedious, but it got me up and out.

Looking different had its useful bits, too. Had my injury been less obvious, I might have kept trying to pass. But the conspicuousness of it was, eventually, freeing. As a kid, I had been very neat and particular about my appearance. Now I wore shredded clothes and let my hair grow out. I wore shorts every chance I got—for a time, comically short ones; it was as though I needed some skin to touch the air. I needed people to see that I wasn't afraid, so that I wouldn't be. I learned not to constantly compare my new body to my old body or to other people's. Instead, I could engage in the creative process of making my way through the day.

I got close enough to see something of death and come back from the ledge, only to realize that it's in and around us all the time. And now I see this truth in my patients, looking to change and be themselves all at once.

——

Shoshana's Story

I OFTEN WISH I'D KNOWN HOW TO WRITE THIS BOOK BEFORE TAKING care of my dying father, Stanley.

As a child, Stanley was something of a math prodigy. Calculating the infinite riddles of the universe offered an escape from his much smaller life in Brooklyn with my grandparents, immigrants who had a grade school education. At 24, he was hired at Berkeley as professor of engineering. For fifty years, he taught his students the principles of blood flow and jet wakes with a kind, steady hand.

My parents divorced when I was 13, and until Stanley met Beth twenty-five years later, he would come home after work and eat sardine and margarine sandwiches alone in his kitchen nook while reading four newspapers. He had no hobbies. All that mattered to him were his children and the inner workings of his brain.

One night, Beth asked me if I'd noticed how forgetful he'd become. Suddenly it seemed obvious—his forced punch lines after failing to calculate the tip on a meal. It wasn't long before his colleagues politely suggested that he retire. They'd pulled him from the elevator, where he'd stood frozen, not knowing which button to press, the doors opening and closing repeatedly. He was 73.

My dad spent the next five years in and out of the hospital, regressing to an infantile state, with an ambiguous diagnosis: not Alzheimer's but somewhere on the spectrum of dementia, aggravated by depression.

He would sit in the office of a young resident at the Memory and Aging Center and attempt to answer a series of inane questions: *What is today's date? In what state do you live?* He knew that the questions were insultingly simple, yet he got most of them wrong. The thought that all of my father's knowledge would be lost in a vault of dead cells was a death I wasn't prepared for.

When his driver's license came up for renewal, he failed the test and we took his keys away. Little by little, he was stripped of everything that had made him feel confident, independent, free.

There were endless doctor's visits. On one drive, he became increasingly irritated by his weakened bladder, punching the dashboard, ordering us to stop the car on the bridge. By the time we arrived, he was trembling violently and unable to speak. I escorted him down the hall to the bathroom, stood behind him in the stall, and held his waist as he fumbled with his penis. Who was I, daughter or nurse?

We hounded his doctors for a plan, and they rattled off an endless array of possible causes (water buildup in the brain?) and treatments (implant a stent!). Every attempt to cure my father's incurable disease landed him in the hospital again. On one visit, I noticed that his arms and legs were bound to the bed like an animal's. He kept lurching forward, trying to wipe his nose. I begged the nurse to untie him, but she said he was a danger to himself. I drove home screaming.

Some days he'd be well enough to sit on the couch and watch my children play, and it brought us so much hope. I'd hold his hand and tell him what I was working on, and he would smile and say, "Oh, that's terrific!" He still knew that I was his daughter and those were his grandchildren. My son has his face.

We urged his wife, Beth, to request hospice care. But to her that meant giving up, and in her desperation for more time, she told the doctors that my father wanted to extend his life at all costs; he'd jotted it down on a napkin somewhere. A social worker explained that he would never return to his former state. Beth finally relented, and we brought Dad home.

One of the hardest things about taking care of a dying parent is the role reversal: you still feel like that person's child. It's awkward to ask your father to consider wearing diapers, and by the time such questions come up, it's often too late. My father helped us understand the mechanics of life, how fluid and air and energy flow. But he couldn't teach us how to give him the death he wanted.

I remember those years as being full of anxiety and grief but also as a time of drawing closer. My father had always been an intellectual, and while we knew he loved us more than anything, he could be emotionally distant. Now, with his mind gone, words were of no use to us. But there was a universe of feeling in just holding hands.

Now you know a bit more about us.

Who are you? Whether you have a serious diagnosis, love

someone who is getting older, want to make your exit easier on your family, or just want to make the most of life while you have it, this book is for you.

And we have good news: you already know more than you think. ❖

PLANNING AHEAD

Maybe you've already begun making the big decisions about life and death. If not, now is the time to start; ideally, planning for what's to come begins early in life and kicks off ongoing contemplation and conversation, well before you find yourself in an urgent situation with no time for either. If we had our way, along with driver's ed and sex ed, we'd all get a course in death ed before graduating high school. In this section, we cover all the things you'll do well to consider before you have to.

Don't Leave a Mess

Clean out your attic; secrets and lies will catch up with you; say the things that matter most

No matter how much we try to clean up after ourselves, human lives are messy. And when it comes to the end of life, our messes become more consequential.

Part of what we leave behind is material: property, books, clothing—objects acquired over a lifetime. Then there's the immaterial, emotional stuff. Attending to all of it before you're gone ensures that your survivors have the opportunity to focus on *you* and not on how long it took to clean out your condo. As Rabbi Sydney Mintz says, "I have seen the profound difference it makes in the grieving process when someone dies and their house is in order, and when someone dies and their house is a mess."

Thankfully, there's a lot you can do to take charge of the situation, repair what's broken, and leave behind only what you want to be remembered for. And if you set out early enough with the intention to prepare and mend, to clean up the mess, and to earmark the things that you truly value to pass down, it will clear your head, giving you more room to *be*.

——

1. Clean Out Your Attic

UNLESS YOU'RE GOING EGYPTIAN PHARAOH STYLE, YOU WON'T BE taking much more than a suit or dress with you when you die. There is a word for "death cleaning" in Swedish: *döstädning*. As you age, the Swedish expect that you'll get rid of what's unnecessary and tidy up what's left. Simplifying takes time and commitment—don't expect it to happen overnight—but it can bring great satisfaction and even a jolt of pride.

Though the process of sorting through your belongings after you go will never be easy for the people you leave behind, you can make it *a lot easier*. That's why cleaning up is one of the best gifts you can give loved ones. It will save them time, money, and no small amount of heartache. I was certainly happy to inherit my dad's collection of *Whole Earth Catalog*s but not so much his file cabinets full of phone bills and tax returns from ten years ago.

SO MUCH STUFF

It's important to ask yourself why you're keeping all of this stuff. Is it because you still use it and it gives you pleasure? Is it the memories embedded in each piece of furniture or cast-iron pan? Or is holding on a symptom of your resistance to thinking about no longer being here? Maybe you're overwhelmed by the volume of it all and know it's going to take more time and energy than you have to sort through it? Setting aside time to go through your belongings, reflecting on what each item means to you and letting go of what you no longer need, can be cathartic. And there's no rush. Occasional purges can be something you do periodically throughout your life.

YOUR KIDS PROBABLY DON'T WANT IT

Here's a foreseeable truth: your family doesn't need or want most of your stuff. People develop their own tastes, and though they might appreciate what they grew up with, they may not want to replicate it *exactly*. If they do take something, it'll be a few quirky, sentimental items: kitschy coasters from a Las Vegas nightclub; an orange plastic tape dispenser; that one midcentury Danish dresser in need of a new finish. Few are going to go for the big stuff: the brown, curly-edged furniture you think of as antique and boardwalk artwork bought on trips to Florida are likely not going to find a new home with your children.

Prepare yourself for the real possibility that you may not even get to the part where your kids reject your stuff, as they may not be prepared to talk about any possibility of your no longer being there. "Often I'll hear from clients that they talk to their children and the kids say, 'I don't care about your things.' But after the parent dies, it turns out they really do care but weren't ready," says Ross Sussman, a Minneapolis-based estate lawyer.

Grief therapist Julie Arguez had a patient with a terminal diagnosis who had labeled everything in her house. But when her children arrived, they felt ambushed. Why was she accepting her death prematurely? they wailed. "It was really hard for her kids to accept the idea of her physically not being present in their family home," Arguez says. But once they understood their mother's point of view—that she was trying to take care of them—they took the stuff. Mom was pleased.

WHAT TO DO WITH FAMILY HEIRLOOMS

Ask family and friends from time to time if they'd come over and do a walk-through of your home. Tell them the backstory of items that are important to you—knowing the *why* behind a piece of jewelry could be the deciding factor in taking something home, wearing it, and retelling the story going forward.

Here are some simple ways to give away the more meaningful items:

- **A round robin where each heir chooses one thing.** Sussman had a case in which the mother had a fair bit of jewelry, some valuable and some not so much. The daughters didn't speak to each other. They couldn't remember why. So Sussman and a lawyer for one of the sisters made a detailed inventory of everything and then went round robin for each sister to pick something until there was nothing left.

—
TIP
If there are objects that you really want certain children to have, tell them now so it doesn't become a point of contention between siblings after you die.

- **A walk-through of the house with masking tape.** Sussman was invited over to a client's house, and their two kids were there. The purpose was to have each child choose the items they wanted. Sussman would put a strip of tape behind each object, ask who wanted it, and write names on everything. When the parents died, he went back to the house with the children and made two piles of the paintings, sculpture, and all the other valuables they'd marked. Everyone walked away grateful.

SELLING YOUR STUFF

Even if you place great financial value on the things you have gathered over a lifetime (artwork, jewelry, books, furniture), we don't recommend trying to recoup it by spending endless hours finding buyers, negotiating pricing, and arranging handoffs.

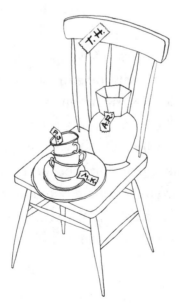

Few things are more painful than the idea of your family fighting over your estate after you're gone. Going through and assigning household belongings in advance will help to avoid conflict later.

Most antiques dealers and auction houses are very picky about what they'll accept. Even a popular midcentury lithograph that's numbered and signed and blah blah blah may be hard to offload. Selling on eBay can be a full-time job when you're wrapping and shipping off packages yourself. But a drop-off at the local Goodwill or Salvation Army takes mere minutes, and your discards may become treasures in someone else's living room.

There is courage in the trash can and a magic to tidying up. But you don't have to go crazy and throw out *everything* that doesn't bring joy when you hold it up against your heart. The idea here is to make the mess manageable for the people you love.

——

2. Now Clean Out Your *Emotional* Attic

EVEN IF YOU MEET RESISTANCE FROM YOUR LOVED ONES, KEEP pushing for more conversation before you die. We're not talking about discussing your next treatment or what to do with your hat collection after you're gone. This is the time to make sure your relationships are in order and that you say what needs to be said to avoid regret at the end of your life. These are the conversations that determine how you're remembered on an emotional level. In practice, of course, it's not always easy, especially if there are wounds that have been left to fester.

SECRETS AND LIES

Secrets are so common that nearly every grief counselor we spoke to has dealt with them. "I have had encounters with adolescent children who knew that something was being kept from them," a great thing, and I've comforted people in their sixties who've never heard that from their parents. It doesn't get easier as you get older."

But more than guidance for what to *say*, this is advice on what to *do*: really love those you love, seek forgiveness in earnest, and, if you can, take time to release those around you to live on. The rest will follow.

RECONCILIATION

Though *your* pain may die with you, the pain you've caused in others won't. Wayne had had multiple affairs throughout his marriage. A distinguished author and college professor, he'd remained aloof from his extended family while he pursued his career and extracurricular activities. His infidelity was never openly addressed, though his wife suspected it. After the deaths of his wife, most of his peers, and two of his three children, Wayne was diagnosed with advanced heart disease at the age of 94. He began to talk more openly with his remaining son about his marriage and how he wished he'd appreciated his wife more and shown her respect. He had never apologized. Now, softened by age and loss after loss, he sought forgiveness from his family. And when they took comfort in the apology, he was released from his shame.

Though last-minute reconciliations aren't always within your power—sometimes the damage can't be undone with a sickbed apology—it's always within your power to try. ❖

> **JOINTLY HELD**
>
> This one is for all the people sharing a household. One mess that will keep on messing with your survivors has to do with billing accounts. Cable, internet, cell phones, club memberships, anything else that bills for services on an ongoing basis; if these are not in both your and a partner or family member's name, that partner will be spending a very long time traipsing through bureaucratic minefields to shut them down or convert the accounts to their name so they can manage them. It can take years to resolve it all. Really. Think of every frustrating call you've had with your cell provider, and then multiply it by ten, and you'll get an idea. By calling these companies now and adding your partner to the account as a joint owner, you can make sure he or she will be feeling relief instead of exasperation.

says Tom Umberger, a social worker who specializes in grief. "Nobody in the family would tell them what the details were, and that made it worse, because it left them to fill in the blanks."

Secrets have a way of revealing themselves, especially in the age of DNA tests like 23andMe and heritage sites like Ancestry.com. Test results are uncovering unknown birth parents, hidden siblings, lost nationalities, and buried religious identities, upending the origin stories that many testers long held to be true. If you don't want your family to find evidence of a secret, get rid of it now, lest you prolong their agony or open new wounds after you're gone.

Erik's parents went through a bitter divorce while he was still

If you're keeping a box of love letters or incriminating photos somewhere, assume they'll be found after you're gone. (And you won't be there to explain.)

in elementary school. His father, Bill, went on to date a stream of women, all unknown to Erik, but landed on a second marriage in his late fifties. After Bill passed away, his second wife took Erik aside and told him she had some news for him: "You have a half brother." He was stupefied. It turned out that a woman his father had been seeing before the divorce had borne a child by him, but Bill had opted to keep the truth from his then wife. The half brother had always known about Erik but had never contacted him out of anxiety. When Bill died, the half brother saw the obituary and reached out to Bill's second wife, hoping that the timing

might be right. The result was that Erik and his half brother became close, able to bond over their understanding of the father who had kept the secret. The happiness they feel together could have included Bill if he had introduced his sons while he was still alive.

DESIGNATE A "CLEANER"

Yes, you can elect a "cleaner" to scrub down your life after you die. That person is a friend or acquaintance whom you trust to shred, erase, dump, and otherwise whitewash any secrets that you wish to keep secret. You can ask that person to go through your home, medicine cabinet, electronic files, and . . . any close where you kept your sex toys.

THE IMPORTANCE OF WORDS

Where do you begin if you've been estranged for a long time have what feels like a Superfund site of toxic feelings to c up? We are big fans of the pioneering palliative care phys Ira Byock's book *The Four Things That Matter Most*. Here a things he's found most people long to hear that can help even long-fractured relationships:

"Please forgive me."
"I forgive you."
"Thank you."
"I love you."

We asked him if he'd add anything, since the h lished fourteen years ago. "It's so useful for a parer child, 'I'm proud to be your mother, I'm proud to ' he told us. "Oh boy, is that the gift that keeps or

The Bottom Line

DON'T LEAVE A MESS

It's not an easy thing to do, but cleaning out your attic buys you and the people you love a lot of freedom; freedom from the unnecessary suffering of sorting through baggage, both the psychic kind and the actual suitcases full of stuff. Get the armoires out of the way, and do your best to say what you want to say. Lighten your load so you can be more present for the rest of your life.

Leave a Mark

Bequeathing money; capturing your story;
writing an ethical will; leaving a letter

*L*egacy is a loaded word. There's an air of self-importance to it, as though we have to invent cold fusion or have a building named after us; as though we have to deserve to be remembered. We define legacy as leaving a mark—a trace of who we were in the world. For some, that will mean using assets to fund a scholarship or a trust for the kids; others will have fewer material, but no less valuable, things to hand down.

When they're asked, it turns out that people care more about inheriting stories and values than stuff. The Allianz Life Insurance Company of North America surveyed baby boomers, and only 10 percent thought it was "very important" to inherit financial assets or real estate from their parents, while 77 percent of all respondents said that receiving and providing "values and life lessons" is very important.

This doesn't have to be extra work. If it feels overwhelming and you don't have the energy for any of it, take comfort in knowing that your legacy is already carried by someone out there in the world. If you've been alive, you can't help but leave a mark. One woman told us that every time she smiles, she feels her father beaming through her.

——

Your Legacy

YOU HAVE SOMETHING OF VALUE TO GIVE. MAYBE IT'S A FOLDER OF quotations that you've collected over the years, a collection of favorite recipes, works of art, a slideshow, a movie, a poem, or some other invention that's all your own. Jane was a prolific reader and career librarian who ended each day with a book in hand. Throughout her career she worked to ensure that libraries were accessible to everyone. Her father was a librarian as well and her mother the fastest reader in the family. After she passed away, her husband found a typed list of more than five hundred of her favorite novels with the author, title, and a brief synopsis of each—an unexpected gift. He circulated it among her friends and family, encouraging them to pick something to read, and that list created both a connection to Jane and a way to honor her love of reading.

LEAVE YOUR MONEY

Money doesn't have to be part of your legacy, but charitable donations are a noble way to express your values. This long-practiced tradition of giving back can underscore who, or what, has influenced your life. And your deliberate thought and care will enrich your place of worship, a local animal adoption center, hospice, or homeless program—whatever you care most for and find meaningful.

FAST FACT
Most nonprofit organizations, academic institutions, and companies have processes set up to accept bequests.

If you have the inclination and resources to leave money to organizations, you'll hear the word *bequest*. That is, a thing of value given through a will or trust, to be doled out after you've died. You can bequest cash, securities (stocks), or property through those documents, ensuring that your assets will be transferred to the cause of your choice upon your death. You can also designate your favorite cause as a beneficiary of your will/trust.

remember me.

collections + keepsakes

grandma's meatloaf

lasting letters

a place to sit

the family Bible

plant for
the future

look at that hair!

The things that fill your days—what you read, cook, wear, and collect—carry your story and are worthy of being handed down. What will be important to others is that it was important to you.

WHAT YOU CAN GIVE

- Cash (either a lump sum or an "annuity" that will be paid out yearly until the full amount runs out; more on annuities and their tax benefits below)
- Stocks and bonds
- Retirement plans and IRAs
- Life insurance policies
- Your car or other valuable property

SET UP A SCHOLARSHIP

Want to help support future students at your alma mater or those studying to work in your field? Anyone who's been the recipient of a scholarship will tell you how life-changing it can be. You can do this as a lump sum donation set to transfer at the time of your death or you can work with a charity or school to design an annuity. This is essentially a contract where you pay a certain amount to the organization each year and that money is invested. You receive a fixed amount back either quarterly or annually for the rest of your life. Bonus: you'll get a tax deduction for part of the donation.

FAST FACT
If you leave an IRA, the full amount will go to the organization *without* taxation. So if it's worth $40,000, the organization will receive $40,000.

CREATE AN ENDOWMENT

If you want to make sure your gift continues giving for years to come, you can set up a continuing scholarship. Note that each institution sets its own rules for how much you need to donate to endow an annual gift. Because the money you donate is invested and (fingers crossed) continues to grow, endowed gifts go on long after your death, without an endpoint.

OTHER WAYS TO GIVE

There are enough possibilities to fill a book all its own. Consult a financial planner for more than this short list.

- **Donor advised fund.** This is an account that you set up but it is managed by a nonprofit organization. You contribute to the account, which grows tax-free, and you can recommend how much (and how often) you want to distribute money from the fund to a specific educational institution or charity, but in general you cannot direct how you want the organization to use the gift.
- **How to give without touching your bank account.** You can give real estate in the form of a primary residence, vacation home, timeshare property, farm, commercial property, or undeveloped land. The property must be held longer than one year, and you get a federal income tax charitable deduction for the favor and avoid paying capital gains tax (as you would if you sold it). You no longer have to deal with that property's maintenance costs, property taxes, or insurance. You can deed the property directly to an organization or ask your attorney to add a few sentences in your will or trust. If you don't want to move out of the house, you don't have to. With a "life estate" the donors transfer title to the property to the charity of their choice while retaining the right to live in the house for a specified period of time or for the rest of their lives.

As with creating your will, it's best to consult a financial or estate planner about how to do this properly. And after all that, we want to reassert that it's fine to take pleasure in spending every dime you make while you're alive on what makes you happy.

LEAVE YOUR STORY

What made you *you*? Telling the story of your life and leaving a record of experiences, people, and ideas that matter to you gives those who love you a feeling of continuity from one generation to the next.

"The minute you sit down to do this, there are going to be all sorts of voices in your head, like 'nobody really cares,' and 'you're not old enough,'" says Susan Turnbull, the founder and principal of Personal Legacy Advisors of Manchester-by-the-Sea, Massachusetts. One way to get around those voices is to imagine that you have been left with a story written by a great-great-grandmother. How revelatory would it be to see the world through her eyes? Once you reframe the exercise as a gift of time and place and family values to future generations, you might feel less self-conscious about it.

TIP
Telling your story can be as simple as creating a list of evocative questions and recording your responses.

Who was your first crush, what was your first job, what is the first time you remember being afraid? When was the first time you got into trouble? What was your room like growing up? What were your parents like? Where were you happiest? Whom did you admire? Here are two easy ways to record your (or a loved one's) stories for future generations:

- **Use a story capture service. StoryCorps,** for example, records forty-minute conversations between you and the person of your choice and places them in the archives at the Library of Congress. You can also download the StoryCorps app and record stories yourself. **StoryWorth** sends you or a loved one questions every week and asks for a quick story, which is shared with you. A year's worth of stories are collected and printed in a book with a picture on the cover.

- **Make a family tree.** Genealogy sites such as Ancestry.com and the National Archives make tracking your family tree a collaborative exercise. And you can request that the next generation add their branches after you're gone.

Clear an hour of time to write out your story or to capture audio or video on a phone or with a video camera on a tripod. On a recent trip with my mom, over breakfast in the hotel, I asked her about growing up in New York, and recorded her response as a voice memo on my phone. She ended up talking for an hour. However you record your story, include it in writing or note the link to an electronic audio file somewhere in your "When I Die" file. You'll read more about that later.

LEAVE A LETTER

Frish Brandt started transcribing letters as a way to leave last words with someone you love, while volunteering with a local hospice agency. People liked the service she provided, so she set up Last[ing] Letters to offer it more widely.

Brandt asked me if I'd like to write a letter, and I decided to direct it to my 11-year-old daughter, Cleo. I didn't know how to start, so she prompted me: "What would you want to say to your daughter if you couldn't tell her in person?" Things I hadn't planned to say started gushing out. She kept asking me questions. My throat tightened and I had to stop a few times, but when it was over, she took ten minutes to arrange her notes and read them back to me in the form of a letter.

Here's what it said:

Cleo,

You are incredibly strong and can weather anything. In your life there are likely going to be times when that strength is challenged. You may feel like the world is testing you, doubting you, perhaps doesn't see you the way you see yourself. Remember this: You are capable of anything.

If you can see the world as a series of open doors rather than closed doors, there's nothing you can't do.

I learned my bravery from my mother who never heard the word no. A crazy matriarchal spirit comes through our line. There is art in there if you look for it. Your great grandmother Pola could take any misshapen lump of clay and draw a spirit out. You will carry that forward.

As a child I felt like I was being chased and you have that same fear. There is some value in that fear because our time is not unlimited and, in a way, we are being chased by death and have like five minutes here, so do all you can.

Sometimes I felt like our family had a lot of strife. I worried about it . . . I worried about not modeling well what a loving family could look like. I hope you know how deeply your father and I love you.

Cleo, we are on a small blue marble in the sky. Look up, and as all-consuming and overwhelming as life may feel, remember that we are just a small part of everything.

Life is a really grand experiment and I have no doubt that you are ready for it.

I love you,
Mom

I printed it out, folded it up, and slipped it into the file where my husband and I keep our wills and trusts. I felt a huge relief in knowing that it was there for my daughter to discover (though she'll likely read it here first). I'll be curious to see how the letters to my children shift as I get closer to death. It will always be too soon to tell your story and let people know how much they mean to you, until it's too late.

You can do this yourself. Rather than sitting down with a blank piece of paper and high expectations, try writing in a low-pressure format you're used to, like an email or text to yourself, and then printing it out. The question you're answering: What do I want to make sure they know? You can give the letter to your loved ones now, store it with your will and other important documents, or deputize a friend to give it to them after you're gone.

LEAVE AN ETHICAL WILL

Okay, we know what a legal will does, right? But what about an ethical will? This is your way of transferring immaterial things to loved ones: **your life lessons and values.**

FAST FACT
There are ethical wills that are over 3,500 years old. Jacob was said to have orally delivered the first one to his sons, as relayed in the Old Testament.

An ethical will is a complement to your will, not a replacement. "I like to say it's your values alongside your valuables," says Dr. Barry Baines, the author of *Ethical Wills: Putting Your Values on Paper* and a hospice medical director in the Twin Cities. It can act as the explainer for why you made certain choices in your legal will: why you gave your car to the youngest daughter, say (all the other kids already had one). And the exercise of making one is good for you, too: Baines found that 77 percent of his patients felt their emotional well-being improved and 85 percent felt their physical well-being had improved after completing an ethical will. They reported having a deeper connection with loved ones, felt more positive about themselves, and felt they had "more purpose in their life."

Susan Turnbull, who helps people prepare ethical wills, had a client who had a lavish estate that he hoped would last for many generations beyond him. He wanted to tell the story of his ancestors, who were immigrants, in his ethical will. "You'll get some money from me when you're 25," he wrote. "You need to know where the money comes from—that's the true wealth." He wanted his descendants to understand the values that had driven him to persevere and earn his fortune.

Remember, making an ethical will doesn't have to be a big deal. It can consist of things you're already doing—collecting quotes you like, or journal entries. Here are some tips to make it easier:

- **Begin by asking yourself about your values and beliefs.** What did I do to act on my values? What did I learn from grandparents / parents / spouse(s) / children? What am I grateful for? What are my hopes for the future? What life event have I learned a lesson from? To me, the love of my family means _____. The values I hold that I got from my ancestors are _____.
- **Decide what format you're going to create it in.** Using your phone or computer is fine, but make sure it's technology proof. Don't entrust your will to the cassette tape of the future; it's best to leave a printed version, too.
- **Read a few ethical wills** so you can learn by example. Dr. Baines's site, Celebrations of Life, has several. ❖

The Bottom Line

LEAVE A MARK

You were here. Even if you write no letters, capture no stories, don't fund a scholarship, and have nothing but moths in your pockets, you will be remembered for something. Your personal legacy may hinge on nothing more than your interactions and words. Some of the people we've met who've left the most profound legacies had nothing to their names but a deep well of kindness that they and others drew from.

Yes, There's Paperwork

How to prepare a will and trust; what to put into your "When I Die" file; choose someone to manage your health care and finances

D eath has its own paperwork.

　　We wish we could say we'd found a way to make end-of-life planning quick and clear, but the truth is, it's difficult—both in feeling and in practice. Emotionally, it's not easy to entertain a suite of life-and-death scenarios, predicting how you'll feel and articulating what you'll want. In practice, you're filling out legal documents, written in arcane language, that require several warm-bodied witnesses to become official. Since we can't make it painless, we're at least going to define the terms and tell you what to expect.

It may help to keep in mind that there is something useful and good in filling out these forms: The process will steer you toward important issues, and offer you an opportunity to wield control. Where life can feel out of whack, this is a real way to whack it back. You'll be protecting your own wishes, and in doing so, you'll also be making life a lot easier for your heirs. Here's the paperwork that helps you define what you want at the end of life:

1. Advance directive
2. Durable power of attorney for finances
3. Will
4. Revocable living trust

All of these forms are meant to *document* important conversations. They are not substitutions for the discussions you should have with your doctor and loved ones, who, when armed with a thorough sense of your personality and beliefs, will be able to speak for you in ways no boilerplate form ever could. And in general, these are *series* of conversations you should be having over time as you and your health change. Over the course of your life you may change your mind about any and all details within these documents, so you may complete any one of these forms multiple times.

——

1. Advance Directive

THIS IS A LEGAL DOCUMENT THAT NOTES YOUR HEALTH CARE WISHES should you become terminally ill and unable to make health care decisions for yourself. It's a tool you can use to direct your medical care at a future time when you can no longer think and communicate for yourself.

ADVANCE DIRECTIVE OR LIVING WILL?

In most states they're the same thing. An advance directive is *a state-specific legal document* that you can get from your lawyer or the hospital or download yourself. The advance directive forms for every state are free—just search online, download, print, and complete one to keep with your important paperwork. (If you live or spend significant time in more than one state, you may want to complete a form for each.) It will ask you to:

- Elect a "health care agent," a person who will make medical decisions for you should you not be able to speak for yourself. (Note: some states have separate forms: one for the advance directive and one for the agent)
- **Make your end-of-life care wishes known,** including what approach to treatment you prefer (anything ranging from medically aggressive to comfort-focused care) and what specific interventions (such as resuscitation and artificial nutrition)

you want, in the event that you are unable to communicate those wishes yourself

- **Say whether or not you want to be an organ donor**

Every state has its own advance directive laws and requirements, so make sure you are using a form that is legal in yours. In most states, there are limitations on who can be your health care agent. For example, **your health care agent may not be your doctor or someone who works for your health care system.** Usually, your advance directive form **must be signed in the presence of two witnesses, neither of whom can be your agent.**

If you have an estate-planning lawyer, he or she will be able to sign and provide a second witness (like a paralegal). In some states you must also have a notary to make the directive official. No, they don't make it easy, but those protections are in place to make sure no one is filling out the form pretending to be you or manipulating you into making choices.

As long as you are able to make your own decisions, **you may revoke any portion of the advance directive—or the entire document—at any time.** You can do this by telling your agent or doctor that you revoke it, by signing a revocation, or simply by tearing up the advance directive and writing a new one.

TIP
If you are downloading the form, ask neighbors or friends **not named in the document** to be your witnesses and find a local notary online.

If you designate your spouse as your agent, that designation may automatically be revoked by divorce or annulment unless you specify otherwise in the document. Check your state's laws, as they vary.

HEALTH CARE AGENT JOB DESCRIPTION

The single most important function of an advance directive is that it requires you to elect a health care agent (also called a health care proxy or surrogate). That person will make medical decisions for you should you not be able to do so yourself. Asking someone you trust to be your agent, and discussing with him over time what kind of care you do and don't want, are what matters in the end.

The reason that this decision is so important is that even the most detailed advance directive would not be enough to address all the nuances of every situation you'll find yourself in and how you would wish to proceed when decisions need to be made. Here are the major rights your health care agent will have and decisions that person will be able to make for you if you have lost the capacity to make decisions for yourself:

- Access to your medical records
- The right to consent to or refuse consent to any care, treatment, service, or procedure that would affect a physical or mental condition
- The right to select or discharge health care providers and institutions
- The right to approve or disapprove diagnostic tests, surgical procedures, and medication programs
- The right to approve, withhold, or withdraw artificial nutrition and hydration and all other forms of health care, including cardiopulmonary resuscitation (CPR)
- The right to sign up for organ donation, authorize an autopsy, and direct disposition of remains

CHOOSING THE RIGHT PERSON AS YOUR AGENT

Our recommendation for a good health care agent is someone who:

- Is 18 or older and legally able to make decisions for you
- Is reachable by phone or in person
- Knows you well
- Will be unafraid to ask questions and be willing to advocate on your behalf, even if it goes against convention or against the wishes of others in the family
- Feels comfortable acting as a diplomat and helping family members communicate
- Is comfortable making emotional decisions under stress

You can add other people as nonprimary agents (secondary and tertiary agents, as backups), if your state allows it. If your primary agent is otherwise tied up with his own health issues or maybe has moved or died, your backups will be on call to step in.

In some states, you can also stipulate that all the agents (if you choose several) collaborate on your care decisions. If you trust them to talk it out and come to a consensus, that can feel just right. But you should still name the ultimate decision maker in case a consensus can't be reached.

Whomever you choose as your health care agent, make sure to ask them if they're comfortable taking on the responsibility. I've had people try to sign me up as their agent upon meeting me at a party—one of the professional hazards of being a palliative care doctor—and casually mention it after the fact. Not the way to go.

Asking someone to be your health care proxy is not a casual text; it's a serious conversation or a series of them.

PROTECTING YOUR AGENT

Being someone's health care agent is a tough job, especially if family members are at odds. You can protect your agent by:

- Talking to your family about your wishes and what you've discussed with your agent
- Explaining to other family and friends why you've chosen this person to play this role

If you fear that your relatives might disagree with your agent and try to sway your doctors in another direction, make it clear that you want your health care agent to resolve any uncertainties that could arise when interpreting your wishes. A way to write this down is: "My agent should make any decisions about how to interpret my wishes and should work with my doctor on when to apply my living will."

Even with perfectly completed paperwork in hand, your advance directive could be forcefully challenged by other family members. If this happens in the hospital, their administrative team may deem the situation at an impasse and ask the courts to weigh in. Retired probate judge Peggy Houghton has seen it all: "The estranged child shows up and says 'I want everything possible to keep my mother alive,' even though the directive says no external measures, and the hospital will not follow the directive—they want [the court] to tell them to do it." Talking to everyone in your family about your wishes and ensuring that they understand and respect your choices will go a long way toward preventing such a situation.

FOR PARENTS

When your children turn 18, they will have to complete their own version of this paperwork to name you as their agent, or you will no longer automatically have access to their medical records or have the legal right to make decisions about their care should anything happen to them. This is due to the Health Insurance Portability and Accountability Act (HIPAA), which requires the protection and confidential handling of your personal health information once you are an adult.

YOUR BEST AGENT MIGHT NOT BE YOUR PARTNER

The person you elect does not need to be the person closest to you. Though it seems obvious that you'd want to elect a partner

HAPPY BIRTHDAY !

(time to choose a health care agent)

Advance directives aren't just for your grandparents. The moment you become an adult, at age 18, is when you should consider filling one out.

or child to whom you are deeply attached, remember that attachment has its perils. There are many heartbreaking decisions at the end of life, and they can come in rapid-fire succession, short-circuiting your agent's ability to make rational decisions based on your wishes. If you are afraid of emotions ruling the day, a close friend or lawyer may be the best person to carry out your wishes. And if you're worried about hurt feelings, remember: you can add loved ones as second or third agents; that way, they will feel included and your voice will still be protected.

YOU'LL BE THE ONE TO BRING UP YOUR END-OF-LIFE WISHES

If you're waiting for your doctor to put his hand on your shoulder and say with great solemnity, "It's time to get your affairs in order," don't.

The reality is that fewer than a third of doctors report having had any training in how to talk to patients about their end-of-life wishes. Only 23 percent of people say they've talked to a medical provider about who would make decisions for them if they were incapacitated. You're likely to be the one who has to bring it up.

FAST FACT
Medicare now reimburses doctors for discussing advance care planning in an office visit.

END-OF-LIFE DECISIONS AREN'T MADE ALONE

For some of you, your wishes may matter less to you than the wishes of the people you love. Or, rather, your highest wish may be that your loved one's wishes are met. Here's a story that illustrates the point.

Rebecca Sudore, a geriatrician and palliative medicine physician whose career is devoted to studying and developing tools for advance care planning, decided it was time to have a frank conversation with her grandma and grandpa as her grandfather became increasingly frail. As described in an article published in *The Journal of the American Medical Association*,[1] her grandfather told her he'd had a good run—that he loved his wife of sixty-five years and was not afraid of dying. He told her he was tired and didn't want any mechanical intervention. "No breathing tubes! No shocks, and no pushing on my chest. Just let me go." He was willing to try treatments that would make him feel better (comfort care), Rebecca says, such as wound care and pain management, as well as the treatments he was already getting. But, he said, "If they are giving it to me just to give it to me, then forget about it."

At that point, Rebecca turned to her grandmother, who would be the ultimate decision maker should her grandfather become unable to make his own choices. "Well, darling," she said, "of course I would tell the doctors to do everything possible to keep my husband alive." Rebecca was stunned. She'd just had a lovely, candid, and specific discussion with her grandfather about his wishes. Hadn't her grandmother heard what he'd said?

She then asked her grandmother to tell her what she had heard her grandfather say, and her grandmother repeated his wishes but said she loved her husband too much to let him go. "If he is with me just one more day, it would be worth it to me," she told her granddaughter. It would be worth it to her even if he were "hooked up to machines and not able to talk to me."

Rebecca then turned back to her grandfather and asked, "Did you just hear what Grandma said?" He said he did. She asked how he felt about her going against his wishes and requesting a feeding tube, ventilator, shocks, and other treatments he had said he did not want. "Is that okay with you?" she asked in disbelief. Her grandfather said it was. "I am ready to go, but if it helps your grandmother to feel that she did everything possible for me, even if it is because she doesn't want me to go, that is okay. She is the one who has to go on living with her decision. If this is what she wants, then this is what I want because I love her."

Rebecca realized in that moment that her grandfather's wishes *were* being honored; above all else, he wanted a death that his wife could live with. Relieving his wife's emotional burden was more important to him than all else, and he was willing to grant his wife leeway or flexibility in making medical decisions for him.

For all of the focus on patient autonomy, none of us makes decisions in a vacuum. What we want is often shaped by the people we love and the context of our lives. Giving the people we love agency and choice in our care is something that may feel both right and useful.

TIP
Consider having and documenting a discussion about leeway with your health care agent in advance.

IF YOU *DON'T* COMPLETE AN ADVANCE DIRECTIVE

If you *don't* elect a health care agent and there comes a time when you become incapacitated, doctors will typically seek decision guidance from family members, or will decide on their own. In complex or contentious cases, there are laws in place to determine who that person will be. In many states, it will be a friend or family member or a court-appointed guardian the court feels will act in your best interest. Better to pick for yourself while you still can than have the choice made for you.

If you find yourself in a situation where you are not ready to choose an agent or don't feel there's someone you trust to make decisions for you, that's all the more reason to talk about your wishes with your doctor and make sure the doctor has them written down or in your electronic files. But because the forms are

For Caregivers

Not everyone is eager to discuss the end of their life, and springing the topic on someone over a casual coffee might feel like an ambush. One way into the conversation is to bring up someone in the family or a close friend who died and ask what they took away from the experience. Often it's easier to say what we don't want.

Say something like "Remember when we visited Aunt Genie in the ICU? She had five tubes coming out of her and didn't seem to know where she was. That was really hard to see, but maybe that was what she wanted. How did you feel about that? Is that what you'd want?"

One approach is to use the opportunity of a holiday meal, maybe not at Thanksgiving dinner itself, but while enjoying leftovers. If this is a family discussion, make sure you and your siblings talk about it beforehand, too, so you don't trip into a family feud. Here are a few possible opening lines:

- Instead of starting with a direct statement such as "We need to talk about what you want when you die," which will stop all conversation cold, try asking them to share a story about their life. Once you get reminiscing, it's easier to move to a discussion about values and wishes.
- Use your own wishes as a springboard: "Mom, it's important to me that you know what I would want if something happened to me." Share first, and then ask them if they've thought about their own wishes.

often a series of check boxes that do not describe *why* someone chose what he did, the forms alone can be only so effective.

IN THE CASE OF ALZHEIMER'S DISEASE/DEMENTIA

You are well within your rights to tell your health care agent about, and write instructions for, what you want concerning feeding and treatment should you develop dementia.

You might say, "If I become unable to make decisions about my health due to Alzheimer's or other dementia (be as specific as you can to avoid misinterpretation), please do not administer any curative treatments or medications, such as antibiotics, should I become ill, except to keep me pain-free and comfortable. I do not want to be forced to eat or drink or have the reflexive opening of my mouth to be interpreted as giving my consent to being fed."

If this sounds leading, it is. In my years working in a hospital, I saw too many people with a terrified look in their eyes, their bodies broken down beyond repair, unable to know where they were or what was happening to them, while we dutifully poked and prodded away. Judging from their expressions and the feelings in our own stomachs, our attempts were more akin to cruelty than to healing.

It may seem like excessive planning to write your wishes down in case you get Alzheimer's one day, but when you consider that one in three seniors dies with (and many from) Alzheimer's disease or another form of dementia, it's actually a very good investment. Although research is well under way, we currently do not have any treatments to halt or cure Alzheimer's. Because of this, in the end stages of dementia, the best route for most is to not get in the way of the person's body as it is trying to die, and to make sure comfort is paramount.

You or your family can also state that you are not to be taken back to the hospital the next time something goes wrong as long as you are comfortable, in a safe environment, and have access to palliative or hospice care. All of these things can be stipulated in an advance directive.

MEDICAL ISSUES WITHIN AN ADVANCE DIRECTIVE

Some advance care documents will ask you specific questions about what specialized medical interventions you do or do not want for yourself, and it's imperative that you understand the consequences of what you're choosing before checking any boxes.

Organ Donation

One choice that you make in an advance directive is whether or not you want to donate your organs to a person in need or to medical science when you die. A few points of clarification here:

- **Being an organ donor does not affect whether or not emergency crews will resuscitate you if you've been in an accident.** The prospect of your organs being of use to others does not trump your own health.
- **If you want all your major organs to be donated after you die, you'll have to be in a hospital at the time of your passing.** People who die at home are not within range of equipment that keeps the organs viable and safe for the intended recipient.
- **If you die at home, you can still donate your body to a Willed (Whole) Body Program for medical science. These types of donations need to be arranged with the school or program of your choice by you or your representative** *before* death occurs. Once you register, your information is saved and they'll

provide instructions on steps to take at the time of death as well as a phone number that is monitored 24/7.

- **If you choose organ donation, and die in the hospital, your body will be whisked away almost immediately after you're declared dead.** We're not suggesting this should dissuade you from choosing to donate—on the contrary, we see it as a noble, important, and generous act—but this little-known part of the process is something to talk over with your family so everyone is prepared to let the body go quickly.

Greg Segal, a cofounder of Organize.org, an organ donation registry, met a single mother who had a 16-year-old son. The son came home from a health class at school one day and said he wanted to be an organ donor. She was taken aback, as she was not a donor, nor had anyone in her family ever been. Two weeks later, her son was hit by a bus and died. In his final moments, the hospital asked her if she wanted to donate his organs. He wasn't yet registered as a donor, but because they had talked about it, she knew that was what he'd want. How could she not honor his wishes? The mother is now best friends with her son's organ recipient; they spend Thanksgiving together. And it all came from a single conversation. Your decision to donate can save up to eight lives with your transplanted organs and enhance many others with your tissue.

Life Support and Resuscitation

When death is imminent, do you want doctors to place you on life support, such as a breathing machine (mechanical ventilator, or "vent")? And when you die, do you want doctors to attempt to bring you back? Or would you prefer to let nature take its course and all professional efforts to be geared instead toward your comfort? These are heavy questions with lots of consequences for you and your family, and unless you are absolutely certain of your answer, they are context specific and need to be discussed at length with your doctor and over time as your health changes.

Artificial Nutrition and Hydration

Another question you'll be asked when preparing an advance directive is whether or not you want artificial nutrition and hydration. The answer isn't as straightforward as you might think.

Tube feeding typically involves placing a small tube up your nose and down your throat into your stomach. The tube can also be inserted directly into your stomach through the skin. Liquefied nutrition and/or water is passed through the tube and into your gut, bypassing the need to swallow. It is also possible to be given nutrition and water intravenously. Whether by feeding tube or by vein, the cases for and against are much the same.

Tube feeding has been shown to extend life in some situations. Feeding tubes can serve as a bridge either to more life or toward more time to figure out whether or not a traumatic event is going to be survivable. But in late stages of terminal illness, artificial nutrition and hydration can actually become a problem. **In this context, the body's rejection of food and water is a symptom of death approaching, not the cause of it.** Interrupting this natural shutting-down process with a feeding tube runs greater risk of hurting than of helping. When a body cannot process it, food or fluid will cause trouble: bloating, delirium, shortness of breath, and pain; so the body is being smart by saying no. At this point feeding tubes will not extend life.

So why is this a difficult issue? Practically speaking, the difficulty is entirely about when to draw the line. When has your body begun to shut down for good? What exactly constitutes the

organ donation:
one last act
of KINDNESS

Choosing to be an organ donor may be the most direct way you can save a person's life. In the United States alone, twenty-one people die each day waiting for an organ transplant.

"late stages" of illness? You'll need a doctor's assessment at that time to make that call, which makes it hard to imagine and decide with certainty now.

This situation highlights why advance directives are difficult to complete and why the most important thing you can do is to designate a person who knows you well to work with your doctors in real time.

YOUR CARE AND HANDLING INSTRUCTIONS

Though official paperwork can go a long way to ensuring you receive the end-of-life care you want, our overall well-being is the sum of a thousand tiny choices we take for granted that won't be addressed by any official forms. People are often hesitant to ask for small quotidian things to be done for them, but these can make all the difference. Do you prefer to take baths or showers, and how often? How do you take your coffee? Are there songs that will reel in good memories? Are you a side sleeper? To make sure you get your needs met, think about writing "care and handling" instructions for yourself. Taking the time to write these things down in your advance directive notes will do much to help caregivers take care of you.

MEDICAL FORMS TO COMPLEMENT AN ADVANCE DIRECTIVE

For those already living with a serious medical condition or advanced age, a POLST form should be completed, and a DNR form should be discussed and completed if appropriate. Unlike an advance directive, these forms need to be signed by a doctor to be valid. The fact that they are signed by a doctor is what makes them more rigorous and likely to be honored by health care institutions.

Physician's Order for Life Sustaining Treatment (POLST)*

The POLST is a one-page, double-sided form that asks you to mark your preferences for the most common medical interventions: CPR, intubation, etc. **It is a document that should be completed when you are seriously ill or approaching the end of your life.** Completing one requires a conversation with, and signature of, a physician. The power of the POLST is that it's a medical order and protects both patient and provider. **You do not need to have an advance directive to complete a POLST, though it's best to have both.** As of now the only states that do not meet the National POLST Paradigm criteria are Vermont, Maryland, Nebraska, and Massachusetts. That just means they have a different type of form for patients to complete to make their wishes known. If you are elderly or know yourself to be in the late stages of illness, especially when your body is growing weaker no matter what you do, having a completed and signed POLST form is the best single thing you can do to protect whatever wishes you have for your own end-of-life care.

TIP

Keep a copy of your completed POLST form handy in your home—taped to your refrigerator or someplace people would easily see it in an emergency—and on your person if you're traveling.

Do Not Resuscitate (DNR)†

You'll often hear the term *DNR* in a hospital setting. It instructs your care team not to do cardiopulmonary resuscitation when your heart stops beating. (This resuscitation could be in the form of compressing your chest, shocking your heart, and inserting breathing tubes to keep your body alive.)

*Also called MOLST, SMOST, TROPP, MOST, POST, LaPOST, COLST, IPOST, or WyoPOLST, depending on your state.
†Also called Allow Natural Death (AND).

—
FAST FACT
There is also a separate out-of-hospital DNR form for people who do not want to be resuscitated if they should die at home or away from a medical location.

A doctor's signature is required for the forms to be valid and for you to order a corresponding DNR bracelet or necklace.

PUT YOUR PAPERWORK SOMEWHERE SAFE AND OBVIOUS

Once you've done the hard work of getting your wishes down on paper, make sure they don't end up in a box on a high shelf where no one would think to look. Consider doing the following:

1. **Copy or email your completed forms and give them to your health care agent and other family members, and to your doctors (all of them).** Many of the electronic medical systems that your doctors and hospital use can upload your directive so it becomes a part of your chart.
2. **Register them online with the U.S. Living Will Registry or MyDirectives.com.** Documents can be stored in the cloud so they're accessible from anywhere with an internet connection.

——

2. Durable Power of Attorney for Finances Form

YOU MAY NEED SOMEONE TO MANAGE YOUR FINANCIAL AFFAIRS, should you become incapacitated. That person will be able to sign checks and other financial documents for you and pay your bills, so make sure it's someone you trust (and someone who has a good nose for financial matters). Some states will require a letter from your doctor or some other named person stating that you were unable to take care of it yourself.

Your agent has power over your finances while you're alive, but only if and when you are not able to say or do things for yourself.

The idea of turning over all of your accounts to someone may make you shudder; it's hard to have to imagine and it's no small decision to make. Do you have a friend or family member who's highly responsible with her own finances, maybe even a banker or accountant? Ask that person! It can be the same person who holds your power of attorney for health care in some states, but you may feel better about splitting the assignments.

———

3. Will

A WILL GIVES INSTRUCTIONS FOR HOW TO TRANSFER YOUR ASSETS and property, meaning who gets what, and when. This matters if you own anything at all. But you really need to invest in a will only if the property is in your name alone. If it's jointly owned with your spouse or child, it will automatically be transferred to him or her upon your death. You can also create a transfer on death (TOD) deed for the property while you're alive to give it to a specific beneficiary (person or organization of your choice).

A will is generally less complicated and less expensive to create than a trust (which we'll discuss later). **In your will you'll name the person you want to manage your stuff after you die (an "executor").** The executor notifies your survivors of how the stuff will be divided and to whom it will go. (Spoiler alert: that process may require some sleuthing, so pick someone whom you trust to handle it.) You'll also choose guardians for any children under the age of 18.

WHY A WILL IS NOT BULLETPROOF

Even with the many protections that a will puts into place, human behavior is hard to predict and there can be all sorts of complicating factors as families change shape.

Though we can't cover all the ways in which things can go wrong, trust us when we say that when someone in the family is dying, it tends to bring up a lot of unfinished business. There's no shortage of litigation between family members who feel slighted by a parent or spouse's decisions, or who harbor old resentments. Just because siblings are in their sixties doesn't mean that childhood wounds are healed. And when people are under duress or grieving, it's like pulling off a scab. So although wills are designed to keep people from fighting, even the most inviolable paperwork can't force families to work together and may widen rifts. A poorly written will can also lead to disputes.

Do you have a partner you've been with for twenty years whom you expect will take care of you as you age, but you've never married? Virginia Palmer, an estate planning and trust lawyer at Wendel, Rosen, Black & Dean LLP, says that if you're not married and you don't put your partner into your will or trust or provide for him or her through some form of beneficiary designation or joint tenancy, he or she will most likely be left out in the cold. Palmer has had only one case in thirty-five years where the decedent's family honored the deathbed wishes to provide for a girlfriend.

You may see your kids as the most generous and thoughtful people in the world, but by the time they've paid off all of your bills they may not want to share and may defend their decision by saying "If Dad had wanted to protect you, he would have put you in his estate plan." Here are a few other things to watch out for:

what goes INTO a will?

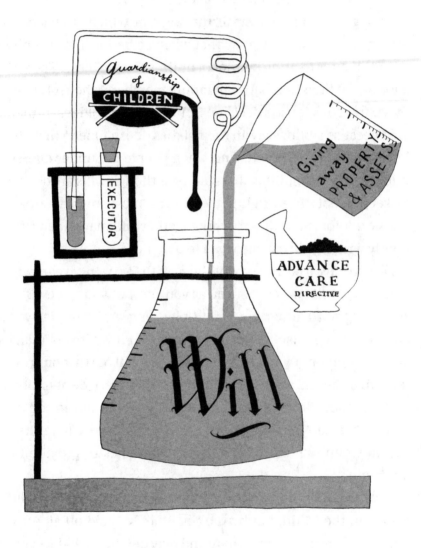

People often confuse wills and trusts. Make sure you sit with someone who knows how each document works and what is right for you.

- **In-laws.** Often it's not the siblings who are driving the nego-tiations but the in-laws. "Time and time again, if I've got four kids who get along decently and if I can keep their spouses out of the picture, I can get [an estate mediation] done," says Bren-ham, Texas–based estate lawyer Laura Upchurch. "As soon as the spouse is allowed in, it falls apart."

- **Blended families.** The calculus of decision-making changes when you're on your second marriage and have two sets of kids. Choosing a kid from the first marriage as your executor can seem like an act of favoritism.

  When it comes to blended families with many step- and half siblings, parents may want to elect primary, secondary, and tertiary executors of the will so no one feels as though they've been cut out altogether.

You can also assign children different roles: one as power of attorney for finances; another as your health care agent; and a third as the executor of your will. You can explain why you gave them those roles in a direct conversation (Gina is good with money; Chuck knows how to deal with doctors), or by writing your ethical will (read about that in chapter 2, "Leave a Mark").

All that said, even assigning equal roles won't prove you love everyone equally if they have amassed years of evidence to the contrary. The goal is to avoid a long, protracted conflict when you're dying or after you're gone, and only you can know how best to do that.

TALK TO YOUR KIDS ABOUT YOUR WILL

Telling your kids in advance what you've chosen to do in your will—even writing them a letter explaining why—is the most honest, loving thing to do, even if they don't agree with your choices. If your children know what's coming, there's no seismic shock: they can prepare, ask you questions, and make their peace with it or at least have it out directly with you instead of with their siblings in a court of law. You don't have to share every last detail about the amount of money involved or where it is going if you think that's going to be a difficult conversation, but do share the principles behind your will so they understand your intentions.

Karen M. Stockmal, an estate lawyer at KMS Law Offices in Berwyn, Pennsylvania, had a client who was the primary breadwinner in his second marriage of more than twenty-five years. His wife had adult children from a prior marriage, and he had two children from his first marriage. His will divided his assets between his two kids and his second wife. He had named his son from the first marriage as the executor and reviewed the plan with his kids.

Everyone was on board until he was diagnosed with a terminal illness, at which point he and his second wife changed his will to add her as coexecutor and give her a great deal more of the pie. He never told his children.

When he died, they grieved together and then went to look at the will. But his second wife told them, "Oh, that's not the right will, we changed it." Surprise! His kids were irate. They sued her and the estate, claiming that their father didn't have adequate mental capacity and that his second wife had manipulated him into making the changes. Perhaps they could have found some middle ground with their stepmother if their father had talked it over with them before he died. But he didn't, and it felt like a betrayal from the grave.

Parenting never ends. It won't be easy to tell your kids if you're making changes they won't like, but it's still your responsibility as their parent. They will always identify as your children, and expect you to be the grown-up in the room. If you are open and honest, it's up to them to come to terms with it—or not. One thing is certain: a change will be much less forgivable if you pull a fast one, exit the scene, and leave them to deal with it on their own.

MAKING A WILL ONLINE

If you live in California, Maine, Michigan, New Mexico, or Wisconsin, have a simple set of assets, and can't afford a lawyer, you can download a free statutory will and fill it out yourself. You can leave your assets to heirs that way. The downside is that they're one-size-fits-all forms and cannot be customized. **If you're in a rush to get your paperwork done, there are online services that allow you to download documents immediately or as soon as you can fill out all the online forms (see Resources). But be warned, they may not cover all contingencies.**

HIRING A LAWYER

If you're taking care of all of your estate planning and prep paperwork at once (will, living trust, advance directive, durable power of attorney), **we highly recommend working with a lawyer.** Proper planning doesn't come cheap, but it will be far more costly for your family after you die if you don't do your paperwork in advance.

If you're uncertain whether you need a lawyer or not, email a few and outline the size of your estate or set up a thirty-minute

meeting and ask for a road map for your situation. Another question to ask is who in the office would handle the work, as paralegals have lower rates.

Expect to spend a couple thousand dollars to get your paper-work done if you have a simple estate, more if it's large and complicated. Many of the attorneys we spoke to said a good chunk of their business comes from fixing wills and trusts drafted by people who thought they could do it themselves. If you don't have the resources to get this done, don't give up. There are legal aid organizations that will help you.

Most bar associations also have a pro bono panel where you can get a consultation for $35 per thirty minutes; they will often draft paper-work for a simple will and for powers of attorney documents for free.

—
TIP
Search online for "legal aid estate planning" to find pro bono or reduced-rate estate attorneys in your area.

——

4. Revocable Living Trust

A LIVING TRUST IS A LEGAL DOCUMENT IN WHICH YOU PLACE YOUR assets (bank accounts, property). These assets belong to you while you're alive, after which a representative you choose, called a *successor trustee* (a family member, friend, or lawyer), transfers the assets to your beneficiaries (spouse, kids).

So a trust involves three parties: you, the trustee(s) who agree to manage your assets, and the beneficiaries—those who will become the new owners of your stuff. A trust is "revocable," meaning that as long as you've got your wits about you, you can change it at any time for any reason. It becomes irrevocable when you die.

LIVING TRUSTS VERSUS WILLS

We wish we could give you a solid, unambiguous answer on whether you need a living trust, a will, or both. Annoyingly, it depends on how large your estate is, and what your local laws say. If you have property that's owned solely by you, along with other significant assets, it's best to do both. Though the trust seems like the more effective "doer" of the pair, a will does some important things that a living trust can't. **If you have minor children, for example, and want to name a guardian who will take care of them in the event that you die before they turn 18, in many states you must use a will.**

In nearly every state, **a living trust will ensure a quick transfer of your property and assets to your chosen beneficiaries and spare them having to go to probate court.** Probate court is never a walk in the park, but in some states, such as Pennsylvania, it's a quick transaction, while in others, for example Florida, it can drag you through years of administrative hell.

If you have a modest, uncomplicated estate, you may want to skip the legal costs of preparing a living trust. Any jointly owned property (where the title is under both your name *and* your spouse's or child's) will automatically transfer to the other owner when you die. But if you have more than one child, you may want a trust in place to make them both beneficiaries.

FAST FACT
Life insurance and retirement accounts, such as 401(k)s and IRAs, that have a beneficiary listed transfer automatically upon death.

PREPARING A LIVING TRUST

There are many do-it-yourself options out there, as well as online legal resources where you can learn the legalese and educate yourself about estate planning, but it's easy to screw up. Fixing your mistakes requires redoing the entire document from scratch, or going to court, which may end up costing you more than if it had been done properly the first time. "Just don't go to a trust mill," says Virginia Palmer. "Paralegals acting without an attorney's guidance will do a basic form of trust, and you will think you are done. We end up having to do a lot of cleaning up of the mess afterward, including forms that are downloaded off the internet." Let us repeat ourselves: **We highly recommend hiring a lawyer to help you create a trust.**

You can find small solo practitioners who'll complete your will and trust for around $2,500. Palmer estimates that you'll pay $3,500 to $5,000 in attorney fees for a trust and the necessary ancillary documents, such as a pour-over will, assignments, and deeds. And large law firms charge up to tens of thousands for more affluent, complicated estates. Of course, if you have the assets to justify that kind of estate planning, you should be able to afford it.

Are you in a second marriage with kids? Do you have properties in several states? Do you have a child with special needs? Make sure to ask your attorney if they have dealt with your set of circumstances.

TIP
The National Academy of Elder Law Attorneys has a searchable online directory of estate planners.

FUNDING YOUR TRUST

Your trust is like an empty wallet unless you complete the final step of funding it. Here's how to do that:

1. **Retitle your accounts in the name of your trust.** Your lawyer should prepare a memo for you or write a letter on your behalf to your financial institutions, asking for this change. So "Sarah Smith's Checking Account" will become "THE SMITH REVOCABLE

LIVING TRUST Account." It's a paperwork hassle that must be hassled through.

2. **Transfer all of your accounts and property into the trust.** Enlist a friendly bank representative to help. He will ask you to sign ten or so documents to make sure all of your checking and savings accounts are transferred into your trust. He will likely ask to see a certification of trust, which will be part of the packet you got from your lawyer.

3. **If you have a joint account, bring the other person—their signature can't be phoned in.** If you're lucky, your bank will have a notary on the premises.

4. **Your lawyer will transfer the deeds for any property you own.** You'll get the original deed back in the mail a few weeks later. (If you ever refinance and are required to have a deed putting the property back into your name, make sure there is a subsequent deed putting it back into your name as trustee.)

5. **Remember, qualified retirement plans don't go into your trust.** These include IRAs, SEP, and 401(k). The IRS considers putting any of these into a trust to be equal to changing the owner of your IRA or 401(k) to the name of your trust, and you will be taxed.

If you don't fund your trust, your lawyer will end up telling your kids or other inheritors, "I gave her instructions and she never followed them!" and then charge your children to take the estate through the probate process. Good for the lawyer, bad for your kids.

WHAT IS PROBATE? (AND HOW TO AVOID IT)

When there is no trust, an unfunded trust, or your will includes property solely owned by you—like your house and car and bank accounts with no beneficiaries (the legal term for these is *probate assets*)—your survivors will have to go to probate court to settle your estate. Here's what you need to know:

Legal fees can suck up an estate's value. In many states, probate can be a long, painful, inheritance-draining process.

A judge will appoint an executor to handle your estate—your spouse or child or closest relative. That person will then file papers in court that list your property, debts, and beneficiaries. Once that's done, he or she will have to pay your credit card bills, taxes, and any other debts you owe from your estate.

Your executor may have to do a lot of sleuthing. If you haven't given your executor all the information about what you owe and to whom, they'll have to figure it out themselves by going through your mail and papers. (With inherited estates, that's true as well; the difference with probate is that a court is involved.) Then they'll have to notify credit cards and banks of your death with a form letter. Your creditors have about three to six months from the date those letters are issued to request payment.

The executor may have to sell your real estate, stocks, or other assets to cover debts before distributing any cash to family, organizations, and so forth. In most states, immediate family members can ask the court to release short-term funds so the money's not entirely tied up for the year or longer this takes to play out.

If there is no will, the paperwork can get crazy. The estate of the deceased will be split between a surviving spouse and children, so you will need a marriage certificate as well as the birth certificates for the children to prove their relationship to the deceased.

Laura Upchurch had an 85-year-old client who left half of her estate to one person and half to those of her brothers and sisters who survived her. It turned out that not a single sibling survived

her, so that half of the estate passed on to her nieces and neph-
ews, numbering forty-nine children and grandchildren, including two who had been taken in by the woman's sibling.

Upchurch then had to go back and find out if the children
taken in had ever been legally adopted, which required finding
their birth certificates and whether the woman's sibling had ever
been listed as a parent. Because they *were* adopted, their records
had been sealed, so Upchurch had to obtain a court order from
1962. She then had to present the descendant's birth certificate
and the sister's birth certificate to establish the links in the chain
of heirship.

The moral of the story: If you have any assets to leave behind,
not doing your will and trust dramatically complicates the grieving process and drags your family through unnecessary misery.

———

Wasn't That Fun? Now Let's Do It All Again

A WILL AND LIVING TRUST ARE NOT SET-IT-AND-FORGET-IT KINDS OF
documents. It's a good idea to revisit your documents every
year when you're filing your tax return. If they're not up to date,
make the changes then and there. If you sell the family home
and buy a condo, and the old house is what's in your will, it could
create complications that would require the courts to resolve.
And don't forget to update beneficiary designations as you have
(or marry into) more children.

———

Put It All in One Place

WHEN PALLIATIVE CARE PHYSICIAN IRA BYOCK'S MOTHER, RUTH, DIED suddenly, he and his sister discovered a small card file box on a counter adjacent to her kitchen in which she had carefully organized all her papers, account numbers, pending transactions, and everything else they needed to complete her affairs and distribute her belongings. It was an incredible gift to them during a time of emotional turmoil. Ira and his sister both felt as though Mom were reaching out to lovingly support them from beyond. "This was not a Buddhist master's awareness of death," Byock says. "It was a Jewish mother's love for her children." Keeping everything together in one place provides a useful point of entry into your life—one that will save your loved ones time, money, and heaps of unnecessary suffering. Here's a list of things to assemble:

WHAT TO PUT INTO YOUR "WHEN I DIE" FILE

☐ Advance directive that's signed (and notarized if necessary)
☐ Lawyer and accountant's contact info
☐ Birth certificate
☐ Will and living trust (with certificate of trust)
☐ Durable power of attorney for finance
☐ Life insurance policy plus agent's name and contact info
☐ Military service documents
☐ Bank account plus any safe-deposit box information
☐ Investment information
☐ Real estate documents and deeds
☐ Debtor information (credit cards, loans, membership dues)
☐ Copy of driver's license and Social Security card (or number)
☐ Marriage or divorce certificate

when to REVISIT your advance care planning

buy or sell a house

turn eighteen

have a baby

get married... or divorced

retire

get sick

Get in the habit of periodically checking your paperwork to ensure it still represents your wishes and current situation.

- ☐ Location and combination of any safes in your home
- ☐ Tax information
- ☐ Passwords for phone, computer, email, and social media accounts (we recommend using an online password manager to collect them all, sharing the master password with someone you trust, and then designating emergency contacts within the program who are allowed to gain access)
- ☐ Letters to loved ones (see chapter 2, "Leave a Mark," for more on this)
- ☐ Funeral and burial plot documents and funeral insurance
- ☐ Instructions for your funeral and final disposition
- ☐ Helpful home details: location of car keys, gate codes, hide-a-key location, and garage door openers ❖

assemble a

"WHEN I DIE" file

Do the people who matter to you know your account numbers and passwords? Keep your documents together and make them findable.

CHAPTER THREE

The Bottom Line

YES, THERE'S PAPERWORK

Getting your plans down on paper requires some investment and busywork, but you will feel lighter having done it, as if you've finally unpacked a suitcase you've been carrying around for years. Though you can't avoid death, this is one place where you *do* have control. This is yours.

Can I Afford to Die?

The costs at the end of life; what happens to debt; long-term care insurance and Medicaid

L et's talk about money.

Being terminally ill can cost a small fortune. Even if you have plenty of cash socked away and top-tier medical insurance, the bills stack up quickly. Multiple operations, weeks spent recuperating in a hospital, and rehab in a facility will be more expensive than choosing the route of symptom control and support in the home.

Of course, no one wants to make treatment choices based on budget. It's difficult to call something a "choice" when it concerns your health. But all of your health care decisions—the obvious ones and the less obvious ones—have financial consequences and it will be up to you to bring up costs with your health care provider and figure out what will be covered by insurance versus out-of-pocket.

Good news is so often wrapped in bad news, and vice versa. We either have too much money to qualify for support services (such as Medicaid) or too little to get by. Though it's impossible to predict how much you'll end up needing to cover expenses, if you start early, you can prepare for a time when your costs may balloon. The first hurdle is figuring out what will, and won't, be covered by insurance.

———

What's Covered by Medical Insurance?

THIS QUESTION PRESUMES THAT YOU HAVE INSURANCE IN THE FIRST place, which plenty of us don't. And if you suddenly find yourself with a serious illness, lack of coverage becomes a bigger problem. Even if you decide not to pursue treatments, you can incur huge medical costs for tests and doctor visits just to get to a diagnosis.

LOOK INTO OBTAINING MEDICAL INSURANCE

- **Marketplace:** Visit HealthCare.gov and complete an application. You may be eligible for a federal subsidy
- **Medicaid:** Visit Medicaid.gov or call your local Medicaid office to see if you qualify for this type of coverage
- **Insurers:** Go directly to the medical insurers' websites. Many allow you to obtain quotes online

If you have access to a social worker or case manager, he or she will be particularly well suited to help you navigate your options. A visit with an independent insurance broker is another great option.

It's important to understand, right up front, what your insurance will and won't cover. Just because you have the Cadillac of insurance policies doesn't mean it will cover every $30,000 procedure you have. Your insurance may rule against reimbursement or against counting the cost of a treatment toward your deductible if they determine that the treatment wasn't medically necessary or that it was too "experimental." Often it's the very prescription medications or specialists you're looking for that are excluded or that require an insurmountable copayment. Check in with your insurance rep or ask someone at your doctor's office to do so before you begin any new treatments; that will give you peace of mind now instead of a panic attack later.

——

Hidden Costs

ASIDE FROM WHATEVER BIG THINGS YOUR INSURANCE POLICY WON'T cover, there are other out-of-pocket expenses that you should be aware of when looking at your whole financial picture. Many are the small or day-to-day necessities, which will add up quickly. Here are a few hidden costs to keep in the back of your mind:

- Nutritional supplements; organic and specialty foods
- Diapers, bed pads, new sheets
- Hearing aid batteries and other adaptive equipment
- "Alternative" treatments such as homeopathy, acupuncture, and massages
- Lost wages from missing work: your take-home pay, or that of your primary caretaker, may be cut if your hours change or disappear altogether

——

Paying for Care

LET'S START WITH THE OBVIOUS WAY TO HELP COVER costs: *save*. It may be late in the game for some of us, but for those who still have time, put as much money aside for medical-related expenses as you can. Here are some ways to pay:

- **Health Savings Account (HSA).** This is a savings account that allows you to set aside money on a pretax basis to pay for medical expenses before you reach your deductible

FAST FACT
Medical costs are the single biggest cause of personal bankruptcy in the United States, *even among people with medical insurance.*

and for other out-of-pocket costs; be sure to check with your insurer (or HR officer or accountant) about how much you can sock away and for how long.

- **The "accelerated death benefit" in your life insurance policy.** It's a grisly name, but it allows the owner of the policy to withdraw cash before death, generally around the last six months of life. Doing so diminishes the funds that will flow to your beneficiaries when you die, but you may need the money now and this is one way to find it.

- **Life insurance with a long-term care component.** This is a hybrid policy that requires a large one-time premium; the money can go toward a death benefit for your heirs, or a percentage can be converted to purchase long-term care.

- **Negotiate!** If you're struggling to make payments on medical bills, be sure to discuss your situation with the finance department. They won't advertise it, but hospitals, clinics, nursing homes, and other institutions are sometimes willing to work out a payment plan or negotiate the debt lower. They can be impressively flexible, especially when you ask in advance of piling up invoices. Same goes for your doctor's office; ask the administrator if they can go to bat for you with the insurance agency. Most have had lots of phone time discussing issues exactly like yours and may be able to help with lowering a payment or getting something covered when it initially wasn't.

——

Long-Term Care Insurance (LTCI)

THE GOOD NEWS: LTC INSURANCE COVERS ALL SORTS OF EXPENSES not covered by health insurance, like aides who help you get through the day, or the costs of a nursing home.

The bad news: The industry miscalculated how great the need and cost for care would be later in life—especially now that we're living longer—making it a financial sinkhole for the insurer. As a result, fewer companies are underwriting these policies and with more restrictions at a higher cost to you. Some things to be aware of when considering LTC insurance:

- **It kicks in only once you lose the ability to complete two or more of six activities of daily living (ADLs): eating, bathing, dressing, getting to and from the bathroom, continence, and walking by yourself.** You'll need a clinical professional to sign off on that claim.
- **You may not be eligible.** Are you a woman with osteoporosis? A man with a cane? Someone with cognitive impairment such as dementia or Alzheimer's disease? You can be denied coverage based on a preexisting condition.
- **Whereas they used to last a lifetime, most plans now cover only two to three years.** So, if you are looking at a ten-year period of illness, you'll likely be covering seven or eight of those years.

——

LTCI Quiz

EVEN IF YOU QUALIFY, IT'S NOT A QUESTION OF "DO YOU NEED IT?" BUT rather "Can you afford it?" Ask yourself these two questions to help determine if LTCI is right for your personal situation:

1. Are you concerned about protecting your assets for those who will inherit them? Yes/No
2. Are you able to invest a large sum of up to and over $100,000? Yes/No

If you answered yes to *both* these questions, LTCI may be the right choice for you. If you answered no to either question, be prepared to spend whatever money you have on treatment and direct care rather than paying into long-term care insurance.

——

Can I Rely on Medicaid?

THE SHORT ANSWER IS YES. AS OF THIS WRITING, THE MAJORITY OF people *are* able to count on Medicaid. It pays at least some of the nursing home tab for 62 percent of residents. The common misconception is that you need to be completely bankrupt to be eligible. You don't. As with many social services, the Medicaid benefit is overburdened, understaffed, and perennially on the political chopping block, but it can be a powerful safety net for those in need, covering care for patients in whatever place they call home—a hospital, nursing facility, or home itself.

ARE YOU ELIGIBLE FOR MEDICAID?

- You are allowed to have no more than $2,000 in the bank.
- You can have an automobile and your primary home and still qualify.

That said, if you have resources, Medicaid should be seen as a last resort, not least because the care options available will *feel* like a last resort. Medicaid is invaluable, but not exactly a cushy policy. It may not cover the doctor you're used to seeing or the medications you're used to taking.

——

Gaming to Get Medicaid

HOPING TO GIFT ALL OF YOUR MONEY AND PROPERTY TO YOUR KIDS and jump on the Medicaid train so you don't drain your children's inheritance? There's a whole cottage industry of consultants who help people do so.

Leah's mother was showing signs of memory lapse in her sixties, and her daughters feared the worst: the onset of Alzheimer's. They all lived far away from their family home and decided it was time to look into a long-term care insurance plan. When Leah talked to the agent, he said she and her sisters should think about divesting their mother of all she owned in case she outlived the insurance plan, which covered up to six years. **Medicaid has a five-year look-back, meaning that Leah's mother would have to have had assets of less than $2,000 for at least five years, or there'd be no government support after her long-term insurance plan ran out.** "He told us to dump all of her assets," Leah says. "Then he said, 'You'll be fine, because Medicaid will kick in.'" But that's risky advice.

If the government finds that you sold off assets and property that equal more than the $2,000 you claim to have now, you could be denied coverage. And if it finds out about it later or it turns out after your death that your estate has the money, your family might be forced to pay the government back.

FAST FACT
When you apply for Medicaid coverage, the Feds will check your finances up to sixty months in the past.

And before you start dumping assets, consider this: using Medicaid if you don't really need it takes away from the population that really does. Remember, too, many doctors and facilities don't accept Medicaid.

And owing to the relatively slight reimbursement associated with Medicaid, some doctors aren't able to give the time or attention they do to patients with better-paying plans. Patients with Medicaid as their primary insurance may go to the doctor and hear statements along the lines of "You're only allowed to tell me about one problem." It can feel as though you're a second-class citizen and will be jarring if you've had more personalized or comprehensive care up to that point.

If, on the other hand, you are a patient who has had no insurance, being able to see a nurse, or to walk into a clinic and have your issues addressed, provides a real sense of refuge. In other words, whether Medicaid feels like a demotion or a godsend depends on your starting point.

———

Death and Debt

ACCORDING TO ONE RECENT STUDY, 73 PERCENT OF AMERICANS WILL die in some kind of debt. If you're worried about this exact situation, know that the Federal Trade Commission has rules in place to ensure that your family doesn't have to pay your debts out of their own wallet. While your individual relatives will not be personally held responsible for your debts after you die, your estate *is*—so money and assets that you thought would go to your heirs will be combed through and used to pay any outstanding bills. Jewelry, cars, and even coin collections will be sold off for cash if necessary. Heirs of the estate don't have to pay out of pocket, however, so if there aren't funds to pay the debts from the estate, creditors may be cut short.

There are a few exceptions to this rule: if your relatives cosigned anything like a loan or a credit card, they will be accountable for your debts. The laws of debt payback have some discrepancies that vary by state. Here's a breakdown:

- **In a community property state:** A deceased person's spouse may be responsible for paying some health expenses, but generally bills will be paid out of the estate first.
- **In a filial responsibility state:** Adult children *may* be required to pay for a deceased parent's unpaid medical debts, such as those to hospitals or nursing homes, when the estate cannot.

FILIAL RESPONSIBILITY AND COMMUNITY PROPERTY STATES

FILIAL	BOTH	COMMUNITY
AR • CT • DE • GA • IA • IN • KY • MA • MD • MS • MT • NC • ND • NH • NJ • OH • OR • PA • RI • SD • TN • UT • VA • VT • WV	AK • CA • ID • LA • NV	AZ • NM • TX • WA • WI

But these debts can be negotiated. Patient advocate Lisa Berry Blackstock, in California, has had cases where she negotiated the debt down to 5 percent of what was being billed. We can't repeat it enough: each circumstance is different, the courts in your state may disregard the laws on the books, and state laws change, so do some homework or enlist a lawyer or a medical billing patient advocate to help you. ❖

The Bottom Line

CAN I AFFORD TO DIE?

When you look at the shockingly high cost of health care, it's easy to feel as though we're all already bankrupt. And even if you're not actively treating an illness, there are plenty of other ways to drain your bank account, including having to pony up for assisted living or home help. But there's hope: having read this chapter, you're already well ahead of the game. If you're saving for retirement, it's time to add end-of-life costs to that list.

DEALING WITH ILLNESS

This section addresses the period when death begins to move from abstraction to reality—a period of living with a condition or illness that can't or won't be cured, one that may stretch from days to years. We'll walk you through this, from the moment of receiving a diagnosis to the practical and emotional challenges that can shape your decisions for your treatment plan.

Doctors often use the phrase *goals of care* to describe your plan. But for our purposes, it's much bigger than whether or not you decide to take on that fourth round of chemo. You're going to have to make a lot of choices over the course of an illness, and you'll need a good foundation upon which to do so. This process isn't just about logistics; it's deeply personal.

I'm Sick

Getting the news; communicating
with doctors about your prognosis;
how to deal with the shock of it all

S ometimes it happens quickly. You're sitting in a tiny clinic room or lying in a hospital bed, and the doctor begins to speak. Maybe you get a call, and the floor drops from under you. More often it happens gradually, a series of inflections on your way to realizing the truth of what you're dealing with.

Moving from "healthy" to "sick" is a process. First comes a diagnosis; then, at some point, the news that it's not curable or the realization that you're not interested in trying to cure it anymore. There will be time to freak out, deflate, process, reorient, learn, and come up with a response. But today—the day you get that dose of hard news—is a moment all its own.

——

"It Felt Like a Bad Acid Trip"

I'VE SEEN SOME BEWILDERED EXPRESSIONS OVER THE YEARS: ALL manner of contortion; explosive tears; facades coming down or going up; surprising calmness or politeness; shades of pale yellow, khaki, green, and red in the faces of my patients and their families. Eyes darting about. Mental fuzz sets in: it's as though an emergency shutoff valve arrests the flow of information and allows only a small trickle of what's being said to get through.

Andrea, a petite blonde in her sixties, is on her third cancer diagnosis. Recently, we were sitting in the tiny exam room at the clinic, and she was thinking back on the moment she had received her first batch of bad news: "My world tilted, never to return to normal again," she said. "It felt like a bad acid trip, totally unreal. The second before I was fine, and then I wasn't. I had no context to understand what I was being told or how to deal with what I was hearing."

——

A State of Shock

A SKILLED CLINICIAN WILL STATE IMPORTANT INFORMATION MULTIPLE times and ask you to repeat what you've just heard to increase the odds that you've understood it. But even if your doctor does her part, your brain might twist things around to protect you from a truth it's not ready for.

Weird emotions and thoughts creep in, too. Maybe you start scanning your past for any and every way you could have brought this on yourself: cause, effect, *give me a reason*. It's an old human habit: find something to blame. Blame the environment. The stress of modern life. Your parents and their crummy genes. Maybe it was all that drinking and smoking. You could have eaten more broccoli and taken the stairs. Or maybe you were straight as a pin and did all the "right" things, and now you're wondering *why*?

Maybe there's a surprising sense of relief, something at last that explains why you've been feeling this way. Maybe you feel nothing—a void. It will take some time for your mind and emotions to catch up with your body.

——

Surviving Today

ONCE THE DOCTOR HAS DELIVERED THE NEWS, AT SOME POINT SHE'S going to get up and leave the room and go on to the next patient. Ideally, you will not feel forced to leave or do much of anything. You are in a vulnerable place, and you are going to want to jet-pack yourself anywhere but here. But now may be a perfect time to do nothing at all. If you're feeling wobbly or your mind is racing in circles, stay put and call someone to come pick you up, or ask the staff to make that call for you. Ask if there's a quiet place for you to sit and gather yourself. It's not an overstatement to call news like this traumatic, so treat yourself with all the care and safety that trauma requires.

Making rash decisions is one way we flee. But if you can help it, don't throw yourself into situations that you'll regret. First: feel, watch, listen. Try to slow your mind down. Here's some advice:

——

DO	DON'T
• Go somewhere comforting: to the park, the movies, home, wherever you feel safe and secure.	• Quit smoking or drinking. (Tomorrow, maybe, but don't take away your coping mechanisms today.)
• Call the people who will be supportive.	• Get a divorce or buy a house or a boat or a Lamborghini or a tiger.
• Indulge in whatever feels familiar and good: a pint of beer or a pint of ice cream or both.	• Post it on Twitter or Facebook. Not yet, anyway.
• It's fine to look at the internet if you need to know more about your illness, but curb that desire. You don't need to explore every angle tonight, and you're going to need a clear mind to wade through all the junk out there.	• Get hammered, drive 120 miles per hour, and get a DUI.
	• Commit to particular treatments, neither the conventional nor the far-out stuff. Not today.

day of diagnosis:

DOs

treat yourself

call someone

go to a park

DON'Ts

tweet

drive drunk

get a pet tiger

The urgency you feel to do something—anything—is a fight-or-flight reaction and a good cue to slow down. It's right and good to seek comfort, but not the kind you'll regret later.

Crying Wolf

THOSE OF YOU ALREADY LIVING WITH CHRONIC ILLNESS, SUCH AS heart failure or lung disease, may have heard many times that "this might be the end" only to find that after a brief hospital stay or a course of some treatment, you were back in action.

If you've been getting hard news with some regularity, it may have lost its punch. This is why it's best to neither clutch at these declarations nor ignore them. In general, throughout this odyssey, it helps to hold things lightly but with attentiveness. The danger of not taking a prognosis seriously is that you'll put off things that are important to you—telling your kids that you're proud of them, letting go of grievances, dealing with your will—and then, suddenly, it will be too late.

——

Diagnosis Unknown

SOME PEOPLE NEVER GET AN OFFICIAL DIAGNOSIS. THEY HAVE NOTHING to look up online; no support group; nothing specific on which to focus. This is a special torment all its own. We can grapple with just about anything, it seems, if we know what it is. A diagnosis offers a tidy bundle of information: how to treat it, whether it's curable, how long might you have to live, and confers a kind of validation for feeling the way you do.

Doctors should go down the list of all known things that could be causing your symptoms. Barring an answer, you might hear them conclude with the phrase "failure to thrive," which is another way of saying "your body is not doing well, but we don't know why." Or, if you're older than about 70, we might chalk up your difficulties to "old age."

For those of you in this situation, the way forward is much the same as for people with a diagnosis: be attuned to your body. With or without a diagnosis, you and your doctor should be tracking your body's *function* and doing so over time.

Look back over the past few weeks or months. Do you find it harder to walk? Have you been shorter of breath lately? Are you finding it harder to control your bladder or bowels? Have you been losing weight for no apparent reason? Any bouts of confusion? Getting out of bed less and less? Changes like these are what should inform the course of treatment. Perhaps the "treatment" is moving to a nursing home. Or hiring an aide. Maybe you simply treat the symptom, even if you can't know its underlying cause. No matter what, the goal is to support you and your body over time.

——

Why Doctors Don't Say the D-Word

AS YOUR DOCTOR IS EXPLAINING THE "HARD NEWS" TO YOU AND YOU'RE trying to focus enough to even understand the words she's saying, you may notice that there's no mention of that one very important word: death.

Left to their own devices, doctors too often avoid the D-word and fall back on euphemisms—whether from a desire to ease the blow to the patient or family, or a desire to ease it for themselves. As a doctor, I hear myself say, "Time is short." I say it even when I know it's not really helpful.

Why do we do this?

Many people harbor a kind of superstition: say it and it becomes real; don't say it and it won't. And very few people want to talk through the details of how disease comes to overwhelm a body—it's devastating for patients and their families and sad for doctors, too. Doctors often don't talk about death because they don't want to destroy hope. Hope is a powerful force: it wills us out of bed in the morning and helps us put up with the difficulties of treatment and of being a patient, of living in a world we don't totally understand and can't control.

As helpful a force as hope can be, false hope can do harm. Propping up improbable outcomes and using indirect language tend to make things worse for everyone involved. Communication can get so murky that patients often don't even realize that their illness is terminal. Phrases such as "We're going to beat this thing" can be confusing—beat the disease, beat the pain, beat the fear? Or "There's always something we can try"—to cure the illness, to ensure longer life? What?

It turns out that there's no evidence that being honest about a terminal condition destroys hope and plenty to suggest that it can bring patient and doctor closer.[1] In fact, openly and supportively discussing bad news most often winds up feeling like a relief to the patient. Most have a gut sense of the truth of their situation, and not talking about it can be its own burden. So the issue is not *whether* to discuss the truth but *how*. ❖

The Bottom Line

I'M SICK

Learning you have a life-limiting diagnosis is a radical moment. It will take time to wrap your head around this new reality. You've just been introduced to the thing that will bring about your death one day; don't expect to arrive at equanimity immediately. In fact, don't expect much at all from yourself right now. You're just at the beginning.

CHAPTER SIX

Taking Stock

Questions to ask yourself: What's my situation? What's important to me now?

I t's time to think about this new reality and figure out what your priorities are now. That said, it's rare that a treatment decision actually has to be made right away. More often, you'll have time to mull things over. Take it. Look inside and around yourself. Think about where you are, where you'd like to go, and what you'll need to get there.

——

Feel and Think

I OFTEN SEE PEOPLE IN THIS MOMENT WANTING TO HAND THEMSELVES over to a doctor who they think knows more than they do. The desperation is understandable, but be careful to not give yourself away too easily. Even if you want the doctor to make decisions for you, that doctor needs to understand what is most important to you so that she can tailor treatments and treat you with respect.

When first meeting a patient and their circle, I've learned to ask a range of questions that help me see past the disease and understand the patient as a person; questions that get at their history, their beliefs; what makes them tick and what makes them bristle. Only with a more intimate understanding are we able to support patients in ways that will actually help.

Consider the following questions to get a sense of yourself now. This is the first step on the way to arriving at a personalized plan for how to proceed. These questions are best answered in dialogue and at multiple junctures over time. Use them as conversation starters with your family and your doctor:

1. **What have I been doing with myself?**
   When we're stressed, we tend to revert to base, familiar territory. Pay attention to how you're coping now, and consider

how you've coped with difficult things in the past; you are looking for clues on how you might want to move forward this time. Keep an eye out for both the positive (constructive) and the negative (destructive). Have you been drinking a lot? Getting happily engrossed at work? Knowing this will help your doctor determine the parts of your routine that should be nurtured and protected and what should be dialed down.

2. **What do I find myself thinking about most?**

Often the worries that surface tip you off to what needs attention. Maybe you can't stop thinking about what will happen to your spouse's health after you're gone, or how you're going to get the kids to school on chemo days. A good next step might be to get your partner a physical, or work on the carpool schedule. Or maybe you keep thinking about visiting someone or someplace, so you might make that trip a priority. Whatever it is, your mind is trying to tell you something. Start somewhere. The idea here is to ease your burden wherever possible to free up time and space.

3. **When and where during my day do I feel the best? When and where do I feel the worst?**

What are your daily patterns? What people, places, activities, and things might you avoid, and which might you seek?

4. **How has my mood been?**

If you're angry, where is the anger directed? If you're sad, how are you handling it? If you're strangely giddy, you either have everything in perspective, or you may be in denial. Your mood offers you and your loved ones cues about what needs attention and how to respond. Asking yourself this question is an invitation to let it out.

5. **What am I most proud of? What do I like about myself?**

What are your strengths or interests? Identifying those will help you make decisions absent fear or nihilism. Look for aspirations: Who do I want to become? Is there a trait or a habit I'd like to change? There is always room for growth.

6. **Have I ever lost someone close to me?**

If the answer is yes, thinking about how they made their way to death may help you consider your own choices. Do you have old grief or fears from that experience? The past will color your choices, so take a moment to sift through whatever thoughts and feelings bubble up. If the answer is no, then you might expect to have more questions for your doctor, or to not know what to ask in the first place. It's a good idea to make that confusion clear.

— —

What's Your Situation?

WHAT STAGE IS YOUR DIAGNOSIS, AND WHAT EXACTLY DOES A "STAGE" mean anyway? And how about the rest of your life: Where do things stand with your overall health, home life, finances, and social life? When it comes to treatments, what are the options? This is a time for reflecting out loud with people close to you; with all the consequential decisions to be made, it's all the more important that you're on the same page with your circle, including your clinical team.

1. **What do I understand about my diagnosis? What do I know about treatment options?**

This is generally one of the first questions any trained palliative care clinician asks when meeting a patient. Asking and answering this question is a great way for you and your doctor to get aligned.

2. **Am I having any symptoms?**

   Pain, nausea, trouble sleeping, constipation? Feeling "off" in some way? If so, these are important calls to action for your clinicians. If you're feeling lousy it's very difficult to make the best decisions for yourself. To whatever degree possible, getting on top of your symptoms should be an early priority.

3. **Have I been able to talk to anyone about this, and if so, how did that person respond?**

   What's your social situation? Do you have people you can turn to? How much help do you have around you, and how willing are you to reach out and use it?

4. **Do I feel I can talk openly with my doctor?**

   If you can't trust your doctor, it's time to either work on that relationship or find a new one. You may have to hit the yellow pages to find a new physician or ask friends whom they recommend; or ask the clinic staff if there are other physicians in the practice you might switch to. The doctor-patient partnership is a critical one, and your previous doctor should only be supportive of you finding the best fit.

5. **Where am I living?**

   Are your bare necessities covered? Do you have a roof over your head, and can you rely on that roof for the foreseeable future? Is your home easily accessible to emergency care and others coming to you? To whatever degree possible you'll want to feel safe and secure, and you'll want to have access to care and support.

6. **What are my assets? What insurance do I have?**

   What do you have to work with? Check your assumptions about the costs of care. Being proactive and thinking about your finances early can avoid serious problems down the road. Whatever you have, start there.

Answering these questions will help you get a handle on your situation and where you want to make changes. And if you're feeling as though you don't know enough or have enough, try not to worry—everyone feels that way, no matter what they have or know. It's always about making the most of what you have.

———

What's Most Important to You Now?

THIS ONE QUESTION SHOULD BE THE CENTRAL GUIDING FORCE IN YOUR care plan. It might seem like an easy one at first, but it can be hard to answer, not unlike "Who are you?" Here's a list of questions that will inform your answer:

1. Which of these is my first priority: amount of time left, or quality of time left?
2. How much time do I want to spend with family and friends?
3. How much faith do I have in the health care system? In my doctor?
4. Do I have dependents, and what do they need from me?
5. What are the financial costs of possible treatments versus no treatment?
6. Where do I want to be when I die?
7. What are my opinions regarding life-support measures?
8. Do I want to make health care decisions, such as treatment choices and whether or not I want life support, or do I want others to make them on my behalf?
9. What does my faith or belief system dictate, and how important is that to me?
10. What type of funeral or memorial do I want?
11. How do I want my remains handled?

It's possible that what's important to you now has nothing to do with treatment. A hospice nurse told me a story about how her father, a lifelong academic, just wanted to stay at home and be comfortable enough to watch Red Sox games. She was surprised about this choice given how complicated and cerebral he ordinarily was. It brought her such relief to know her father was getting what he actually wanted. Keep in mind that your treatment decisions will affect everything on your list above because of the demands on your time the treatments invariably make.

I had two conversations about goals of care with Randy, a 27-year-old with metastatic mesothelioma. He was young and otherwise healthy, so we worked on his fatigue and pain regimen and then talked each other into gearing up for a long treatment course. Randy received an initial dose of chemotherapy just a few days after his first dose of brain radiation—the first attempts to outmaneuver his cancer. Even though his cancer was terminal at the time it was discovered, there was just enough of a chance that these treatments could slow the disease, push it back. That was his first goal. And it wasn't hard for everyone to adopt an aggressive stance, no matter what the chances.

A few days later, Randy was back in the hospital, utterly exhausted. Just the one dose had leveled him. Coming to terms with that reality and looking for a new way forward, I asked Randy what gave him pride. *At your best—your favorite—who are you, Randy?* He answered that he wanted everyone to know how much he loved them. He wanted his death to prove his love of life. Now we had a compass by which to make treatment decisions.

Randy decided to forgo more chemo or any other intensive intervention. He signed up for hospice and moved from his cramped apartment to a hospice house. There he was surrounded

simple pleasures

baseball

music

a bit
of nature

puzzles

a good book

something sweet

You may think the end of life is a time for grandiose moments, but the things that make us love life are often very small.

by family and friends and was comfortable enough to feel and show his love—to soak it all up—in his final days.

Here's a simple exercise that can help you get a bird's-eye view of your care goals:

1. Draw three lines down the center of a piece of paper.
2. At the top of the first column write: MY SITUATION.
   Elaborate on your understanding of your condition and of the resources available to you.
3. At the top of the second write MY GOALS.
   Write what you want to do (this can be anything)—live as long as possible, die comfortably at home, travel, reconcile with loved ones.
4. At the top of the third write TRADE-OFFS.
   What are the trade-offs you are willing to make and not willing to make? For example, are you willing to have a surgery that would take away your ability to swallow food if it extended your life? And does it change your thinking if that trade-off comes with a feeding tube? Or how about treatments that require you be in a hospital instead of home for much of your remaining time?
5. At the top of the fourth write NEXT STEPS.
   What's next for you? A trip? Treatment? Making home safe to stay put? Electing hospice?

MY SITUATION	MY GOALS	TRADE-OFFS	NEXT STEPS

——

When to Reconsider Your Goals of Care

IT'S A GOOD IDEA TO REEXAMINE WHAT'S IMPORTANT TO YOU ANYTIME you find yourself at a crossroads, or whenever something significant has changed, such as:

- You need to decide whether to pursue a particular treatment
- Your disease has progressed or shifted and you've been told your illness is at a new stage
- **The details of your life have changed.** You have lost or are changing homes; have become newly insured or uninsured; have had a child
- **Your ability to care for yourself has changed.** You've become dependent on others for basic acts like grooming or hygiene or getting out of bed; or others in the home have become dependent on you because they're sick or disabled
- **Your perspective has shifted in a significant way.** Religion has entered or left your life; or you've had an epiphany about what really matters to you in the end ❖

Now What?

Prognosis and the flow of information;
major chronic diseases and their patterns;
working with your doctor; navigating
treatment decisions; saying no

N ow that you're clearer about where you stand, it's easier to make choices. This is the point in the process where your goals of care turn into action. There will be crossroads all along the way, some of the most significant of which have to do with decisions about medical treatments, including whether you want to start or stop them. Making these kinds of decisions is key to living the rest of your life on your own terms.

——

How Much Time Do I Have?

AS YOU HEAD INTO THIS NEW FUTURE AND ALL THE DECISIONS IT WILL ask you to make, you might be curious about your prognosis. A *prognosis* is a prediction of the likely course of a disease or ailment. And naturally, we all want our doctors to ease us into the future with certainty: *How much time do I have? What will life be like along the way?* But no matter how well trained and kind and experienced your doctor is, definitive answers to these questions are just not possible. Life's more interesting and variable than that sort of certainty will allow. At this point in the advancement of medical science, the best anyone can do is offer an educated guess, based on pooled experiences and clinical judgment. Here are some things to keep in mind when discussing prognosis:

TIP
Applying population trends to you, the individual, is tricky. None of us is the average person all the time, and all of us beat the odds sometimes.

- **Though doctors occasionally *underestimate* how long a patient has to live, they are more likely to *overestimate* it.** This has been studied widely over the years. The longer a doctor has known a patient and the more often she sees that patient, the more overly optimistic her guess is likely to be. It's as though the depth of the relationship—affection—puts a rosy hue on the doctor's thinking.

- **A prognosis is more accurate when it's based not just on tests but also on your *functional status* (what you can and can't do in daily life).** That is, it takes into account how much time you're up and out of bed, and how effectively you're able to tend to the basic activities of getting through the day like using the toilet, eating, and dressing. How much you are eating and how often can also say a lot about your condition. These variables need to be taken together in the context of your particular disease and your particular life.

- **Prognostication is more reliable when functional changes are noted over the course of several doctor visits rather than gauged from a single point in time.** You're looking for changes to whatever has been your baseline. For example, if three months ago you were jogging five miles per day and now you're in bed most of the time, that's significant and different from someone who was previously chronically immobile.

- **Doctors aren't infallible in their prognoses.** But it's reasonable to expect that your doctor knows what's knowable, has offered the most up-to-date treatment, and will address any discomfort that may arise over time. Having so many necessary unknowns to contend with, you can see why a good doctor is a companion and advocate, not merely a technician. This is a very achievable bar; your relationship with your doctor is a great place to focus your attention and self-advocacy.

- **No one's going to get too specific, or at least they shouldn't.** In hospice and palliative care we are trained to not tempt fate by trying (pretending) to be too exact. You might hear your team use spans instead of something definitive, such as *hours to days*, *days to weeks*, or *weeks to months*.

——

How Much Do You Want to Know?

SOME PATIENTS WANT TO KNOW EVERYTHING THERE IS TO KNOW about the state of their illness, and some people want to know nothing at all. And for others, the bar is somewhere in between.

Stephen Scheier lost his wife, Amy Doppelt, to cancer in 2010. I was one of her doctors in the final days. Amy was actively dying and asleep most of the time our team was involved, so, as happens sometimes in palliative care and hospice work, I got much closer to the spouse than to the patient.

Steve came to realize how fortunate he had been to have Amy control what she learned about her condition and when. It wasn't more or less *information* that she had wished for but rather a hand on the spigot, and Amy knew how to take control by force of personality and with plain, clear communication. She understood that information could help her but could also hurt if she wasn't yet ready to hear it. Beyond the basic facts of her diagnosis and treatment options, she let Steve and the team know when she was ready to hear more. Research backs this up: unless you're prepared to address the situation head-on, knowing details about your prognosis can easily make you feel worse and *less* capable of making decisions.[1] The very same news can one day be paralyzing and the next, illuminating.

In the year after she died, Steve came up with a basic tool that he hoped would one day help others summon the deftness Amy had possessed. Both patients and clinical staff stand to benefit.

——

OPTING IN/OPTING OUT: A CONTRACT WITH YOUR CARE TEAM

Here's Steve's script. Feel free to use it to communicate with your doctors. You might even print it out and take it with you to your next appointment.

I wish to participate in my care and to always operate from a position of "informed consent." That being true, I also understand that information on prognosis can be difficult for health care practitioners to offer and for patients to accept. In order to facilitate communication with my physician I choose one of the following four options:

☐ **OPTION 1**

Tell me everything. I want to know about my likely prognosis including the recommended course of treatment, my life expectancy, and the challenges inherent in the treatment option I decide to pursue.

Be direct and kind with me. Spare me no important details. I want to know what your experience and training can tell me about what is ahead of me.

☐ **OPTION 2**

Do not presume that I want to hear about my prognosis. When various decisions need to be made over the course of my treatment, please ask me then whether I want to hear prognostic information.

☐ **OPTION 3**

I want to participate in my treatment, but I do not want to receive any information on my prognosis.

☐ **OPTION 4**

I don't wish to know any information about my prognosis, but I authorize you to speak with _____ about my case and answer any questions that person may have about my likely prognosis and treatment.

Once you've made it clear to your doctor how much you wish to know, don't let him off the hook until you're all agreed. This is a moment where you or your family may need to be assertive.

———

Pattern Recognition

GERIATRIC AND PALLIATIVE CARE DOCTORS USE THE PHRASE *trajectories of decline* to describe patterns that illnesses tend to follow over time. Yes, the phrase sounds dire, but it might be helpful for you to understand that there are patterns to how our bodies respond to illness and age, and these trajectories have been observed by many doctors in many patients over time. Hold these patterns loosely; they are generalizations and refer to the functions of our bodies, not necessarily how we might feel or think along the way. They are useful in helping you predict how this illness is likely to play out, in broad, physical strokes, which in turn will help you make decisions along the way.

These patterns refer solely to your physical functioning. They have nothing to do with your spiritual or emotional growth; those can go in all kinds of directions.

CANCER

The first pattern is typical of terminal cancer diagnoses. Details will depend on the cancer type and how early it's caught, but today's treatments are allowing people to go about their daily business and manage even incurable metastatic cancer over long periods of time—sometimes many years—before a threshold is reached where the disease accelerates and your body's ability to function in the face of the illness quickly declines. When this time comes, there is practically nothing to do to control the disease, though much to do to support you through to the end.

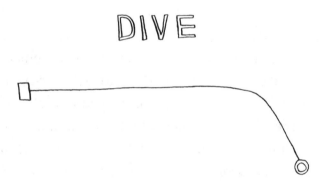

HEART, LUNG, LIVER, OR KIDNEY DISEASE

The second pattern is typical of diseases of the heart, lung, liver, or kidney. It follows a windier course and often lands you in and out of the hospital for frequent tune-ups, where you can cycle from death's door to alive and well and then back again. Over time, the increasingly tired body's ability to bounce back begins to wane as the disease grows more intense.

ROLLERCOASTER

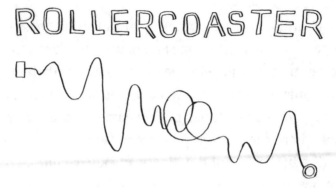

ALZHEIMER'S DISEASE, DEMENTIA, AND OTHER NEURODEGENERATIVE DISEASES

The third pattern is more typical of progressive neurological illnesses such as Alzheimer's and other kinds of dementia. This path is marked by slow decline in cognitive and bodily function. Energy steadily fades. You can expect a similarly slow arc of decline with the frailty of old age (dying of "natural causes"). It's often something simple that brings death: breaking a hip in a fall or aspiration pneumonia from muscles too weak to swallow. In other words, something that seems relatively small becomes the last straw.

FADE

How Much Treatment?

—
TIP
In practice, most treatment decisions are made based on what the doctor believes[2], not the patient, so you do need to assert yourself.

—
TIP
Before pursuing any treatment, be sure to ask your doctor what they mean by "treatable." Expectation management is key.

THIS IS OFTEN *THE* QUESTION, SINCE TREATMENTS, with their side effects, logistics, and particular combos of ups and downs will have so much to do with your day-to-day life. This is why treatment options need to be checked against your own priorities, which will most certainly shift over time. Checking in with yourself and your team, again and again, is how you'll arrive at the "right" answer for you.

Another thing to keep in mind is that your functional status (discussed early in this chapter) is key to gauging what treatments your body can withstand, just as it is to sussing your prognosis. Your functional status will help reveal the line between choices that are daring and futile, wise and foolhardy. People tend to rely too much on what tests tell them rather than paying attention to what their bodies are trying to say. Ignoring this is precisely what leads to "overtreatment"—that is, treatment that hurts more than it helps. This is one reason why tending to your symptoms along the way is crucial. Feeling as well as possible will keep you as active as possible, which in turn will allow you more treatment options. And feeling good plain feels good.

In general, for any illness, there's a range of treatment. Most people experience the middle of this range, electing to have some treatments and saying no to others. Identifying the two extremes can help you get your bearings: on one end is no treatment (which

you DON'T have to pick a side

Do your best to get the divisive language people use out of your head. Making decisions is hard enough without all of that outside noise. You are the boss of you.

can mean stopping treatment or never starting it at all); on the other is experimental treatment (which can mean "I'll try anything").

——

Stopping (or Never Starting) Treatment

FIRST OF ALL, GET THE "GIVING UP" LANGUAGE OUT OF YOUR HEAD. Saying no to treatment just means choosing a different path. Yielding to what will be—and what is out of your or anyone's control—is different from giving up.

Edith and Tim were both in their eighties and had been dating for some years. Their days unfolded in unison; they lived down the hall from each other in an assisted living facility, regularly attended church together, and were diagnosed with the same serious heart problem at about the same time.

Edith responded to her diagnosis by becoming more social. She declined the surgery that was offered her, aware of its risks, especially at her age, and opted instead to spend more time celebrating life with friends and family. Her pastor, Reverend Luke Jernagan, asked her during one visit how she kept such a brilliant affect. She smiled and said, "Because I know I'm in the Lord's hands." Her faith was freeing; it filled her life with trust and goodwill.

Her boyfriend, Tim, went a different way. To him, the diagnosis did not compute. He'd been a good man to others, went to church, worked hard, and prayed. So the way Tim saw it, why was God punishing him? He chose to have the surgery but expected a certain result for his troubles, and more treatment brought more expectation. He felt owed. When he didn't get the results he expected, he became angry and surly. Reverend Luke recalled the different scenes at the place where they lived. Instead of laughter and song coming from Tim's room as it had from Edith's, it was a tearful nurse's aide, having just been berated for nothing. Tim was miserable where Edith was contented. Edith and Tim died about the same time, but with wholly different experiences.

If you're unsure, and getting lots of advice to keep going when you don't want to, pause and listen for a moment. Maybe you're overwhelmed and just need a break. The truth could be that you're in a lot of pain or racked by some other symptom, like nausea or constipation or fatigue. Maybe what you really need is relief from the *burden* that treatment is putting on your family, a burden that might be lightened by a frank conversation between you and your family and doctor. That conversation could lead to more help, so check in with yourself.

Our medical system is wired to extend life—as defined by the presence of a heartbeat—whenever possible, no matter how uncomfortable the means. You may have already felt this from the way your doctor talks to you, presuming you'll want that next procedure no matter how slim the benefit or how great the toll.

The medical system isn't in the business of telling you what sort of life is worth living; that's your call. Just because a doctor or family member thinks you should do something doesn't mean you must. Similarly, just because you *can* do something doesn't mean you *should*.

I've met countless patients who, despite their own wishes to die comfortably at home or go travel the country or do anything

FAST FACT
Although you can't demand a particular medical treatment, it is always your legal right to say no to a treatment or to delay its start until you're sure it's what you want.

but sit in a hospital, could not get themselves to choose the care that would best serve this wish simply because it smacked of quitting. In truth, saying no to treatment can be a courageous act that frees up time and energy for all sorts of meaningful moments that might otherwise be spent distracted in a chemotherapy room, emergency department, or intensive care unit.

———

Experimental Treatment

MELBA, 61, HAD BEEN LIVING THE RELAXING RETIREMENT BEACH LIFE in California with her husband, Ian, when she was diagnosed with metastatic pancreatic cancer. The prognosis was stark: maybe six months, no matter what treatment course she chose. But she resolved to try anything and everything in case someone somewhere had found a cure or treatment that would give her more time to spend with her husband and children. She traveled to Houston for infusions of a trial drug; she flew to Mexico to meet a doctor who promised miracle results with coffee enemas; she spent precious hours in the air traveling around the country hunting for sunnier third and fourth opinions, or for someone who would at least tell her something she wanted to hear. All the while, her body was falling apart.

Ian and her kids were exhausted by the efforts. They missed their wife and mother, and begged her to take a new tack. They pushed for hospice care, but she saw that as a sure death sentence and would not hear of it. Her can-do-it-ness and optimism morphed into frenzied distraction. Melba's final months were spent going in circles in doctor's rooms and healer's clinics when she could have been at home enjoying her husband and children, *which was what she said she cared about most.* She spent her last week of life in the hospital, delirious from uncontrolled pain, with a family who hadn't yet forgiven her for the choices she'd made.

When you've tried the initial recommended treatments and your illness is not responding to them, you may find yourself becoming increasingly willing to try anything. The list of possible drugs and therapies is practically endless and getting longer as medical science advances, making it only harder to know when enough is enough. And as you go down the list, the courses of action tend to be more aggressive, less certain, and more fraught with side effects. At the end of this list comes the experimental stuff. It's important to remember that clinical trials and other experimental treatments are just that—*experimental*, and geared more for research scientists than for you, so they can learn from your experience.

Even if these new treatments have gone to market and are no longer considered experimental your doctor won't have loads of experience with them, making it harder to know what to expect from the treatment, and harder to interpret what effect it's having on you.

Some of you will want to contribute to advancing science and that's a perfectly good reason to keep trying the next thing. Sometimes people need to cross the line to find the line. I've worked with many patients who, after all sorts of debate about what *could* happen, just have to try that next treatment and see for themselves. If it isn't serving them well, they'll stop. This isn't the path for everyone, and indeed it may be grueling and even risky for an already weakened body. But for some patients, trying every option gives

TIP
Bear in mind that going for more aggressive treatments often means more time in the hospital. A strong desire to stay out of the hospital, or to die at home, is plenty good enough reason to say no thanks.

them the confidence they're looking for: knowing they pushed it as far as they could.

Still, if your doctor knows experimental treatment wouldn't help you and may hurt you, she has an ethical obligation to *not* offer it. Given the fact that doctors generally wait *too* long to draw this line themselves, and given that overtreatment is the norm, if she's saying "no more," take it seriously.

——

Ambivalence Is Normal

ARE YOU AMBIVALENT ABOUT WHETHER OR NOT TO CONTINUE treatment? When was the last time you felt 100 percent about anything? Ambivalence is not wishy-washy or weak—it's rational and normal.

When you take into account the ambiguous efficacy of various treatment options and all the trade-offs you need to consider, it's almost impossible to be certain you're making the right choice. Talk it out with people you trust. Sleeping on a decision is one of the great clichés that works, even if you think you're sure. And beyond reasoning through the facts and trade-offs, pay attention to your intuition; it's a powerful tool to pull you through.

——

The Trouble with Momentum

MOMENTUM CAN BE A USEFUL FORCE, OR IT CAN BE HAZARDOUS. Getting into a groove can help you move through life's challenges, but take care to pause once in a while. Wheels are set into motion with every treatment decision you make and, when it comes to health care, these wheels can be big and heavy and take on a momentum of their own. One treatment slyly begets another and then another. With your head down, likely exhausted but plowing ahead, you may not notice when you've passed the point of no return.

The signs of death's approach can prove too subtle when you and your team are consumed with the minutiae of managing the treatment protocol and getting through another day. (Maybe tomorrow, you think, will be the day your hard work pays off and the treatment finally starts to work and you get to feel better.) This commitment can help you marshal the energy you need to deal with treatment, but it's also possible that you'll look up and find you've chewed through the time you have left. One of the hardest transitions is moving from an aggressive, disease-fighting mode to one where comfort becomes the priority, as is the case entering hospice. It can be hard to change gears, to know when to downshift, so often we don't.

If this is what you want—treating the disease until the very end of your life—*that's absolutely fine*, go for it! You have our support and should count on the skills and services of the system to help you do so. Just know that stopping a course of treatment can feel harder than not starting it in the first place.

One way patients and their families and physicians sometimes handle this pressure to escalate care is to decide together not to. That is the language physicians use: *no escalation of care*. These words draw a line in the sand, saying we're going to keep on this current track and give it all we have, but will stop before sliding into that next treatment or transfer to the ICU. The line could be no more trips to the hospital, or no more intravenous therapy, or no more invasive treatments. Be sure to discuss the idea with your doctor. Of course you and your team can always revisit where you set that line, but in drawing it you've protected yourself from unconsciously sliding down a chute you wanted to avoid.

——

Dealing with Doctors

AS DEATH COMES INTO VIEW AND MEDICAL OPTIONS BECOME FEWER and less effective, the conventional notion of *expertise* shifts. It's no longer the sole domain of the world-famous specialist or treatment center. Experts may know more about your illness, but you know best who you are and how you want to live until you die. This is a relationship, not a chain of command with you playing the subordinate, so neither of you is off the hook.

——

What Doctors Wish You Knew

WHAT IS REASONABLE TO EXPECT FROM YOUR DOCTOR? IT MIGHT HELP you to have some sense of where your doctor is coming from. Here are a few insider tips to optimize the relationship:

- **A primary care doctor is invaluable.** This could be an internist, a family practice doctor or nurse practitioner, or a geriatrician. They aren't easy to find these days, we know. In a better system, primary care clinicians would be more highly valued and every patient would have one. But bouncing between specialists, without the glue of primary care, means there's little sense of continuity and more cracks to fall through. And that means you might not get all that you need to be as well as possible.
- **Doctors have no idea who they are supposed to talk to.** There

may be many people in the room, including family, friends, and well-wishers, and your doctor doesn't know any of them. Who do you want to include in the communication loop and who do you *not*?

- **The internet is wrong (much of the time).** Information is not fact-checked and is presented or viewed out of context, which can send you down energy-sucking or downright dangerous alleys. A fruitful way to use the internet is for educating yourself broadly, to prompt questions for further discussion with your doctor.

- **Clinicians rely on their colleagues.** There's a whole team keeping the total picture of you in view, so one person may not know every detail about your condition, nor will there be only one person on the team with whom you communicate. Many patients with burning questions wait far too long to hear back from their doctor when the question could be more readily and maybe more thoroughly answered by their nurse or another team member.

- **The health care system is messy and unintuitive.** Doctors cringe at it too. When it comes to the system's shortcomings, try not to confuse your doctor with the system in which he or she is laboring, if only so you know where to place your frustration.

- **Clinicians get tired.** They are people—mortals like you. They know you have great expectations and they want to meet them, but they are constrained by myriad institutional issues and by responsibilities that you don't see, to say nothing of the limitations set by the laws of nature. No matter how exasperated or exhausted they become, they really do care.

———

What Doctors Wish You Would Ask

YOUR DOCTOR WANTS YOU TO GET WHAT YOU NEED, SO TELL HER what that is. She needs to know what's not making sense to you, so ask questions. You should be able to discuss almost anything with your doctor, and the good ones wish you would. Take the lead. Here are some questions to ask:

1. What is this treatment meant to do? Is it going to cure me? Make me live longer? Make me feel better?
2. What side effects can I expect from this treatment? How long will they last? What can be done about them?
3. What does "success" look like for this treatment? Is there any risk to trying it? Can I stop it once I've started?
4. How long until I know if the treatment is working?
5. What are the alternatives? What happens if I don't do this?
6. Should I consider hospice? If not now, when? Would you be surprised if I died from this illness within a year? If your answer is "no," should we rethink hospice soon?

I sometimes get the feeling that patients are trying to hide parts of themselves from me—what they're feeling and what they're worried about. This could be because I haven't earned their trust, but sometimes it's because they are hoping to not disappoint me. Imagine that: patients protecting the person who is there to protect them. But hiding your true needs from your doctor only makes it harder for you to get the doctor's help.

——

What Patients Wish Their Doctors Knew

MOST PATIENTS WANT THEIR DOCTORS TO KNOW THAT THEY HAVE complex feelings and busy lives, and not endless amounts of time. Patients may have different goals from what the doctor presumes. They may have different beliefs or come from a culture with expectations and treatments different from what Western medical science dictates. They want their clinicians to know what is knowable and to be honest about what is not; to be open and respectful of other ways of thinking; to use straightforward language; to acknowledge and address emotion; and to help support their families, too. This is what data and experience say. What do you wish your doctor knew? Tell her—the sooner, the better. ❖

The Bottom Line

NOW WHAT?

Illness will affect you. Treatment will affect you. Everyone has some control, but no one—not even that crackerjack medical team—has *total* control. So deciding what to pursue and what to forgo should be an ongoing conversation among you, your people, and your clinical team. Your job is to consider the trade-offs when there's a choice to be had and to do your best to accept that there's no certainty of anything.

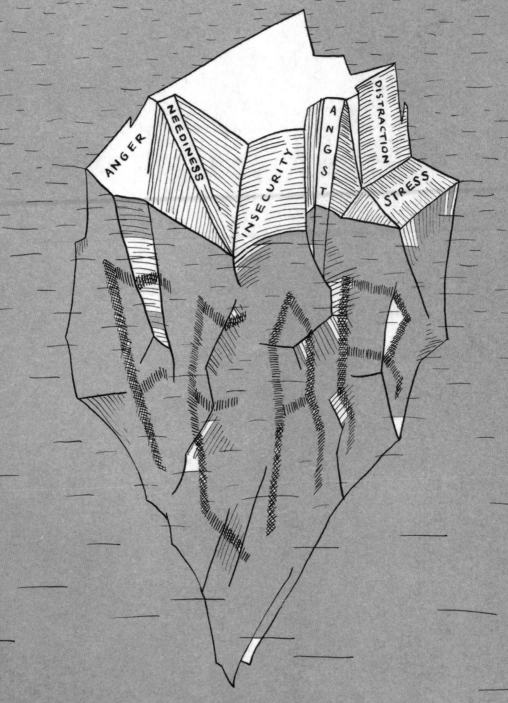

the ICEBERG of fear

Coping

Dread and other complex emotions;
coping techniques; thirteen
constructive approaches to try

"I'm not afraid of death, I just don't want to be there when it happens."

—Woody Allen

W hen you think about the end of your life, are you afraid? Are you sad? Curious? Confused? Maybe you're numb or quickly distracted. You may try to talk yourself out of your feelings, as though the problem is merely an attitude issue; you may get down on yourself for feeling the way you do. Whatever you're feeling, there's no shame in any of it. These feelings, at root, are both protective and instructive; they will tell you a lot about yourself, about what's important to you, where you are vulnerable, and what needs attention. Death is a big deal, and the body knows it.

Our hope is to help you to find a way to be engaged—interested, even—in how you feel about death, rather than cowed or too terrified to face it. If you can see your feelings for what they are, you are less likely to be whipped around by them (and less likely to whip others around with them). Engaged, you're more likely to feel safe and make better decisions for yourself.

——

Making Sense of Emotions

EVERY EMOTION, EVERY THOUGHT UNDER THE SUN IS IN PLAY WHEN it comes to contemplating mortality. But among them, **three tend to crop up consistently: fear, denial, and grief.** Each of those words really encompasses a cluster of emotions, with lots of overlap among them.

——

Fear

FEAR OF DEATH (MORTAL FEAR) IS THE MOTHER OF ALL FEARS. Psychologists and philosophers call it angst or dread; clinicians are beginning to adopt the catch-all phrase "existential distress." Whatever you call it, mortal fear is in a class by itself because its source is inside us. It's not easy to pin down and deal with in the same way you would a phobia of some external threat like snakes or heights. Unlike snakes or heights, the object of this fear is inevitable: death is a little time bomb planted inside us, but none of us gets to know when, precisely, it will go off. As the Buddhist teacher Pema Chödrön puts it, "Fear is a natural response to coming closer to the truth."

——

Understanding Fear

THERE'S DYING, AND THEN THERE'S DEATH. THE FIRST IS MORE straightforward. Fear of dying comes mostly from what we imagine dying will be like. The good news here is that a frightened imagination is almost always overly pessimistic. From what I've seen at many bedsides, and heard from countless others, dying is very often peaceful. (Harder for those witnessing it than for the person actually doing it.)

FAST FACT
Dying isn't always uncomfortable, and when it is there's much that can be done to make it much less so.

Then there's the fear of death, of being dead. Seneca, the revered Roman thinker, wrote two thousand years ago, "We mortals are . . . lighted and extinguished; the period of suffering comes in between, but on either side there is deep peace . . . we go astray in thinking that death only follows, when in reality it has both preceded us and will in turn follow us."[1] All of the major religions have some tradition and language to remind us of life's transience. "Remember that you are dust and to dust you shall return," goes the liturgy on Ash Wednesday, the holy day of repentance in the Christian tradition. By making death a homecoming, philosophers and prophets have attempted to help us keep our lives in perspective and to remind us that our decisions matter *because* our time is not unlimited.

Coming to terms with death means coming to terms with time—and not just with the fact that the future is suddenly constricted. Yes, there is that fear of missing out, but there is also a fear associated with looking back in time. That fear has a name: *regret*, and what a gnarly beast it can be. You begin to realize the impossibility of correcting the past, just as you realize you won't get to achieve every one of your dreams. One way or another, mortal fear becomes connected to the fear of *not living your life while you have it*. This gets at both the problem and the solution: all our new limitations, both forward and backward, can bring into focus what is still possible.

——

"Treating" Fear

MODERN MEDICINE TENDS TO TREAT FEAR AS DEPRESSION OR "generalized anxiety disorder" and send you home with a prescription for Prozac or Valium. But mortal fear is different: it has nothing to do with mental illness and is a vital force that shouldn't simply be snuffed out. There is important stuff wrapped up in this fear; namely, the search for meaning, one of the greatest compulsions of all. Who am I? What am I doing? Is there a higher purpose to all this? Does my life mean anything? Why me? These kinds of big questions, and the feelings lurking around them, signal a time for investigation. Instead of running away, we'd encourage you to get closer.

——

Denial

IT GETS A BAD RAP, BUT DENIAL IS A POWERFUL FORCE. AT ITS CORE, denial is actually a useful coping mechanism. It would be hard to get out of bed if we had to keep all truth—life's fragility and death's proximity—in view at all times. Left unchecked, however, denial gets in the way, barricading you from the full spectrum of your own life.

From the moment Nancy's husband, Lance, was told he had a brain tumor, he only spoke of getting rid of it. Outwardly, he could not accept any other possibility. Nancy knew how bad things were, but supported his stance, making Lance agree to not google his diagnosis (stage 4 glioblastoma, uniformly fatal). She'd shut herself in the bathroom to cry so he and their kids wouldn't see. Lance worked full-time as the president of his company, took treatment after treatment, and looked after their two kids with every outward intention of surviving. They lived with his refusal to talk about death for a year and a half, and Nancy says it was exactly the right path for both of them.

Though Lance refused to discuss the possibility of death, inwardly he was dealing with it on his own terms. He completed an advance directive; he worked hard to ensure his family's financial well-being; and, after some resistance, he allowed hospice into his home.

Denial is the word Nancy uses to describe Lance's approach, but only because a better word isn't available. After Lance's

For Caregivers

A note of caution: you can do harm by attempting to break through someone's walls in one go. In palliative care, when we see someone "in denial," we don't rush to dismantle it; instead, we work with it by teasing out where it's helping and where it's hurting. Asking reflective questions softens the edges of denial and lets reality enter bit by bit. When your loved one describes to you their position on this or that, you might ask: "Why do you think that?" Or, pushing further, "Do you think there's anything we're missing here?" Or, "Is that way of seeing things serving you well?" That last question gets at the central gist–is the attitude or stance actually helping them? Or is it getting in the way? The judgment is theirs to make, but you, too, will get a feel. Eventually the bigger truth of someone's situation will reveal itself in such a way that the person can take it in without breaking under its weight. And patients, sometimes you'll be the ones concerned about denial on the part of your loved ones; the advice goes both ways.

death, Nancy learned that he'd written of his coming demise eight months before to a friend who also had brain cancer. So, it's complicated.

——

Anticipatory Grief

GRIEF MAY START EARLIER THAN YOU THINK. IT'S NOT UNCOMMON for it to well up at the time of a diagnosis or when energy first begins to flag. We grieve for the losses we now realize are coming as well as for the loss of innocence that happens at the moment illness is diagnosed. We grieve in anticipation of death.

And we grieve all sorts of losses, not just the loss of life: loss of freedom, independence, roles, things, ideas, relationships, and bodily functions. Dealing with any diagnosis or ongoing illness or disability, in ourselves or those we care about, means facing a cascade of losses.

In hospice work, and in the hospital, too, you get used to unprocessed grief popping up all over the place and in many forms. We see it in families finding fault with things over which they have some control instead of directing their anger at the disease (which is less satisfying to complain about), or requesting more voices in the mix until they hear the news they seek. We see it in patients (or coworkers) yelling at staff for no particular reason. We see it in our own weird mood swings. All these behaviors, and more, are grief's proxies.

Grief is a shape-shifter and varies in intensity and form as it winds its way through a person. You can feel your insides wrestling with the loss, trying to reconcile the truth of what's gone with what remains. When confronted with death, grief may feel like a dream state, your mind and body a few steps behind the reality swirling around you.

But grief in advance can be helpful, too, as a kind of practice for what is to come. John had an aggressive type of leukemia, a cancer of the blood cells. After about a year of ups and downs since the original diagnosis, he and his wife Pamela were referred to palliative care. By the time we met they'd endured a bone marrow transplant, which worked only briefly before his cancer returned.

Gloom. Hope. Gloom. While John and Pamela began in earnest to prepare for death, waves of new treatments were coming to market, some of them specific to his subtype of cancer. Hope again. John was game, all the while working through his wishes and preparing for death to come soon. But it didn't. Treatment after treatment worked, each one for a short time. It was like watching someone swing from vines through the jungle, swooping from highs to lows to find another vine dangled just in time to keep him from falling. This was a modern medical story, the kind in which the line between chronic and terminal illness keeps moving.

Both John and Pamela became pros at hoping for the best while preparing for the worst, a way to hold conflicting outlooks all at once. But this process took its toll, especially on Pamela. She had to be ready for his "imminent" death and protect his wishes—the appointments, the apartment, travel, social connections, contingency planning for worst-case scenarios, mixing their nightly Manhattans—all the while appreciating this extra time with him. The succession of surprising good news and extended time cast her into what she called no-man's-land. It was very hard to do, so our work turned primarily to her. In our appointments she became the patient, and John got to be the caregiver.

It didn't feel safe for Pamela to let go of the idea that John's death was around the corner, so for the two and a half years this lasted, she was grieving. Her grief was smoldering, subacute, underlying everything. At times she burst into exasperation, wanting all this to be over, and she'd say as much. But John understood and listened lovingly so that Pamela could find more strength, which she did. When the next new treatment on the list would have required an indefinite hospital stay, a big expense, and no nightly Manhattans, John said, "No thanks." Barely two weeks after stopping that last treatment and three years after his terminal diagnosis, with Pamela and his children by his side, John finally died. Hospice was involved, but little help was needed by that point. They'd made it.

Pamela and John were fortunate to be able to work through their grief together. By the time of John's death it was a familiar companion and Pamela was able to enter her official mourning with nothing but warm, deep sadness and a tinge of pride. We called it "clean sorrow."

Grief, denial, fear: at root, they all have to do with longing. If you stop and think about it, missing someone or something, fearing whatever might remove you from them, and rejecting the idea that you'll ever be apart are all expressions of appreciation. Realizing this link is helpful: it contextualizes the pain and sets us up to feel grateful to have ever had that health or ability or relationship in the first place.

Making these connections takes time but, armed with this understanding, we're better able to live with our harder feelings, instead of running from them. And fortunately, there are tools out there for working through those feelings and seeing through them to the love of life that is their source.

——

Thirteen Constructive Ways to Cope

HARD EMOTIONS WON'T DISAPPEAR ALTOGETHER, BUT WE CAN PUT them to good use—working with them rather than fighting them. Here are a few approaches for you to draw from:

1. SET GOALS

People seem to be able to will themselves to the end they need. Harriet's mother, Edith, had had five different bouts of cancer, all of which had been treated with rounds of chemotherapy or radiation—not easy to endure once and all the more unnerving when repeated five times. After the *sixth* cancer diagnosis she said, "I've had enough!"

Harriet, who is the executive director of the Conversation Project (an organization that helps people prepare for the end of life), took her mother at her word, and together they went to Edith's oncologist and discussed the plan. Edith moved in with her daughter's family so they could be close and take care of each other. There she listened to her grandson as he practiced chanting the Torah in preparation for his bar mitzvah. Day after day she'd sit and drink in his young voice—still breaking sweetly at the high and low notes—hearing the promise of his future manhood in those ancient melodies she knew so well.

She desperately wanted to be there for the moment when her grandson officially came of age, so Edith changed her mind about treatment. She and Harriet returned to the doctor and signed up for chemo. And guess what? It worked for a while, and she lived long enough to be there for the big day.

We can't always summon more time, but to some degree we do will ourselves through life, the way a rock climber pulls herself up with finger holds. Inspiration; purpose: these things are as essential as oxygen. Find reasons to live a little longer and you just might.

2. FEEL THE GOOD STUFF, TOO

"Take your breaks where you find them." I've used this phrase with patients (and myself) a zillion times. Funny how we'll endure all sorts of miseries, but won't let ourselves celebrate the upshots. I catch myself doing this often, and have come to think it's because I'm afraid that if I feel good for a moment, I'll have even more disappointment the next time things get rough again. The reasoning goes: *If I stay closer to misery, I'll have less far to fall.*

But either way, eventually you'll fall. And if you don't let the good stuff in, well, then you will miss out on the good stuff and all the resilience that comes with it.

When David Kelley, a designer and professor, felt beaten down by treatment for his throat cancer, his therapist asked him to write down everything he'd done over the course of the day and rate how much fun he'd had. Together, they examined the list, noting anything that "drove his joy number up." David's therapist then told him to pick three of the things that made him feel joyful and make sure to do them every day. For David, those things were calling a close friend who lived across the country; talking to his kid; and going for a drive in his 1954 Chevy pickup. Figure out what makes you feel good and build it into your day.

3. PRAY

Whether you look up into the sky and see mystery or nothingness or God, prayer affords you an intimate space in which to articulate how you feel and what it is you dare to hope for. You speak, aloud or in your mind, to God or Mother Earth or the universe. Of course, this doesn't mean you will receive what it is you seek, but prayer will help you find your voice.

"Having a conversation with God" is how Reverend Luke Jernagan of St. Peter's Episcopal Church in St. Louis defines prayer. "Letting God do some of the talking allows patients to remember that they're in connection with something greater; something that exists beyond death." Prayer can help you feel that connection with the rest of creation.

Prayer can also be a kind of submission to a larger force. It helps you to settle in, gives you a way to lay your worries down.

From what we've seen at the end of life, the saying that "there are no atheists in foxholes" isn't quite true. There are plenty of faithless and undecided who find peace close to death. And plenty of faithful who do not. The difference seems to be in how practiced a person is in bumping up against what he can't necessarily command or comprehend.

4. BE GRATEFUL

It's easy to tune in to all that's wrong, but noticing the good in the world is therapeutic for you (and those around you).

A woman in her eighties, knowing she didn't have much time left, invited all of her friends over for a fancy luncheon. Like a queen, she sat at the head of the table with a starched white napkin on her lap and invited each friend to come sit next to her so she could tell them face-to-face how fond she was of them and why; how much their loyalty and companionship over the years had meant to her. Being able to say all of those things—to pour out a pitcher of gratitude—was a kind of medicine. She felt so happy afterward.

Gratitude is really a by-product of appreciation. So start by taking life in. It can come during grace at the dinner table, or as a bedtime ritual. Next time you're with a friend, instead of talking politics or illness, make gratitude a topic of conversation. If nothing's coming, start small: "I'm grateful for your company." Feeling prickly, are you? that's okay, too. Be grateful for solitude or grateful that there's something to prickle about. Try to be grateful for whatever you're feeling, that you feel anything at all. For some, death itself represents something to be grateful for.

5. ACCEPT

Sara and Francesca, sisters who took care of their father, Len, at home until he died, say that a big part of Len's legacy is the example he set in facing death. There were several missteps in his early care, and he went from "There is nothing wrong with you" to "You have stage 4 cancer and there is nothing that can be done" in an instant. That news was delivered, rather breezily, by a doctor he didn't know, over the phone.

But Len, who was a sociologist by trade and contemplative in spirit, used what he had learned over the years to process what was happening. "He didn't blame, he didn't feel like a victim, he didn't hide his fear, he didn't lose his wonder, curiosity, or joy—he cried at the drop of a hat." He rolled with every emotion. He accepted all of it, and couldn't wait to see what came next. And, importantly, Len had the same attitude when actively treating his cancer. Acceptance is not only for when you're out of options. It is simply a matter of seeing things for what they are.

His openness made it safe for his family to get used to the idea of him dying. By the end of Len's life, the sisters noted that words like "when I'm dead" had lost their taboo. Not having to dance around the subject was a relief for them, as it was for Len.

6. LOVE (GIVE IT *AND* RECEIVE IT)

Love is the greatest force we know. It can answer any question. In a way, this entire book is about love. Love may be immense, but it often shows up in subtle and unexpected ways.

During her work with the Department of Veterans Affairs, grief therapist Julie Arguez counseled terminal patients who suffered from prolonged periods of lovelessness. She treated a vet, then dying of cancer, who'd returned from Vietnam with PTSD and become alcoholic. There had been bouts of violence in the family in the years after he returned home, and he had been estranged from his ex-wife, who'd died several years before, and from his son, now fifty. Arguez had a sense that the patient wanted to reconnect with his family, so, with his blessing, she reached out to his son and asked if he'd come to have coffee with his father.

The first visit was forced and awkward. Neither knew what to say or do. To Arguez, it was clear that they had a lot in common: both were independent and stoic, showing little emotion. A week later, Arguez invited the son back to help with his father's laundry. The son did so, and then came again a week later, and many times after that, staying longer each visit. At the end of the three months they spent getting to know each other again, the vet asked his son for forgiveness and told him he loved him. "There were all of these hurts, but none of it mattered in the end," Arguez says. The son sat on his father's bed, holding his hand, embracing his face, and saying good-bye. Gestures of love don't have to be grand and cinematic. They don't have to happen in a sudden burst of tears at the bedside as the credits roll. Often love builds, just as it did at the VA hospital, one load of laundry at a time.

7. RELATE

For the first many years, Andrea's response to cancer was to battle it. That metaphor served her well for a while. But war is exhausting, so, upon her third recurrence, she changed the relationship: sidling up to her illness instead of treating it as an intruder.

That choice was a breakthrough for her. It gave her more negotiating power, and more compassion, too, including for her cancer cells. She eventually came to give her illness a name: Gus. She found a toy made of yarn that looks like a goblin with a blue heart embroidered on it, who became Gus. She keeps him in her purse and even talks to him—cheering him when the tumors shrink and scolding him when they grow.

Sometimes she hates Gus, and sometimes she's sweet on him, as in any intense relationship. Gus allows Andrea to be with her disease while also being more than her disease.

8. BE

Patrick, a longtime patient with liver disease and prostate cancer, took a mindfulness-based stress reduction course and started meditating for twenty minutes a day. The change was obvious. He grew less reactive, less depressed, more in control of himself, and more capable of handling what he could not control. Sitting still and following his breath, noticing but not reacting—his new practice gave him a kind of buffer.

When you're mindful, you're watching your thoughts as they come or go, not necessarily clinging to them. You might realize there is a world beyond thought. This means you're better able to tell when your thoughts are helping you or getting in your way. The same goes for your feelings. The basic idea is to become more fully aware, and maybe less agitated. Mindfulness may involve sitting quietly with eyes closed and legs crossed. Or it can come while gazing out a window or on a stroll around the block. It can be anything that pulls your attention to the now, the life that's still here.

9. SEE DIFFERENTLY

Medical marijuana is an increasingly common remedy for chronic pain, and data suggest that it's also useful for the treatment of anxiety, depression, nausea, and insomnia, to name a few. In some of those studies you'll find euphoria listed as a side effect of the drug. That's not such a bad thing if you're looking to change your outlook.

There's an even more recent resurgence of academic interest in the therapeutic potential of psychedelics such as psilocybin (aka magic mushrooms), and a growing body of evidence to support it. MDMA ("Ecstasy") is another drug also being revisited, as is LSD.

The first few hundred study participants to take a dose of psilocybin have reported an ushering-in of wonderment and awe; a sense of belonging to something larger and a loosening of the grip of fear and isolation. Ratings by patients and clinicians after one dose suggested these effects endured at least six months. What's more, there were no adverse effects. Other, smaller studies show similar results.

It is important to note that the participants were not thrill-seekers or counterculturists but people gripped by a fear of dying from their disease or other trauma. The sessions were guided by experienced psychologists in a carefully monitored environment. These are serious tools for serious predicaments.

FAST FACT
One Johns Hopkins University study found that a single dose of psilocybin produced substantial and enduring changes, like decreases in anxiety in patients with a life-threatening cancer diagnosis, as well as increases in quality of life.

From the positive study results to date, it's possible to imagine that psychedelics will make their way to mainstream clinical medicine, but that moment is still years away. For now, psychedelic medicines can be accessed through clinical studies, more of which have begun in the past year.

And of course, the point isn't to escape. The point is to realize that there are other ways to see yourself in the universe so you don't feel the need to escape. These drugs seem to open up new lines of sight. *Perspective.* In illness and disability there is so much that can fall apart, but there's also an opportunity to reconfigure oneself, and psychedelics offer one way to access that power. Falling apart well is a skill that can be learned.

10. PINCH YOURSELF

Feeling something is one of the ways we prove we're alive: *This must be real, I felt that pinch!* And there is so much to feel. Think about how profound it can feel to have the sun on your skin, or taste that first bite of your favorite childhood meal. Or the fundamental joy of being outside. Of bathing. Of moving your body through space, not just to get somewhere, but to feel the work of muscles and bone pushing against gravity. The phrase "What I wouldn't give for a _____ " is usually about a desire for a sensation. Want to feel alive for as long as you are? Pay attention to your senses.

Breathing was harder and harder for Jeanette, not because of smoke damage—she hadn't smoked for decades—but from weakening muscles due to ALS. Now that death was getting close, she resumed smoking her favorite French cigarettes. She described the sensation of smoking as a way to feel her lungs in action. For Jeanette, it was more an act of appreciation than of defiance or self-destruction. And for us caregivers, with her death coming soon no matter what, it was hard not to be happy watching her pull on a cigarette and exhale with a wide smile.

11. CREATE

Throw out the idea that you're "not the creative type." Humans have a remarkable capacity to make things from the raw material life gives us, including, importantly, limitations. If you think about it, getting through an average day is a creative act, filled with improvisation and invention as you come upon hurdle after hurdle. We are an incredibly adaptive species. Go further if you like: use that inborn impulse to write a poem, plant a garden, cook a meal, sing a song, paint a mural. Creation can be wholly internal, too. Just *imagining* something can be potent.

Thekla was a singer and a painter in her seventies who would sometime soon die of lung cancer. She was one of the rare people to admit to their fear. As her breath waned, she turned more toward her painting to help her work out what was happening to her body. She realized her paintings had changed since her diagnosis. Whereas in the past she would paint an image she already had in mind, now Thekla painted with an open one. Still a means of expression, painting also became a way for her to explore what she didn't yet understand; to come to know something of the unknown. Death's closeness opened her mind to whatever came. Curiosity and playfulness replaced pressure, and fear met its match.

12. LAUGH

One day in December, Beth's stepfather, Joe, who was 95 and full of vitality, was crossing the street to visit his neighbor when he fell and cracked his head. After seven weeks in the hospital and rehab, he returned home. Joe had raised Beth from when she was a baby, and they'd spent countless afternoons together leaning into the wind as they sailed the San Francisco Bay. The two of them shared three things: love for Beth's mother, who'd died two years before; being out on open water; and a ribald sense of humor.

When Beth brought Joe home from the hospital, she set him up on a reclining hospital bed in the living room, right under a large painting of his late wife—posing nude. It looked as though he was going to bounce back until he started having seizures. His body temperature dropped and he died within a week. But up until the very end, he was still trying to make Beth laugh. "He was wearing a squirrel T-shirt that read, 'I'm so old I can't even find my own nuts,'" she says.

Laughter can be a tool for putting dread in its place. A longtime patient and I were talking about his daily toils with prostate cancer, his career that had never quite gotten off the ground despite his hard work, and the children who made little effort with him now despite his love for them. And for what? he asked me. We sat in silence for a moment, looking for a suitable answer, and then we both said, practically in unison, "Maybe it's all for nothing." We laughed our heads off. It wasn't his pain that was funny but the absurdity of how hard we work to move forward in life, often ending up in the same place or even a step behind. The joke is only on us if we don't find some way to laugh.

13. CALL A TRUCE

Frank was a remarkable troublemaker who showed up one day in clinic and said, "Hi, I'm dying and I don't want to be afraid. What can you do for me?"

In many ways, Frank was already as prepared for death as he could be. By the time we met, he'd lived more than twenty years with HIV, buried many friends, explored multiple religions, pushed his body and mind in all sorts of ways, served countless others in his work as a river guide for people with disabilities, and now was dueling with metastatic prostate cancer.

We worked through his fear of suffering, mostly by talking and reflecting together and getting very specific about his feelings; it was a process of discovery. Frank got savvy about medications for pain and depression and various other symptoms along the way. He honed his meditation practice. He rededicated himself to his spiritual community and to his family and friends, and they to him. He continued to work on the river, staying present in his body, swimming and rafting as long as he could. When he could no longer muster that energy, he found ways to support his mentees in their own development. He was hilarious and crass and honest. He let others in and knew love. Frank did it all. And it all helped.

But he never totally shook his dread. One day, after years of rolling around in the dirt with fear, we both noticed that something had shifted in the way he spoke of it: there was less anxiety in his tone, and his words softened. There was even some affection in his voice, like he was talking about a crusty, beloved relative. Without realizing it, he'd made fear something of a companion, which defanged it. Fear was more familiar now and so less scary. And with that realization, he called a truce.

It wasn't long after that day that Frank died. Luckily, I got to see him on a home visit in what proved to be the last few hours of his life. He lay there smiling wryly; sleepy, but clear and unafraid. ❖

The Bottom Line

COPING

Death represents the mother of all fears, and there are many ways to cope with it: humor, forgiveness, creativity, prayer, attention, love, perspective shifts, adaptation, and patience, to name a few. Make room for fear, and it won't be so scary.

Breaking the News

How to tell others, including your children
and your boss; dealing with people's
reactions; posting on social media

Hearing hard news is one thing; breaking it to others is another. One of the first challenges you'll face is telling others about your condition. Talking about illness and death doesn't come naturally to most of us. Good communication about sensitive topics requires listening attentively and gauging a person's readiness to talk. Try to remember that awkwardness and discomfort are part of that conversation, as everyone fumbles for the right response.

And mind your assumptions. We tend to project our own discomfort onto others. "When someone is dying themselves, it's classic, they say, 'I know I'm dying, but don't tell my family, they can't handle it,'" says grief therapist Fredda Wasserman. "And then you go talk to the family, and they say, 'We know he's dying, but don't tell him, he can't handle it.'"

——

How Soon Should I Tell People?

ISOLATION COMPOUNDS PAIN BY CUTTING YOU OFF FROM THE KINDNESS and support of others. It's entirely up to you how many people you tell, and when, and what exactly you tell them. But we do encourage you to tell someone you trust in short order. Begin by talking with your closest-in people, usually within the first hours to days after hearing the news. The guiding questions here are: Who can bring comfort and support? Who will help you feel more secure?

Beyond this inner circle, you might take a breath and keep an eye out for the right moment. You're sharing something important that's not easy to say or hear. **You'll often find that you— the sick one and ostensibly the one in need—wind up being a teacher and nurturer.** Here are a few things to keep in mind as you break the news:

- **Prepare yourself.** Start with a gut check: When you tell people, is there some response you're after? Do you want advice? Do you want the listener to take action? Do you want them to simply listen? How about a hug? You may end up blurting it out—even to people you barely know—and that's okay, too.
- **Make sure everyone is comfortable.** This usually means having a seat (or bed) and making sure the room is otherwise free of distractions. If you are in the middle of a fit of pain, best to take a dose of medication before entering into a difficult conversation. Yes, some meds can dull your ability to listen and think clearly, but not as much as intense pain does.
- **Tee it up so they know what's to come.** Doctors call this a "warning shot," such as "I got the test results back today." Or "I've got some hard news to share."
- **Say what you need.** Be direct about the response you're hoping for. Say "What I really need is your empathy." Or confess, "I don't know what I need. Just sit here with me."
- **Meet people where they are.** We mean on the emotional plane. Consider the state your listener is in and work from there—just as your doctor ought to have done with you. Is your listener stressed out after a long day at work? Does she have to run right back to work or get kids to school? When possible, build in some time to sit together or take a walk outside. And don't forget to stop talking and do some listening yourself.
- **Hold some silence.** Let things sink in, and allow responses to come to the surface.
- **Acknowledge emotions.** One of our common defenses is to stay in our heads. Intellectualizing keeps emotions at a distance, which is ultimately only isolating. So break through, with hankies at the ready, and acknowledge the feelings in the room: with your eyes, or your own tears, or a comment such as

"I'm afraid" or "This hurts" or "I'm numb." Establishing this kind of emotional safety between you and the other person is probably the single most important thing you can do.

- **Expect a lot of misguided responses.** When people don't know how to deal with something—like illness or death—it's a common response to hold it at arm's length and judge it. Don't be surprised if well-meaning friends and family start dispensing advice about how to deal with your diagnosis. People will have opinions: You're either in denial, or a mess who can't get out of bed and it's about time you got up and dusted yourself off. Sigh. It's often close-in people who can't accept the news and are most gripped with fear or sorrow or anger of their own and least capable of being there for you in the moment. Try not to take it personally; it says more about their state than it does about yours.

- **Try to hear beyond what people are saying to what they are trying to convey.** Intentions are more important than execution. Often you know in your heart what someone is trying to get across, despite their fumbling; the fumbling and nervousness usually point to how much they care. Hear that.

——

Telling Your Adult Children

MY FATHER, STANLEY BERGER, WAS SO ANXIETY-RIDDEN OVER TELLING my sister and me about his first diagnosis that he kept it from us for two years. He didn't want to saddle our lives with worry. In the end it was his new wife, Beth, who insisted that he come clean. So one night after a family dinner, he sat us down on the couch, looked off into the middle distance, and said, "I have cancer." He went on about how confident he was that he was going to beat it, never once making eye contact.

We were furious that he'd kept it from us for so long, and he sat there quietly and took our ire without uttering a word in his own defense. Then he took our hands in his and we suddenly saw how hard it was for him to deliver this news. He'd always been a somewhat remote, stoic figure. I never saw him cry. And that night, he cracked a little and allowed himself to be vulnerable. With that simple gesture of taking our hands, we understood that all he wanted was to take care of us and for us to continue to love him.

There's no easy way to tell your adult children. You may find yourself wanting to keep it from them, like my dad did, or getting so gummed up that you ask someone else to break the news; or maybe you have such a close, open relationship that you don't think twice and your kids are the first people you call. As with so much about dying, there isn't a prescriptive approach that will work for everyone. You are the best person to know what sort of support your kids will need in moments of loss, but here are a few suggestions to help you prepare:

- **Consider the pecking order.** If you have multiple children, whom you call first may matter a lot to them. Take that into consideration before you pick up the phone. Maybe you convene a family meeting or a conference call so it doesn't bring up old resentments about who's the favorite.
- **Don't delay too long.** If you put off telling your kids you also lose precious time for trying to come to resolutions, for telling them things that you may want them to know, and for saying good-bye. Some parents may decide to postpone delivering the news, whether to spare their kids worry or not disrupt their lives, but your adult kids may be bitter that you made that decision unilaterally without giving them a chance to support you.

- **Choose a decision maker.** As you think through who will take care of you when you're sick, you'll be choosing a health care agent (more on this in chapter 3, "Yes, There's Paperwork"). Once you've done so, if you've passed over the eldest child and given the decision-making power to a younger one, it's best that everyone knows. If open communication can't happen for whatever reason, at least tell your medical team so there's no confusion at the bedside.

As for telling kids who are actually still kids, we'll discuss that a little later (see chapter 16, "Everyone Dies: How to Talk to Kids").

——

Telling Your Boss

BREAKING THE NEWS IS LIKE CUTTING OPEN A PILLOW AND SHAKING the feathers loose—once you've put it out there, there's no taking it back. Knowing that, it's best to have a good grip on what your illness will require of you, along with a plan, before you broach the news with your boss; that way you and your supervisor can come up with a strategy for how your work will be covered in advance, instead of just leaving her to figure things out after the twentieth phone call that you have to miss another meeting. Here's some advice:

- **Do it in person.** Talk with your direct supervisor one-on-one about your illness. This allows for a human moment, helping you to gauge her initial response and determine how best to proceed from there. Ask to discuss what accommodations can be made for you; it might be extra time off for treatments or appointments, or an earlier departure each day.

- **Keep notes.** Take your own notes in this meeting so you have a record of what was discussed. Document any meetings with your boss about your illness and confirm decisions made via email; then you have a paper trail to refer to should questions arise.
- **Beware the prejudices around illness.** Your boss's bias may tend either toward the negative or the positive. Both come with their own perils.

THE NEGATIVE BIAS	THE POSITIVE BIAS
• Your boss may presume you can't keep up with your work. • Plum assignments may go to someone else or be taken away from you and justified as a way to make sure you're not under too much stress. • Your news may confront your boss with her own fears, so she goes numb or avoids you altogether.	• Your supervisor is incredibly sympathetic and wants you to focus only on yourself, which can be further isolating. • She pushes you to take time off when all you want to do is distract yourself with spreadsheets and meetings.

- **Know that you are not required to divulge anything about your health to your employer.** But we still encourage you to consider doing so. If you don't, your manager may come to his own inaccurate and unhelpful conclusions if your appearance changes or you miss work frequently without giving the reason. Keeping it secret can also add to your stress. Once you tell your boss, however, assume that the information is going to make its way to the HR department as well.
- **If you do tell your employer and feel that the information led to**

discriminatory actions, know that you may be covered by the Americans with Disabilities Act (ADA). Talk to your HR department if you feel this is the case. Bear in mind that, in general, HR departments are charged first and foremost with protecting the corporation's interests, so you may still need to seek legal advice outside the company to make sure your rights are upheld.

Don't underestimate the power of empathy of your coworkers and supervisors. You may find an untapped source of support at work.

———

Posting About Your Illness

DYING ONLINE IS COMPLICATED. AS ANYONE WHO HAS A SOCIAL MEDIA account knows, our digital incarnations distort who we are. They have a whitewashing effect.

That effect can make Facebook and Twitter and other networks feel like a problematic place to reveal you are not well. Some people fear that posting about their condition will look like a cry for pity; others see it as indispensable. Though it may seem inelegant to some, joining Facebook support groups and tweeting from your hospital bed can be a fast and sure way to get updates to the people you care about and soak up some much-needed cheer and support in return. We'll leave the decision up to you, but here are some tips about how to notify your larger circle:

- **Mass emails.** Though reply-alls are a running joke at work, they are perfectly acceptable when notifying those in your network of your condition. Make sure to include whether you do, or do not, want questions in response. Without this caveat

For Caregivers

Talking to someone who is sick requires building up a new set of muscles, including gauging a person's readiness to talk; listening well; distinguishing your worries from theirs; and meeting them where they are.

Everyone faces hardship differently, so follow the person's lead and don't assume you know the best way to comfort or help them. To paraphrase Dr. Francis Peabody, a famous early-twentieth-century-American physician and educator: *the best way to show you care for someone is to care for them.* I return to this bit of wisdom nearly every day when I'm trying to figure out how to be with people. Having you sit there and listen may be all they really need.

Here are some suggestions for talking to people who are experiencing a terminal diagnosis.

Things to do:

- Though it may feel all wrong to say it out loud, simply stating that terminal illness is *really hard* can be a balm
- Don't hold back on reaching out with words of encouragement, letting the person know he is loved and making an impression on the world just by being who he is
- Holding a little silence, even a few seconds, can be transformative. It can feel hard to stay in it, but silence conveys all sorts of kindness that words cannot, and it also

For Caregivers (continued)

allows room for deeper emotions—perhaps in the form of better words or tears or a howl—to rise to the surface

- It's best to keep a narrower focus in asking questions. Ask how she is *today* or *this morning* rather than how she is in general
- Ask what you can pick up for him while you're at the grocery store; or if you're headed to the Laundromat, stop by to pick up his load of sheets and towels. If you have a good sense of the person and what he likes or needs, go ahead and bring him that
- Ask if he just wants company. There's no need for conversation. Maybe take in a movie together. Physical presence can be comforting in and of itself
- Reflect with him: it can be poignant and instructive to hold up a mirror to your friend. He needs to figure things out for himself, but you can play back what he's saying, helping him make sense of his thoughts and feelings and you of yours

Things that are probably best not to do:

- Don't try to put a silver lining on the situation or pep the person up with "Think positive!" or "You're gonna beat this!"
- Don't confuse your feelings with theirs
- Don't compare their suffering to someone else's
- Don't try to sound profound. There's nothing less profound than someone trying to sound profound

For Caregivers (continued)

- Don't act out of pity. Empathy and compassion, helpful. Pity, unhelpful. The difference is often simply one of tone. Hearing "You poor thing" may feel humiliating, while "This really stinks" may feel like exactly the right thing
- Don't project your own religious views. This is a quick way to isolate people if they don't share your beliefs
- Don't talk about the person's life in the past tense
- Don't stop showing up after the first month. People often get a bunch of lasagnas in the first few weeks after a diagnosis or the death of a loved one, then nothing in the months later, when they're locked in the bathroom sobbing and could really use some support or are finally ready to receive it

you're looking at a lot of emails to respond to. It's also okay to deputize someone close to you to write these emails on your behalf; just make sure you've approved it before hitting send.

- **Social media.** Posting about your condition is a great way to update your extended community on a regular basis. You may hear from others in a similar situation who will share thoughts and feelings and advice on how to cope. Remember that the way people will respond is impossible to predict.
- **Blogs.** Publishing on a personalized website (see Resources section) is a more intimate way to share updates with a private circle. It can be cathartic to keep a journal and log your thoughts

and feelings in a way that you can easily share by sending a link. And because the page isn't a social space, there's no expectation of a response.

A note of caution: don't inadvertently exclude your actual family. If you are making decisions and plans based on the feedback of your online community, at least let your family and friends know so they don't feel ignored. Kelsey Crowe, the author of *There Is No Good Card for This: What to Say and Do When Life Is Scary, Awful, and Unfair to People You Love*, has seen firsthand how friends of the deceased can use an online social platform to speedily organize activities for their friend's funeral, only to be completely remiss in including the wishes of the deceased's offline family members. In one instance, the funeral's raucous festivities took place while the bewildered family remained sequestered in a corner of the funeral hall.

Be clear about what you need in real life. If you have gobs of followers and online support groups, it may appear to closer friends that you don't need them to show up with a hot meal or give you a ride to an appointment.

Communication is a big part of my job, and I still say dumb things to patients and friends who are suffering.

As Kate Bowler, a cancer patient, wrote in the *New York Times*, no one knows what to say to the news of a bad diagnosis:

> "Most people I talk with succumb immediately to a swift death by free association. I remind them of something horrible and suddenly they are using words like 'pustules' at my child's fourth-birthday party. . . . This is not comforting."

———

Responses May Vary

THERE WILL BE PEOPLE WHO SIMPLY WON'T BE ABLE TO SEE YOU AS you grapple with this; they'll be leery of saying the wrong thing, or respect your privacy to the point of neglect, or will be too afraid to be around disease and death. When friendships fall away, it can feel like you've been roped off behind caution tape. Some friendships may just have to end. But often enough, you can make the people you care about feel it's safe to come closer. Try just coming out and saying "I know it's hard to talk about what's going on, but it's okay to ask me about it. I still want to see you."

If you don't feel comfortable saying that in person, or feel exhausted by the thought of repeatedly telling everyone you know, sharing a blog or Facebook post with that message can be a great shortcut. One very candid post can open the floodgates for friends near and far to gather around or offer virtual hugs.

The last thing you need while dealing with illness, treatments, and existential angst is to have to *manage* your relationships. You may need to let go—of worrying, of trying so hard, of whole relationships. If some people become overbearing, beloved though they may be, it's perfectly fine to hang up a virtual "Do Not Disturb" sign, sending an automated response that you need downtime and are off-limits until you say differently. ❖

The Bottom Line

BREAKING THE NEWS

So much of the roller coaster of living and dying is tied up in communication—or its absence. Do your best to acknowledge what's going on, for yourself and everyone involved. Remember, it's an honor to be on the receiving end of this news no matter how hard it is to say. As Simone Weil said, "Attention is the purest and rarest form of generosity." No matter what words are spoken, being there is the real balm.

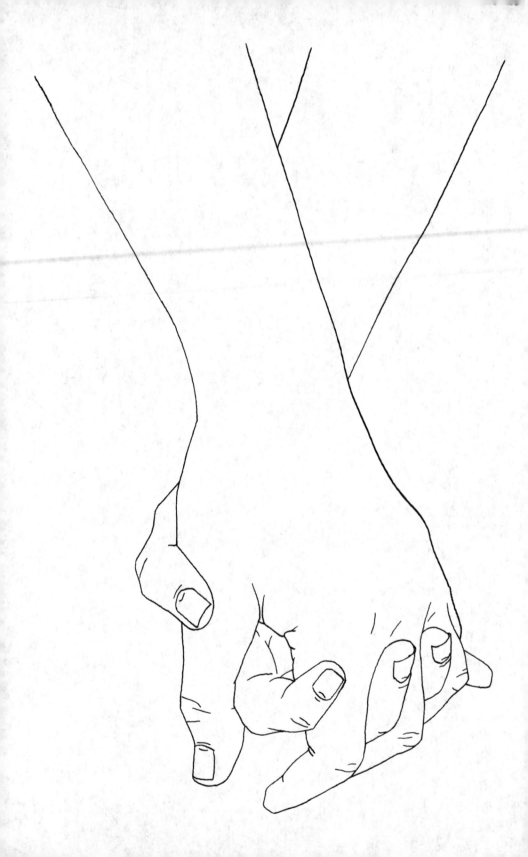

Love, Sex, and Relationships

Relationships in flux; guilt, anger, and other
unpleasantries; choosing to stay together
or not; what is sex now?; don't forget your
senses; connect while and where you can

I llness changes, or at least challenges, everything: certainly our relationships to ourselves and to others. The psychotherapist and palliative care chaplain Reverend Denah Joseph has spent years observing and guiding couples through this phase of life. As she says, "Illness is about the *relationship*. In my practice this is usually the bull's-eye, the tender core where illness is experienced most acutely as both strengthening and undermining our bonds—the most important source of safety, connection, and attachment that any of us has."

Some relationships will grow and thrive under these conditions, and some won't. This chapter focuses primarily on romantic relationships, but be aware that all of your relationships will change, subtly or dramatically, and that everyone in your orbit is affected. Roles bounce around: husband becomes nurse, wife becomes aide, and so on. And all this shifting upsets the balance of your emotional ecosystem.

You don't have to forgo your familiar role entirely. Facing the end can be an incredibly tender time between people. Partners can forgive and be forgiven. Patients can teach caregivers how to be vulnerable or raw. And everyone can show the people they love how much they love them.

——

How Relationships Change

IT'S A SHOCK TO THE SYSTEM WHEN YOU CAN NO LONGER DO THE things your partner depended on you to do—play catch with the kid, take out the trash, not wet the bed. All of the things you took for granted, even the smallest ones, might be stripped away.

Make no mistake, transitioning from the role of spouse or partner to patient or caregiver is a hard one, whatever your age.

When you've lived your entire life under a certain identity—patriarch, matriarch, child, boss, you name it—it may feel next to impossible to assume a new one. The semblance of independence gives way, and that can overwhelm your long-established dynamic and the patterns of your care for each other, and for yourselves.

Acknowledging what's gone in your relationship—missing it, mourning it, whether through words or action or ritual—is powerful, and it's key to living on. This is how you can protect intimacy. Give each other permission to vent and wade through the emotions that come up, even if they're hard or unpleasant. Doing so is a way to offer real support to each other. Being authentic will protect you both from feeling like too much of yourselves is going away. There will be more to go.

Here are a few ideas for sticking together as you go through this. These are for both of you to consider:

- **Rally around things that have little to do with your illness.**
  Insist that you are partners (or a family) more than you are "patient" and "caregiver." Maybe you devote Wednesday night to doing something you have always enjoyed together, such as a game of cards or listening to music.
- **Reflect on what brought you together in the first place.**
  We forget. Remembering the charms you first fell for in each other; the old jokes between you; the routines, places, food, books, or whatever drew you together might still do that now. I'm reminded again and again in clinic how much trouble befalls people when they lose touch with the basics of their lives, most importantly with what brings them joy. If those things just aren't accessible now, the act of remembering together can be powerful by itself.

illness can

ALTER IDENTITY

You may be playing many roles now: daughter, nurse, therapist. The shape-shifting is temporary, but that doesn't make it less difficult.

- **Make new rituals and routines.** What's something new you can do together? Movie night? Reading aloud to each other? Stopping at a park or an ice cream shop after doctor appointments? Maybe a sip of sherry at medication time? One kiss per pill. Prizes for pooping. Make it up. The point is to settle into this new, weird reality together and make it yours.

- **Make sure you both have time to yourself.** Do things independently of each other. This might mean time spent alone or with different people; in silence; with a book; out for a meal. Your relationships with yourself and the wider world are also important.

- **Appreciate each other.** One gnarly thing about being weighed down with symptoms and treatments is that it's easier to miss the subtle sweetnesses happening around you and *for* you. Slow down and notice. Look each other in the eyes. Hold that hug a little longer. These moments settle the nervous system. Try looking for things to learn about yourselves and each other—moments of exchange—and maybe each of you will see how strong you are, living this experience of frailty. You can't choose so much of what you're facing, but you can keep choosing each other, hour by hour.

——

Before Death Do You Part?

YES, COUPLES DO BREAK UP AT THE END OF LIFE. A TERMINAL DIAGNOSIS may bring some people closer together, but it's not likely to fix a relationship that's already in trouble. A breakup—hard under the best of circumstances—can be devastating when you're sick and feeling all the more vulnerable. On the other hand, it can feel cathartic and empowering and smart to let go of a relationship

For Caregivers

Maybe you're the banker and your partner is the chef, or your partner is the calendar keeper and you're the cleaning crew. Whatever your particular dynamic, this sort of wonderful teamwork can mean that certain day-to-day duties are wholly owned by the other person; a relief when you're together and fully functioning, but a source of disproportionate difficulty when the other person is consumed by illness. There are many adults in the world who never learned to balance a checkbook or do laundry; there was no need since those tasks were kindly tended to by the partner.

You may be concerned about taking on your partner's responsibilities but afraid to broach the subject. It's humbling, and it's also difficult, to talk about what your beloved can no longer do or to propel yourselves into imagining the day when one of you is gone. But it's important and kind to do so.

If you're both well enough, take on the tasks of each other's roles for a week or two. If that's unrealistic now, schedule some tutorials from the couch. This will achieve at least two things: help you appreciate your partner, and help you learn what you'll be newly responsible for. This stuff may feel mundane, but that's why it's invaluable—it's the arena where most of life happens.

(or anything) that's not working and is consequently sucking up precious air.

——

Getting the Right Support

IF YOU FIND YOURSELF WANTING TO LEAVE OR IN THE MIDDLE OF A breakup, quickly look for other emotional and logistical avenues of support. Was your partner driving you to your appointments? Who else in your circle can do that?

In addition to telling close friends, it's a good idea to let your clinical team know if you're newly single. They need to understand what's going on with you and may be able to help. And ask your doctor or insurer directly for a recommendation for a social worker. Whether you're seeking counsel on obtaining medical insurance, need help with rides or meals, or could use a friendly conversation, a social worker can unearth whatever resources exist and help you access them.

——

Insurance Custody

ARE YOU RELYING ON YOUR SPOUSE'S MEDICAL INSURANCE? BEFORE one woman split with her partner, she asked him if she could remain on his insurance plan for a limited time. He still cared for her, and it was an amicable split, so he said yes, and they remained connected in that way until she was able to secure her own plan a year later. People strike deals in this way all the time. But when a tidy way forward is not at hand, it's a good idea to reach out to a social worker or case manager. A change in your marital status might mean, for example, that you lose significant income to pay

:its, treatment, and in-home help. But then again, ..gnt now qualify for programs, such as Medicaid, that were not available to you on a joint income.

———

Anger, Conflict, and Other Messy Emotions

THE THOUGHT OF LEAVING YOUR LOVED ONES BEHIND IS HARD TO bear. You may be angry at the universe and everything in it. You may be exhausted or in pain. But is it okay to be crabby? To fight? To tell your partner to get lost when he or she is being insufferable?

The answer is yes. Of course it is. This phase of life is just that—life—and everything human remains. One way to lose each other is to put on kid gloves. Don't deprive each other of the full range of emotion; illness diminishes enough. So, yes, when it comes to expressing yourself, this time should be no different from the rest of life.

If you were a couple that fought before a life-changing diagnosis, that behavior isn't likely to change, and may actually bring a feeling of normalcy—for some couples, arguing is a form of intimacy. Of course, if it starts to happen all the time or turns into cruelty, it can do real damage, pushing away those you need most.

Remember: Behind most complaints is a request. So, what do you really want? Do you want to be alone? Do you need to be told you're still attractive? Are you blowing your stack with your partner because you feel safe with them and not with anyone else? What a great thing to let the other person know.

———

The Struggle Has Its Charms

DURESS CAN BRING OUT THE WORST AND BEST IN US. I'VE KNOWN many couples over the years who swore that illness saved their relationship, usually because it sanded down the jagged edges that had been developing between them or gave them an excuse to finally communicate and dare to need each other.

For Jen Panasik, a 40-something mom with two young kids whose husband had stomach cancer, taking care of her husband brought a renewed closeness and sense of purpose. In fact, the years during which her husband's cancer was in remission ended up being the hardest. "It was actually the worst time for our relationship," Jen says. "He was starting to drink a lot . . . because he was petrified of it coming back. That's how he was dealing with it, instead of talking to me." His behavior enraged her. "I told him, 'Hell no, you're cancer-free, you can't check out, I'm sorry!' I know it's him hurting and he's in pain, but I kept thinking *You should be getting healthy! That's what you should be trying to do, right?*"

The cancer returned after three and a half years, and they were devastated. But the recklessness stopped almost immediately. "In a way, it's easier when we're dealing with the illness, because we feel like we're doing something together."

There is some caution to note here, too. The ups and downs of life with illness will yank your relationship around. The struggle itself—the drama—has its own pull and can become desirable in a strange way, or at least anticipated, leaving you either listless or anxious when it's absent. So stock up whenever possible, on energy or rest or joy. This will help you keep up when things are chaotic, but also to unwind when they are easier. Give your nerves a moment to reset.

——

For Caregivers

Being a caregiver can feel like thankless work. There will be times when you give and give and give and get back only darker moods and more demands. Adding to the strain, your loved one may not have the presence of mind to show you how grateful he is for all you do. This is where talking with other people going through a similar experience can feel so helpful; consider looking into support groups for caregivers, where you can be seen by others.

As for you and your partner together, here's something to try when you start to feel taken for granted: ask for small signs of gratitude or affection; a squeeze of the hand or a smile or a bit of much-needed flattery to get you through the day. Small gestures yield much more than the fraction of time and space they take up. The ailing person feels the burden he's placed on you as keenly as you do, so it will come as a great relief to know what you need and be able to give it. It may also help to remember that we will all be on the receiving end of care at some point; one day we will need to ask for some of that care in return.

Create an Emotional Safe Zone

IT'S HARD FOR A COUPLE TO STAY IN STEP WITH EACH OTHER. WHAT one person needs in the moment may derail the needs of the other. But at any given time, what this all comes down to is *safety*—both emotional and psychological. With the ground shifting beneath you and your body falling apart, that can be hard to achieve. But we need it, all of us, no matter how tough we are. When we don't feel safe, we constrict, run, build walls, or put up our dukes.

Losing your independence is very, very difficult, especially if you pride yourself on self-reliance. Needing more and more help can be demoralizing to the point of despair. It's nearly impossible for a partner to grasp how lonely dying makes a person feel, no matter how loved she might be. Indeed, each role—patient and caregiver—comes with discrete difficulties that are impossible for the other to fully grasp. Try to give each other the respect that situation deserves.

The goal is to feel that you are seen. That you are okay as you are. This state of mind is created and nurtured by the two of you, so the advice here is for patient and caregiver alike: Get basic. Listen without judgment. Drop your defensive armor. Vent. Spare the ultimatums, and focus on the thing between you that you are both in charge of creating: the relationship.

——

The "Little Death"

A state or event resembling or prefiguring death; a weakening or loss of consciousness, specifically in sleep or during an orgasm.

—*Oxford English Dictionary*

WHEN YOU'RE SICK, ONE OF THE FIRST THINGS THAT MAY GET neglected is your physical relationship. It may feel extravagant or even dangerous to afford your body any pleasure, but let's check those assumptions. Dr. Marianne Matzo, a nurse practitioner and researcher who studies sexuality at the end of life, recounted the story of a longtime cancer patient who died while his wife was giving him oral sex. In the hospital, no less. To be clear: her husband died from advanced cancer, not a sex act. The point is that this couple kept active until the very end.

——

Talking to Your Doctor About Sex

CLINICIANS AREN'T ALWAYS GREAT ABOUT TALKING THROUGH HOW sex may change when you're sick. And those changes range from the physical to the emotional: fatigue, grumpiness, a real headache, lack of interest, embarrassment, pain, vaginal dryness, erectile dysfunction.

Men, you are likely to hear from your doctor about whether or not you'll be able to have an erection after treatment, at least from a plumbing point of view. Because erectile dysfunction is so common, and because there are pills nowadays to help, it's become a fairly standard, if incomplete, conversation. That's good, but blood flow is only one issue of many; ask sex therapists, and they'll tell you that sex is far more a psychological matter than a physical act.

When it comes to talking to women about what sex will be like after treatment, things aren't quite so clear. "For a woman with cervical cancer, the oncologist usually recommends

TIP
If you are hoping to be a parent, ask your doctor about all side effects before starting any new treatments, as they may affect your reproductive organs.

radiation and surgery—*but [they're] not going to mention to you that there will be problems,*" says Matzo. "So then, down the road, when she's ready to have sex, she finds out, saying 'Holy hell, that hurts, what happened?'"

If there's any question about your ability to have safe sex, start with your doctor or nurse. They can be very helpful, especially when it comes to the mechanics. Here are some opening lines to break the ice:

- **Start the conversation with:** "I'd like to talk to you about something that's a little personal."
- **If you're in a room with a crowd:** "I have something private to discuss, can we talk alone?"
- **If you aren't sure whether you will be able to have sex (or be interested in it):** "Will this treatment/procedure change my ability to have sex?" And "Is there a way to preserve or improve my sexual function?"
- **If you're worried about safety:** This has to be delivered point-blank: "Is it safe for me to have oral/vaginal/anal sex?"

We realize that all this might be awkward, but breaking through the awkwardness is a huge step in the right direction.

——

Can I Even *Have* Sex?

SEX AFTER TREATMENT WILL BRING A WHOLE NEW SERIES OF sensations. Your body may feel different to you; some parts numb, others extra sensitive. And that's just the physical part. Your sense of who you are—your confidence, limits, energy—may have shifted, too. So a frank conversation with a doctor or nurse is a good place to start.

As Susan Gubar wrote in the *New York Times*, "At diagnosis, quite a few cancer patients spy Eros rushing out the door. . . . It can be difficult to experience desire if you don't love but fear your body or if you cannot recognize it as your own. Surgical scars, lost body parts and hair, chemically induced fatigue, radiological burns, nausea, hormone-blocking medications, numbness from neuropathies, weight gain or loss, and anxiety hardly function as aphrodisiacs." Illness, however, does provide a great excuse for revisiting our bodies and for paying attention anew.

——

There's More to Intimacy Than Just Sex

FOR CHARLIE, A YOUNG MAN WITH CEREBELLAR GLIOBLASTOMA multiforme, a rare form of brain cancer, and his girlfriend, Amanda, intercourse was quickly off the table. "I know he feels bad about not giving me that. But when we tried to have sex a few months ago, he was mid pump and just crumpled on top of me and said, 'I can't do this.' He's exhausted or nauseated most of the time from the treatments he's undergoing—not exactly conditions that put you in the mood." But intimacy comes in many forms. For them, cuddling took the place of sex.

Another of Marianne Matzo's patients, a man who could no longer have an erection, voiced concern that his wife would leave him. Matzo turned to the wife and asked, "What do you think about no longer having sex?" His wife confessed that she was actually relieved to hear it. She didn't need it. "We still cuddle, and we're still close," she said. Sometimes all it takes is talking it through—with or without the help of a therapist—to realize that you are still able to be romantically connected with each other in a new way.

The upshot? Screw sex! It gets a lot of attention, and yes, it can be very hard to let it go for good, but intercourse has never been for everybody. And there are all sorts of variations on intimacy waiting to be explored. Let that be exciting if you can—maybe the nervousness can harken back to a time when you were less familiar with one another. There is a lot of body beyond the groin, and any part of it can become erogenous. Find a patch that doesn't hurt—an elbow, toes, hair, wherever—start with a light touch, and work from there. Communicate faithfully and plainly so you know what's working and what's not. Be patient. Here are a few tips:

- **Make small gestures.** A touch on the shoulder, a hug, a foot rub, holding hands. Anything that feels good in the moment.
- **Don't fear the hospital bed.** Medical interventions and equipment might put physical barriers between you that suggest you shouldn't be touching. Tubes, needles, hospital beds with buttons for everything—don't let them get in your way. A hospital bed need not be a prison. It's perfectly legal to crawl in with your beloved. Those side rails *are* retractable.

- **Ask for privacy.** Wherever you are—hospital or nursing facility or hospice or home—you don't need to justify asking others to take a hike. Just say, "We want to be alone for a while. We'll open the door when we're ready for people to come back in."
- **Tell each other what feels good.** A place to touch or a way to touch. Maybe it's certain language used. Or a thing to wear. Whatever helps you feel light or good or unafraid for a moment. You might think it's obvious, but it likely isn't, so say so, or show so. And of course, tell each other what feels bad, too.

——

Connection Comes in Many Forms

I HAD A PATIENT WHO TOLD ME HE'D NEVER REALLY BEEN COMFORTable with human contact in the conventional sense. You could tell by how he was with people in the clinic, from fellow patients in the waiting room to staff at the front desk. But he wasn't as miserable as they thought he was. For him, connection came through his camera. He loved to go for walks through the city at night and take pictures of spontaneous street scenes. He had an amazing eye for people and objects in relationship to one another, as long as he could keep a distance. His photos revealed an affection for others that few felt from him otherwise.

However you engage the world, pay attention to what moves you. Look for these lifelines wherever they show up. ❖

CHAPTER TEN

The Bottom Line

LOVE, SEX, AND RELATIONSHIPS

"Forever" may be shorter than you thought, but urgency has its gifts. If illness and imminent death give us anything—and they most certainly do—it is vulnerability and the intimacy that wants to follow. Closeness can come from surprising sources and can be achieved in ways you might not have considered before now.

HELP ALONG THE WAY

It's not easy to ask for help, but at some point we all need it, and getting the right kind can be a game changer. There are suites of services available that focus on quality of life for you and those you love. From our vantage point, hospice and palliative care are wildly misunderstood, so we discuss them here, including when to request them, what they can do for you, and how they differ. This section also covers how to navigate hospitals, common symptoms you may be feeling, and why caregivers need care, too.

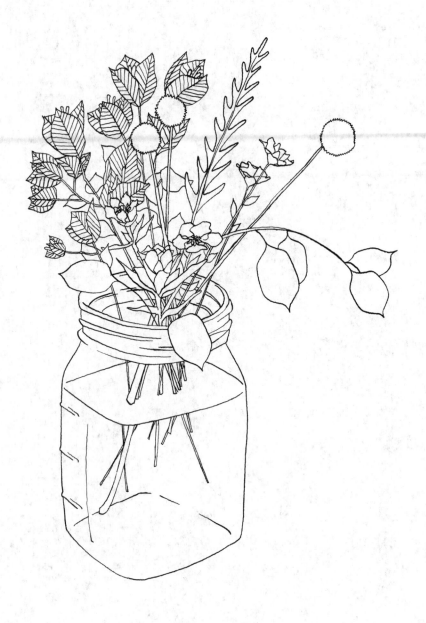

Dynamic Duo: Hospice and Palliative Care

What they are; how and where you get them;
when to get which; how they differ and overlap

Palliative and hospice care are born from the same nurturing instinct: that your physical, spiritual, and emotional care should receive full attention. They are chiefly concerned with how you are feeling.

Palliative care is patient- and family-centered care that optimizes quality of life and treats suffering. It is for anyone at *any* stage of a serious illness, whatever the prognosis, and is intended to be delivered concurrently alongside other treatments, services, and primary care. Most modes of palliative care are covered by medical insurance, are available in most hospitals, and recently have been popping up outside of the hospital, in clinics and even at home. (Note: Some programs are sidestepping the name *palliative care* and calling themselves *symptom management* or *supportive care* services. Same animal, different name.)

Hospice care is designed to treat physical, emotional, and spiritual discomfort for patients with a life expectancy of six months or less. In other words, hospice is a kind of palliative care but designed explicitly for the last stages of life. By this time, aggressive treatment is generally no longer helpful. Therefore, replacing the goal of a cure with that of comfort is generally a condition of your enrollment.

Think of hospice and palliative care as a trusty tag team. Palliative care can start early on, as soon as you feel the need for more support; then, hospice can (literally and figuratively) bring you home. Both are designed to ease suffering and optimize quality of life, and both are multidisciplinary, bringing together expertise from medicine, nursing, social work, and chaplaincy, among others. **The idea is not**

FAST FACT

Hospice care is usually delivered in whatever place you call home and is a defined insurance benefit from Medicare and nearly all other health insurers.

It's a common misconception that hospice and palliative care are one and the same. They are not. While they share a common philosophy and provide a similar range of services, they differ in important details, such as timing and payment.

dying, per se, but living well until you do. In fact, there is abundant evidence that people who receive palliative and hospice care live better than their counterparts who do not. "Better" here means less depression and anxiety—in other words, less stress—and more comfort. There are also enough data now to state with confidence that these types of care don't shorten life, and, in fact, in some cases, they actually help people live longer.

In order to reap their benefits, though, it's best to get palliative and hospice care as soon as you need them. In general, people wait too long to enlist their services and doctors wait too long to refer. The main reason for this is a lack of information. Most people, including many physicians, don't fully understand the differences, so let's start there.

———

Hospice Care

PEOPLE OFTEN THINK THAT HOSPICE IS A PLACE WHERE YOU GO TO spend your last days. Though that's one version, it's comparatively rare. What you get when you sign up for hospice is a team of clinicians *who come to wherever you live* and provide specific types of assistance.

Cicely Saunders is hailed as the godmother of modern hospice. Over the course of her long career she was first a nurse, then a patient, then a social worker, and finally a doctor.

Her approach focused on what she termed "total pain"—a mixture of physical, emotional, and spiritual discomfort, which we now more commonly call "suffering."

FAST FACT
Cicely Saunders founded St. Christopher's Hospice in London in 1967 and was knighted by Queen Elizabeth for her efforts.

This layered understanding led her to create what would become the basic team of any hospice or palliative care program: doctor and nurse tending to the physical; social worker counseling through the emotional; and chaplain attending to the spiritual.

———

The Hospice Benefit

IN 1982, PRESIDENT RONALD REAGAN SIGNED INTO LAW THE MEDICARE Hospice Benefit. So if you have medical insurance, including Medicare, you can rely on access to hospice services at no out-of-pocket cost to you. Since this landmark legislation was enacted, "hospice" refers to both an insurance benefit as well as an approach to care, which can be confusing. You may hear people use the phrase "he's *on* hospice." This means that that person is enrolled in the Hospice Benefit and is receiving hospice care.

The hospice benefit is its own version of medical insurance and takes the place of whatever medical insurance policy you were on. By signing on to hospice, you are signing off of your prior policy (assuming you had one). In most cases, notably for Medicare, it's currently an either/or scenario; however, as we note later, it is possible to "revoke" hospice and have your prior policy kick back in.

If you don't have health insurance at all, whether because you cannot afford it or because you are not a US citizen, most hospital or hospice social workers can help you navigate a relatively quick process to obtain emergency Medicaid, which will then allow you to enroll. For those who still fall through the system's cracks, many nonprofit hospice agencies will accept patients without insurance and provide services as charity or on a sliding scale. Never hesitate to call a hospice agency directly and discuss your situation.

FAST FACT
Even if you are not yet 65 and therefore don't qualify for Medicare, your insurance will have a hospice benefit.

——

How Does One Apply for Hospice Care?

SIGNING ON TO RECEIVE HOSPICE CARE IS GENERALLY STRAIGHTforward and is typically guided by a social worker or nurse from your primary doctor's office or hospital; in that case, the referral sets the process into motion. But you can always call up the agency and ask about enrollment on your own. If you take that route, the hospice will reach out to your main doctor—whether that's a true primary care doctor or a specialist—to confer and initiate the process. Expect to be guided through the logistics and have all your questions answered before signing the enrollment forms. You should never feel pressured to sign up.

A great way to dip your toe in is to request an *informational interview* from a hospice agency to learn more, even far in advance of being ready for the services. In fact, we recommend it. It makes planning for the future much easier, and you'll have a clearer sense of what to expect. When it is time to enroll, someone from the hospice, usually a nurse, will come back to your home with the paperwork to officially get you started. You'll need to sign a few forms, or your assigned health care agent will if you're incapacitated. It's situation dependent, but it can all happen within a day.

Think about hospice early on, earlier than you or your doctor might otherwise consider appropriate. Most of the time, people wait unnecessarily long to enroll in hospice, too late to receive all its benefits. In 2014, 45 percent of Americans (roughly 1.7 million) who died did so on hospice—a number on the rise since inception of the hospice benefit. Since hospice is acknowledged as the gold standard of end-of-life care, this growth is a good thing. But the average time a person spent on hospice was just over two months. Half were only on hospice for 18 days, and one-third were enrolled for a week or less before they died. For some situations, a short stay is just right. But more commonly it just means people are suffering more than they need to. Don't wait for your doctor to bring it up. Ask about it.

——

Qualifying for Hospice Care

To qualify, you must:

- **Be living with a terminal illness.** This means some disease or illness or condition that cannot be cured or one that you are not interested in treating but that will, one way or another, result in death. I've heard patients comment that they aren't qualified for hospice care because they "don't have cancer." The type of illness does not affect your eligibility.
- **Have a physician's certification stating that you will most likely die within six months if the disease follows its natural course.** Enrollment also requires the hospice medical director's certification accepting you into care (in short, two doctors must agree).

A few things to note:

- **Prognostication is difficult and imprecise.** It is not uncommon for a person on hospice to be recertified and remain on hospice for longer than six months.
- **Hospice is for those whose health is in decline. But, it does happen that some people's health *improves* while receiving hospice care.** If the hospice doctor determines a patient is no longer showing signs of decline, regulations stipulate that the person be disenrolled from the hospice program. At such a time, the hospice benefit ends and routine health insurance automatically resumes. That person can always reenroll in hospice down the road.
- **There is nothing magical about the six-month mark.** Our bodies don't somehow change with six months left of life, and one

shouldn't expect to feel different at that moment. It's an arbitrary cutoff legislators thought they had to make in order to designate who would qualify for this high-touch kind of care.

- **"Hospice certification" sounds fancy, but all you really need to do is talk to your doctor about it and he will work with the hospice agency to complete the necessary documentation.** Often, doctors wait too long to refer or resist altogether. So you the patient—or your proxy—might need to push if this is what you want. Ask him, why *isn't* hospice right for me now? When do you think it will be? Remember, deep barriers to facing mortality live in all of us—patient and doctor alike.

- **Be prepared to forgo further curative attempts.** You can still seek treatment for other conditions, just not the terminal one. For example, if heart failure is what's going to end your life— and is therefore your official hospice diagnosis—your doctor can still treat your diabetes or ingrown toenails. To what extent it makes sense for you to treat other problems now is a question for you and your doctor to think through, but know that you're not automatically prohibited from doing so.

  In practical terms, this rule also means that you are no longer going to the hospital. This can be welcome news, and it can feel scary, too—for many of us, the hospital represents a safe house where all sorts of possibilities seem within reach, including cure. That said, exceptions are made when suffering is too intense to be quelled at home; in this case the goal of the hospital stay is to treat symptoms, not the disease. Other exceptions are commonsensical enough: if you fall and break your arm, for example, the hospice will arrange for you to get to the hospital to take care of it.

- **Also know that you can always sign off of hospice if it doesn't wind up feeling right for you. It's called "revoking" hospice.**

By law, your old insurance policy kicks back in, and you'll have lost nothing. You can always come back. So, when in doubt, and the goal is clearly comfort, it is rarely too early to enroll.

——

What You Get Once You Are Enrolled

YOUR NEEDS WILL LIKELY SHIFT OVER THE COURSE OF YOUR TIME ON hospice, and those needs will dictate the routine of the hospice staff who visit you. Some weeks you may have multiple visits from everyone on the list, but if your symptoms are under control and you're feeling pretty good, you might just need a single check-in visit from the nurse and a follow-up phone call or two. If your issues are more related to activities of daily living (ADLs)—that is, you mostly need help with bathing and toileting—then you might see much more of the aides than the nurse. The rhythm of care depends on what's going on with you at that time. Here is the full list of people and services to be drawn from:

- A hospice doctor who oversees care and prescribes medicines for pain and other symptoms. Sometimes this role is shared by a nurse practitioner. This can be your regular doctor (primary care or any specialty) or the hospice's medical director. If you have a preference, make it known, but also know that while you may want your doctor to oversee your hospice, your doctor may not want or be able to, and can opt out, handing over the reins to the hospice medical director. Given the special level of expertise required, this may be a good idea. Note that you'll see much more of the rest of the team than you will the hospice doctor. They're engaged, though mostly in the background, fielding questions from nurses and others, writing orders, and checking notes.

- **A nurse who visits every few days to every two weeks (the official minimum)**, depending on your needs, to touch base with you and your family about your symptoms, and then check in with the doctor or nurse practitioner to refine the plan for your care and make changes if needed.
- **An aide who comes several days per week** for an hour or two to help with personal care (bathing, grooming) and basic tasks at home. Her or his schedule is assigned by your nurse.
- **A social worker or other counselor to help with emotional and logistical side issues.** Support in the form of coordinating caregiving schedules, speaking with you about your family-related concerns, advance planning, help with medical leave for your family members, deciding on funeral arrangements, finding services such as food-delivery programs, and setting up facility moves for respite or long-term stays.
- **A chaplain, trained in interfaith ministry, to provide spiritual support.** He or she can also be in touch with your own clergy or help find someone of your faith tradition to visit you. A chaplain can also be a great ear when you want to talk about everything and anything.
- **A volunteer, if you need one, or request one,** to assist with grocery shopping, gardening, or keeping vigil at the bedside so the caregiver can step out.
- **A physical or occupational therapist, dietician, and speech-language pathologist** (to help with swallowing or communication difficulties). These services tend to be limited beyond a basic assessment but can still be of great value.
- **A grief counselor** provides emotional and psychological care

Chaplains are

INTERFAITH

Chaplains aren't just for last rites and don't require that you be religious or of a certain faith.

to patients, families, and loved ones who are dealing with issues of grief and loss, both during the time on hospice care and following the death.

- **Basic supplies and durable medical equipment (DME)**, such as an adjustable hospital bed, bedside commode, wheelchair, and other medical supplies, all delivered to wherever you are living.
- **24/7 telephone support**, so you have someone to contact at 1:00 a.m. if help is needed. Most of the time a nurse will work to mitigate and treat the situation over the phone, but if not able, they will send someone to you. You should always call the hospice before calling 911. With hospice, the goal is for your symptoms to be treated at home.
- **"Respite stays."** You, the patient receiving hospice care in your home, can go stay in a certified facility (usually a nursing home or inpatient hospice facility) for up to five days at a time to give your family and friends a break. This is meant for occasional use, but in my experience the respite benefit is underutilized. Ask your team about it—it's a great perk for families.
- **Prescription support.** Your hospice doctor and nurse will help trim your medication list to whatever is essential now for your comfort. When living with advanced disease or diseases, it's easy to accumulate medications that may once have been useful for you but no longer are. Many hospice agencies will deliver meds to you, saving you trips to the pharmacy; refills are managed by your nurse, so let them know when you're running low. With the opiate epidemic ballooning, access to pain medication is becoming more restricted, and this can make it unduly hard for people who really need these meds to get them. When you're a hospice patient, you get to avoid some of the clerical hurdles.

- **Around-the-clock nursing care in the home for a day or two if** discomfort is overwhelming or some other crisis pops up. If the suffering is outpacing what can be done at home, the hospice benefit will pay for a short stay in the hospital to get on top of the situation. Your hospice team should stay closely involved, working with the hospital staff to ensure continuity of care, once inside the hospital.

For Caregivers

Despite the impressively large cast of characters available to you while on hospice, the majority of any day is spent without them. Aside from scheduled visits and the occasional spontaneous one as needed, these folks aren't just hanging around the house. In other words, there's still a lot of work left for family and friends. The nurse will teach you the ins and outs of daily medical care for your loved one, but you'll still be tending to the home, dosing morphine and other meds, changing bed linens, helping with toileting and cleaning, repositioning your loved one in bed or on the couch, and keeping a watchful eye out for falls. Look into respite care (see the list of what hospice provides above), and for those who can afford it, consider hiring an aide to supplement what the hospice agency offers. (See chapter 14, "Help! I Need Somebody.")

As a system, hospice is—bar none—the way to get the most services into your home. Because the hospice benefit covers "social" issues as well as medical ones, hospice can also serve you in ways the rest of the health care system can't. For those of us who are alone, the benefit may be only more poignant; hospice is the closest thing to acquiring a family at the end of life. There are limits to what they can do, of course—they can't be in your home all day, every day to dispense every medication or change every diaper—but it's hard to recommend any service more highly.

——

Where Can I Get Hospice Care?

IT BEARS REPEATING: IN THE UNITED STATES, "HOSPICE" DOES NOT refer to a place. It's a *type of care* and will be delivered to you wherever you call home: an apartment, barn, house, trailer, or tent. However, there are a few exceptions in which hospice is both a physical place *and* a kind of care; these are rare but can be a godsend.

RESIDENTIAL HOSPICES

Both types noted below are usually built to feel like home. In fact, many are converted homes. They are mostly small and intimate—often just a handful of bedrooms with some amount of common space and easy outdoor access—created for comfort, not sterility. You'll more likely smell baking bread than bleach, and they tend to be places you want to be in, not flee. Both types will have nursing staff present around the clock and an affiliated doctor on call.

To find one of these places, ask your local hospice agency;

hospice comes to YOU

Hospice comes to wherever you are, and will follow you as you move from place to place. Even if you relocate to a different state, your hospice team can help you find an agency in the new area to assume your care.

even if the agency does not operate such a facility, they will know whether there is one in your area. Case managers and hospital discharge planners are also good people to ask.

Inpatient Hospice

Inpatient hospices are usually owned and operated by a hospice agency. While typically homey, these places are able to provide hospital-level acute care when needed, such as intravenous medications. Inpatient hospice programs are typically designed for a short stay, long enough to get on top of your symptoms before you're discharged back to wherever you call home. They are also able to offer respite care, as described earlier in this chapter. Both types of short stays—acute and respite—are covered by the hospice benefit. If you wish to stay longer, expect to pay out of pocket.

Residential Facility (Social Model or Hospice House)

These places are even less formal than the typical inpatient hospice. It's easy to forget that people are dying here. Residential hospice houses often have storied histories, having grown out of religious or other community organizations. These places fall outside the medical system, which is part of their charm, but since licensure is through your state's department of social services (not health care), services are not covered by the hospice benefit or any medical insurance. Long-term-care insurance dollars (see chapter 4, "Can I Afford to Die?"), however, can be put to this purpose. Many such places raise philanthropic dollars to defray costs and can offer pricing based on your ability to pay, but expect to pay something out of pocket. Residential facilities collaborate with local hospice agencies to provide the medical care but are owned and operated as an independent organization. Most people move in and stay until death.

WHAT ABOUT NURSING HOMES?

In general, if you're living in a nursing home you can still get hospice services there. But do note that the nursing home and hospice agency are typically separate organizations. Ask right from the beginning how those two teams will interact with each other. Will the hospice team recommend medications that the nursing home physician has to order? If so, who should you speak with if you have questions, or if an urgent need arises? The services the hospice team provides are there to supplement the nursing home care. The nursing home should not provide any less care, and the hospice team should still be offering their full range of support, including 24/7 access and help from a personal care attendant. If it feels like the nursing home staff and hospice staff are having trouble coordinating their services you should call attention to the matter and ask that they take a look at who is doing what; everyone involved *should* have their eye on giving you and your family the best care possible, but it may require your own advocacy.

TIP
If you're feeling that your care is in disarray, request a group meeting with both your hospice care team and the staff at the nursing facility to work it out in person.

———

Choosing a Hospice Provider

IN GENERAL, HOSPICE IS CURRENTLY MUCH MORE ACCESSIBLE THAN other types of palliative care programs. The majority of the US population lives within thirty minutes of multiple hospice agencies, so, depending on where you live you'll likely have a choice. Some questions to consider when comparing agencies:

- **Who owns it?** Hospice agencies are independent organizations, not part of a branch of the government. From survey data on quality, across the industry as a whole, nonprofit hospice organizations perform better than for-profit ones. It's not a fixed rule, but it's a data point worth considering when comparing organizations. We certainly believe that *service* is a better motive than *profit*, but it's too simple to suggest for-profit enterprises are inherently bad, and not-for-profits inherently good.
- **What is the staffing ratio?**

    ○ **How many doctors are on staff per patient?** A low patient-to-doctor ratio is best
    ○ **How many patients do nurse case managers carry?** Same idea here, lower ratios are preferred
    ○ **What percentage of patients receive nursing and social work visits in the final two days of life?** A high percentage is what's best here, but note that 100 percent isn't realistic. Sometimes death comes unexpectedly, even in hospice care

Another reason to think about hospice early on: you'll have time to ask around and get a sense of which organization provides the best care. Of course, ask your clinical team for an opinion (especially nurses and social workers) and better yet, you probably know someone who's used hospice services before, maybe a friend or a friend's family member.

——

Hospice Is Not Infallible

AS WITH ANY SERVICE, QUALITY WILL VARY. EVER BEEN TO YOUR favorite coffee shop and it's obvious that everyone called in sick and one poor person has been left to ring everyone up *and* make the drinks? Hospice is a business, too, and is affected by the same mundane staffing issues as any other: illness, vacations, car trouble. The difference here is that a long wait for a bad latté will never be comparable to a late nursing visit when you are in desperate need of help. The hospice system is a part of our stressed health care system and that means it is stressed, too. Burnout and turnover are significant problems across the industry; meanwhile, training programs struggle to impart the sort of knowledge and grizzled experience that good patient care requires.

We're big fans of hospice and feel strongly that the world needs more of it. But since we've gone to such lengths to tout its benefits, we also feel the need to acknowledge that hospice programs sometimes fail to live up to their promises. In general, the great majority of people are very happy with the hospice care they receive, and satisfaction data bear this out. On those occasions when things don't go well, it is usually due to communication breakdowns, wayward expectations, or resourcing issues. But not always; some programs are just plain inept.

We mention this to arm you with the background information to ask good questions and guard against disappointment on top of all the other emotions you are dealing with.

You can learn a lot about a hospice agency by talking to other families who have enlisted their help. Here are some questions to ask:

- Did the hospice agency inform you about the care plan and what to expect from the disease? Did they keep your loved one comfortable?
- Did you have a consistent point of contact? Was the team consistent?
- Did they extend emotional support to you and your family?
- Did you consider other programs? Why did you choose this one?
- Did the hospice stay involved after the death to help your family through grief?
- Do you have any regrets?
- What do you wish you had known before choosing hospice?

And if you aren't gelling with your team, you can request a change in personnel; they may not always have the staff to accommodate your request, but any decent organization will try their best to. They're not selling widgets; they're in the compassionate service business, and this is too important a time in your life to just make do.

———

Palliative Care

PALLIATIVE CARE IS AN OLD IDEA THAT HAS BECOME AN OFFICIAL clinical discipline. It owes its origins to hospice. Legend has it, one morning in the late 1970s, Dr. Balfour Mount, a Canadian surgeon and hospice pioneer who studied with Cicely Saunders, came up with the phrase *palliative care* while at his sink, shaving. He was trying to expunge the unpleasant connotations the word *hospice* had accrued (something like *home for the wretched*), and landed on the less frightening *palliative care* to describe the work he did. *Palliate* means "to ease." Here's how Medicare defines palliative care:

Palliative care is **patient- and family-centered** care that optimizes **quality of life** by anticipating, preventing, and treating **suffering.** Palliative care throughout the continuum of illness involves addressing physical, intellectual, emotional, social, and spiritual needs and facilitates patient autonomy, access to information, and choice.

This should be what all medical care provides, yet, as of now, health care isn't organized this way. So palliative care came along to offer a different orientation: to heed your wishes and alleviate your suffering. There is no qualifying test for suffering and there is no one-size-fits-all definition of quality of life. You, the patient, are here to guide the clinicians as much as they guide you. Kindness and respect in this approach to care are not just niceties but its central tenets.

The field developed in the 1960s and '70s with a focus on end-of-life care. But eventually the real goal became clearer: helping patients feel as well as possible *anywhere* along the path of illness, *including* (but not limited to) the very end. **There is no mention of death or time limits in the definition of palliative care.**

——

How Can You Get Palliative Care?

JUST ABOUT ANY TYPE OF DISTRESS WILL QUALIFY YOU FOR PALLIATIVE care, whether it is pain or nausea; whether it is caused by anxiety or dread, communication breakdown, or family burnout: it is available for any kind of suffering experienced *in the course of a serious illness.*

Some palliative care programs require a physician's referral, but many do not. Individual palliative care programs will have their own limitations and eligibility requirements. For example, the clinic where I work sees only people with cancer.

You probably won't have multiple programs to choose from, though that should change in the coming years. When you do find one, ask about the specific services they're able to offer, how frequently you can expect contact, and which team members will cover which types of issues. You should also ask about costs, as insurers will require copays, at least, for some or all services.

——

How Palliative Care Works

IT'S IMPORTANT THAT YOU HAVE AN IDEA OF WHAT TO EXPECT. FROM one program to the next and one person to the next, there is sure to be a range of quality and polish, and at this early stage in the field's development not every program can provide all services listed below. But whatever the range, when palliative care is functioning as it should, you give up nothing and gain much. Here's the full scope of services:

- Discussions with the patient and family about goals of care and help in making sure that those goals are documented
- Management of pain and other symptoms
- Assistance making sure you have and understand how to use all your medications
- Communication about your medical conditions and what to expect as those conditions progress
- Emotional support for patients and family caregivers
- Help coordinating care delivered by all your providers and as you move from one setting to another (from hospital to nursing home or private residence, for example), especially

communicating with them about how things stand with symptoms and your evolving goals of care

- Referrals to community resources for assistance with social and practical needs (such as medical supply stores, meal delivery programs, peer support groups)
- Spiritual support
- Bereavement services for families

——

Types of Delivery

IN THE HOSPITAL SETTING, A PALLIATIVE CARE TEAM MIGHT WORK with you intensively for a few days, helping with any of the above issues. Here you're likely to meet a team: MD, nurse, social worker, and chaplain, at least. They might be with you throughout the hospital stay or just for part of it, depending on what you need. The team might also return if you end up in the hospital again, when familiar faces can be so soothing. Hospital-based palliative care tends to be intense, brief, and confined to the walls of the hospital.

FAST FACT
A small but growing number of programs offer in-home visits, either in person or by videoconference (via your computer or smartphone).

Programs based outside the hospital are gaining traction in clinics, in patients' homes, in nursing homes, and via telemedicine. Services will usually take place in a clinic setting (an office). You may be less likely to meet the whole team than you would in the hospital; much of the interdisciplinary work is done in the background. You might just see the doctor with visits clumped over the course of a few weeks, if your situation is temporary, or you might see the doctor once every month or two, though over the course of many years. As with much of outpatient health care, your relationship with it tends to unfold over a period far longer than your time in the hospital.

——

Where Can You Find Palliative Care?

THOUGH THE FIELD IS GROWING FAST, SERVICES ARE PATCHY, AND especially scarce in the Southeast and in more rural settings. As of now, there is one hospice and palliative medicine physician for every 13,000 people diagnosed with a serious illness. So keep an eye out for palliative care programs, but don't necessarily expect that you can find one near you yet.

You can ask for palliative care wherever you are. Whether you're in the hospital or visiting clinic, ask your doctor or nurse whether they have a program. Even if you're feeling pretty good and don't need their help, it's great to know what's available. If it isn't available, your request will register and help the field grow to meet the need. You might also contact your local hospice organization and ask if they offer palliative care services or know of a group or hospital in your area that does. ❖

PALLIATIVE AND HOSPICE CARE: A SIDE-BY-SIDE COMPARISON

	PALLIATIVE CARE	HOSPICE CARE
Timing	Any stage of serious illness, any prognosis.	Life expectancy 6 months or less.
Integration with other health care services	Intended to be delivered concurrently with all other treatments and services.	In most cases must forgo further curative-intent care for terminal illness as condition of enrollment.
Cost	Covered by medical insurance but not as a defined benefit (mostly; the insurance industry is actively experimenting with novel ways of covering it). You'll likely have copays.	Defined insurance benefit from Medicare and nearly all other health insurers. Generally all-encompassing, and no copays for you.
Availability	Mostly in hospitals (80 percent of the hospitalized population in the United States has access to a palliative care program). Data are lacking for palliative care delivered outside the hospital, but it's clear that there are not enough programs to suit the need.	Mostly at home. Widely available (more than 5,500 in the United States), but underutilized (63 percent of enrollees use hospice for less than 30 days, including 36 percent with length of service 7 days or less).

The Bottom Line

DYNAMIC DUO: HOSPICE AND PALLIATIVE CARE

Palliative care focuses on your quality of life as well as your family's, managing the symptoms and stresses of serious illness. You can qualify for it anywhere along the arc of illness, not just at the end of life. Hospice, a type of palliative care, is the gold standard for end-of-life health care. Qualifying has its limitations, but once you do, hospice is the way to get the most services delivered to you wherever you call home. As a general rule, within our context of serious illness, *the sooner, the better* for both.

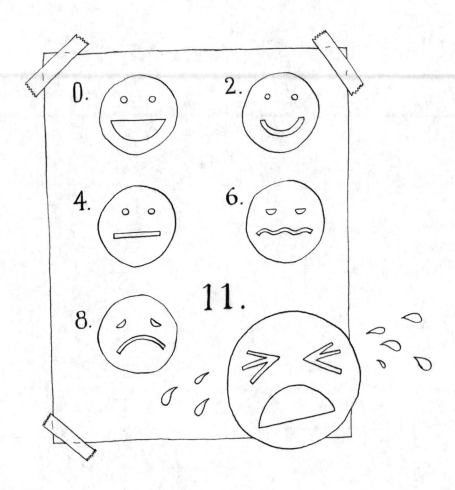

Symptoms 101

What you may feel and experience over
the course of advanced illness

Andy's cardiologist referred him to us for help with nausea. He'd tried a few medications but nothing worked. His heart was the main problem. After years of untreated high blood pressure he had developed congestive heart failure in his late sixties.

The morning I met him, Andy was (distractingly) hilarious, cracking deadpan jokes the whole time. But the distress on his wife, Rose's, face suggested there was more going on. He was one of those guys you had to watch and listen to carefully. He'd bury important information in what sounded like throwaway comments. I asked him about his appetite. "I can eat like a horse," he said. Rose, nearly in tears, started to tell me how moody Andy was at the dinner table, the place that had always been their center of connection and joy. Once she had opened up the conversation, Andy shared how much he hated this nausea—the thing that was killing his formerly generous appetite.

Constipation is a scourge and one of the main causes of nausea, so I asked, *How often are you moving your bowels?* "Jesus, Doc, you don't want to hear about that!" Andy shot back. Pause. Then: "Well, I haven't been eating much of late, so I don't need to go as much." He'd not had a good bowel movement in more than a week. And before that one it had been more than ten days.

It turned out that Andy had been prescribed low-dose morphine for the shortness of breath common to severe heart failure. The drug was right for him—he was breathing much more comfortably now—but he had nothing to treat the constipation that invariably comes with opiates. Complicating things further, the medication his cardiologist had prescribed for nausea was itself constipating.

Mystery solved: nausea caused by constipation caused by medication side effect, necessitated by breathing problems caused by an ailing heart. Andy needed to be on a specific kind of laxative every day, for however long his breathlessness required opiates. And since it had been so long since he'd had a bowel movement of any significance, that day he'd need two enemas to get things moving. Symptoms often intertwine, caused or exacerbated by the medications that are helping on other fronts. But untangling that knot isn't always obvious. It requires thorough communication among everyone involved. Most symptoms and side effects are treatable. Missed signals, less so.

——

Most Discomfort Is Treatable

HOW ARE YOU FEELING? WHATEVER THE DIAGNOSIS, IT'S THE SENSATION that gets our attention. When unattended, loud and obnoxious symptoms can drown out everything else in life. But much can be done to turn down the noise and bring relief, and even a brief reprieve can be revitalizing.

But let's check our expectations. "Fixing" discomfort is only sometimes possible. With incurable illness generally comes incurable symptoms. If the source of the symptom isn't going away, like cancer or organ failure, the symptom likely won't, either. So, the more realistic goal is to get to a state where you're comfortable enough to not be consumed by the symptom.

——

Acute Versus Chronic Symptoms

ANY SYMPTOM MAY BE ACUTE OR CHRONIC. THE DIFFERENCE HAS TO do with time and urgency.

ACUTE SYMPTOMS

Acute symptoms are brief and severe, telling us that something is wrong. Acute pain, for example, is a helpful signal that alerts us that something has changed and we should stop doing what we're doing. In this way, pain can protect us and prevent damage. And if a new symptom is severe—in other words, has you screaming—it's a good idea to call your doctor or hospice agency right away. If those calls aren't cutting it, then you might need to take a trip to the emergency department. Any of the symptoms listed in this chapter can present acutely.

CHRONIC SYMPTOMS

Acute symptoms might set off alarms, but chronic ones can be a lot more annoying. **Chronic symptoms are experienced over time (months or longer), often persisting despite attempts at treatment, and don't require an urgent response.** In other words, taxing as they are, chronic symptoms don't pose an immediate threat to your health, so a trip to the ER for chronic pain, for example, won't likely get you very far. With no immediate action to take, chronic symptoms can be more of a challenge than acute ones.

Those who don't know chronic pain will have a very hard time appreciating the full scope of its effects. Unrelenting, smoldering symptoms chew through our physical, emotional, and psychic reserves, leaving the most cheerful among us in a foul temper and short on will. There can be a demoralizing component—*I know something is wrong, but I feel powerless to stop it*—and in such moments, our body might feel like a failure or an enemy.

The upshot is that time itself can help: time for you to try different treatments, and time for you to become familiar with all sorts of sensations. I often hear "I'm not sure if the pain got better or I just got used to it, but either way I feel better." As with chronic illness, eventually, you'll do yourself a favor by working with your symptoms rather than trying to flee them. Much discomfort comes from resistance.

———

The Truth About Symptoms

THE EXPERIENCE OF SYMPTOMS IS COMPLEX AND VARIES FROM ONE person to the next. No two of us are exactly alike, and we will not experience symptoms the same way.

You're the best judge of what's working for you and what isn't. You get to say whether symptom treatments are helping or not. Unlike many disease treatments, clarity about effectiveness is not the stuff of testing or blood levels. When treating symptoms, if you feel better, then keep doing what you're doing. If you do not, talk to your team about other things to try. Your doctor may be the one who's able to tell you whether a treatment is working on your illness, but you're the expert on how you feel.

Medications can cause other symptoms. Most medications have side effects. Pain meds in particular can make folks feel dopey or sluggish, leaving you wondering if what you're feeling is due to the disease or the meds. The only way to find out is to stop the medication and see, but stopping meds might send you into a tailspin of discomfort, including withdrawal, so discuss it with the team and, if you get your doctor's go-ahead, schedule a trial.

There are many ways to take meds, including by mouth, nose, vein, skin, and rectum. Very few medications can be delivered by all of these routes, and each comes with its own suite of practical issues. For instance, getting IV medications at home is very difficult due to safety and regulatory concerns, the skilled labor needed to inject the drug, and costs. And many medications do not come in a form suitable for nose or skin. So medicating at home usually means being limited to oral or rectal routes, and when you're unable to swallow reliably, practically speaking, this just leaves the rectum. This might be off-putting, but the rectum is actually a very effective means of dosing many of the medications commonly helpful at the end of life, and if you're uncomfortable enough you'll be glad for the option.

——

Keeping Track of Your Symptoms

IT CAN BE VERY HELPFUL TO MAKE NOTE OF A FEW THINGS IN RELATION to your symptoms. All of these will help you and your doctor find patterns and guide treatment. Keep these in a notebook or on a computer, just as you would a diary or journal:

- **Timing:** When does the symptom come on? Note both time of day and duration.
- **Association:** Does it happen when you're in a certain position? Doing a certain activity? When you eat a certain food? With other medications?
- **Severity:** Is it mildly annoying or so bad you can't concentrate on anything else?
- **Fluctuations:** What makes it better? What makes it worse?

——

Alternative Treatments

PHARMACEUTICAL MEDICINE IS THE DE FACTO DRIVER OF US MEDICAL ...ction of the book has a medical bias; but this is only one lens through which to understand and treat symptoms and the illnesses that cause them. If you are interested in exploring other methods, seek out naturopaths, herbalists, traditional Chinese healers, and integrative medicine clinicians, to name a few. Most US doctors will have only a basic appreciation for nonmedical treatments, at best, so you may need to look outside the hospital or clinic. Nonetheless, your doctor may know someone to point you to, as may other patients or support groups or friends. Ask around.

...rcent pa...ts are using some form of alternative medicine, but only 30 percent admit that to their doctor.[1]

——

A-to-Z Symptom Primer

ALMOST NO ONE WILL EXPERIENCE ALL OF THESE SYMPTOMS, AND almost no one will experience none of them. For each symptom described below, we've also included a basic list of treatments. Note that we've only included treatments for which there is *some* scientific evidence or expert opinion of effectiveness. You will undoubtedly hear, online or by word of mouth, about other treatments that are not mentioned here. There may well be other things that help, but the hard part is finding proof that they actually work. For that reason, we've kept our lists conservative. Herbal and non-pharamcological treatments tend to be milder and safer than pharmaceuticals, though anything you ingest has potential for side effects and could react poorly with other drugs.

So use these medication lists as a reference guide to prompt further discussion with your doctor, *not* to self-diagnose or self-medicate.

While many options on these lists won't be right for you specifically, it's important that you know that every symptom we mention has multiple choices for treatment, so be sure to not hold back how you're feeling from your clinical team, and be prepared to try a few different things at different doses. Good symptom management requires a stepwise approach. Your doctor will likely try the safest and mildest drugs first, then together you'll ramp up from there.

For Caregivers

It's hard to watch someone you love suffer. That's the nature of empathy—their pain becomes yours. See if you can channel this heat into other things that might help. Distract your loved one (and yourself) with conversation or a television show; entertain by telling stories or jokes; scream together at the top of your lungs. Pour that empathy into action.

But there will be limits to what you or anyone else can do. You might be upset with them for not doing this or that, or just for hurting. Sometimes the greatest service you can provide is to drop the judgment and let it all be. See chapter 15, "Care for the Caregiver," for more on how to look out for yourself.

ANXIETY AND DEPRESSION

These two have to do with your *mood*. Anxiety is an overall sense of worry or fear or difficulty concentrating. Depression is also common, showing up often as lethargy or having no interest in anything. Of course, all of these signs and symptoms are a normal part of being sick; it's just a matter of degree and to what ends you wish to go to treat them. Sometimes, what feels like anxiety or depression is really boredom or frustration. When we're ill, we may inadvertently cut ourselves off from the sources of inspiration and joy we need to function well. So the first order of business is to make sure that, rather than going straight for medication, you wouldn't fare better putting yourself in front of something you care about.

Herbal and nonpharmacological options: Professional psychotherapist counseling; distraction (safe activities such as going outside, taking in a good movie or book, games); meditation; breathing exercises; guided imagery; physical exercise; yoga; energy healing (Reiki, Healing Touch, tai chi, qigong); music therapy; animal-assisted therapy; massage; acupuncture; craniosacral therapy; essential oils (lavender, citrus, clary sage, bergamot, ylang ylang); herbs (like milky oats seed).

Medications include: Antidepressants; benzodiazepines; psychostimulants; cannabis.

CONFUSION

In clinical lingo, the term is *delirium*. A person with delirium may be unaware of place or time. It is very common in hospital and institutional settings, especially in intensive care units (ICUs); anywhere unfamiliar to the person, or when the sleep/wake cycle is interrupted. Delirium can result from infection (urinary tract infection); neurological conditions, especially of the brain (brain tumors, dementias); insomnia; poorly controlled pain (or other symptoms like constipation, depression, or shortness of breath); medication side effects; liver or kidney disease.

Often delirium evolves from subtle to obvious over the course of days or weeks. In clinic I sometimes ask patients if they've noticed any periods of confusion or fuzziness. Strange dreams and waking dream states can be harbingers of a brewing delirium, too. Often, however, it's family members who make mention of confusion or vague personality changes. Delirium is generally a waxing and waning state—so on any given day or week, there may be periods of clarity mixed with periods of confusion. It may tend to worsen—or be more obvious—at night (sometimes referred to as "sundowning").

Delirium is not something you can control and is nothing to be ashamed of. It's common for people to know something is not quite right with their thinking (and to hide that fact). People, whether patients or caregivers, may be too embarrassed or too afraid to mention early signs.

FAST FACT

In some instances, delirium is subtle, producing a *hypoactive* state, meaning that you may appear very sleepy and still. Other times, delirium is agitating and causes a *hyperactive* state, in which case it's more obvious.

Herbal and nonpharmacological options: Ambient essential oils (rosemary, vetiver, citrus, basil); craniosacral therapy; animal-assisted therapy; acupuncture.

Medications include: Antipsychotics; benzodiazepines.

CONSTIPATION

Often overlooked by clinicians treating people with serious illness, constipation can cause or exacerbate pain, nausea, loss of appetite, shortness of breath, fatigue, and even delirium. It's a common side effect of many diseases as well as of the most prescribed medications—opiates, for example, even at minimal

For Caregivers

Since delirium means the patient is largely unaware, it's typically up to you to intervene and alert the doctor. Delirium often warrants medical treatment, but there are some things for you to try, too:

- **Attempt to correct the person's sleep/wake cycle.** Encourage wakefulness during the daytime, including exposure to sunlight, and sleep at night. Going for a walk, getting out of the bed and into a chair—any form of (nonpainful) physical activity—will help. And be sure they stay as well hydrated as possible.

- **Conduct a casual conversation.** This can help organically reorient the person, and also help unearth where the problem lies. Keep the conversation basic: "Have you seen the nurse this morning?" Or "Isn't it a beautiful day?" The idea is to help the person stay oriented. Talk about familiar people, current events. Remember, though, that the person isn't in control of his thoughts, so take care not to judge or unwittingly embarrass him; being flustered by "incorrectness" only makes matters worse for everyone. Follow the lead of his mood: if the discussion is causing agitation, pause and redirect; if the person is engaged and comfortable, keep the conversation thread going.

- **Surround the person with familiar objects.** Photos or a

For Caregivers (continued)

favorite quilt or artwork. (And don't forget their eyeglasses or hearing aids.)

- Place a clock within sight or make sure the person is in a room with a window. This helps a person reorient without having to ask.

doses, nearly always cause people to become backed up. Immobility, nervous system dysfunction, and dehydration are other common issues contributing to constipation. Here are a few other things to keep in mind:

- Whatever your normal bowel habit was before getting sick, that should be your goal now. The gastrointestinal tract is lined with glands that are always secreting fluid, and cells are perpetually turning over and falling into the gut. All that stuff needs to keep moving, all the way out, no matter how little food you're taking in. If a daily bowel movement was your routine, then it should still be, no matter how much or little you are eating. The exception is in the final days of life, when the effort needed to move the bowels may be impractical and unhelpful.
- Sometimes people report having diarrhea, when in fact it might merely be the watery part of the feces seeping around impacted stool.
- The longer one waits to take action, the harder the stool becomes and the more difficult it becomes to move. If it has been

more than three days since your last bowel movement, you may require an enema or even manual disimpaction (using a finger or special tool to loosen and retrieve stool; if possible, this is better left to skilled professionals).

- Unless you're able to take in copious amounts of water, don't use fiber supplements (such as Metamucil) when taking opiates; fiber makes the stool tacky and can make it *more* difficult to move your bowels, especially if you're dehydrated.

Herbal and nonpharmacological options: Hydration; warm water with fresh lemon or lime juice; chewing on fennel seeds; ambulation/mobilization; abdominal massage; acupuncture; acupressure; reflexology; prune juice; biofeedback and other relaxation techniques; homeopathy; flaxseed oil; herbs such as senna or triphala.

Medications include: Laxatives (multiple subclasses, including bulk, lubricating, osmotic, stimulant); prokinetics; lubiprostone, misoprostol, methylnaltrexone, tegaserod.

DIARRHEA

From a medical perspective, we'd rather your bowels move too frequently than not frequently enough. Sometimes we actively encourage diarrhea, as with advanced stages of liver failure, in order to keep toxins from building up in your system. But any new-onset diarrhea (chemotherapies are a common culprit) should be discussed with a clinician before starting over-the-counter medications; it may be an incontinence problem requiring aggressive skin care and ointments, or be a cue to change other medications or doses. Plus, when self-medicating the bowels, it's easy to swing too far in the other direction and cause constipation.

Herbal and nonpharmacological options: Slippery elm; aloe vera juice; carob powder; probiotics; fermented foods; bland foods such as bananas, rice, or toast; electrolyte and fluid replacement; chamomile and peppermint tea; over-steeped black tea.

Medications include: Bismuth subsalicylate/Pepto-Bismol (a great place to start because Pepto doesn't stop your bowels from moving, it just binds the watery stool and slows it down); tincture of opium; loperamide/Imodium and diphenoxylate/Lomotil (for more serious or intractable cases, these can be very helpful but warrant caution since it's not hard to overshoot and stop your bowels moving altogether).

DRY MOUTH

Xerostomia is the fancy word for this. Dry mouth is a common and unremitting symptom of advanced disease. It can be due to dehydration or poor circulation; breakdown of glandular function of any cause; too much bacteria in the mouth; or it can be a side effect of medication. Check with your physician that an infection—such as thrush—isn't to blame.

Herbal and nonpharmacological options: Drink warm tea and lemon (to help cut through dry, thickened plaques); try mouthwash; stay hydrated; acupuncture; lip balm; artificial saliva products (like Biotene); suck on tart candies or lozenges or ice chips; foods like watermelon ice, frozen blueberries, ground-up cashews with a little bit of water or avocado, olive oil, and salt; swab the mouth with glycerin.

Medications include: Secretagogues.

FATIGUE

We're not talking about needing a nap or an energy drink. Resting doesn't make a dent in this kind of exhaustion, and the energy required to get through a day increasingly cannot be replenished.

But there are so many causes that it can be hard to know what to treat. Anemia, for instance, can cause fatigue, as can insomnia and infections. Depression can present as fatigue. Pain and other symptoms, especially when untreated, can cause fatigue, and vice versa. Confusing matters further, many medications for pain and other symptoms can cause fatigue, too. Chemotherapies, some blood pressure medications, and antidepressants, among myriad others, can also result in this intense sapping of energy.

Herbal and nonpharmacological options: Exercise (do what you can, if only a walk around the block, or to the door and back); a change of location—use your bed only for sleep; social engagement; breathwork; yoga; massage; energy healing (Reiki, Healing Touch, tai chi, qigong); caffeine; essential oils (citrus, lavender, rosemary, bergamot, peppermint); animal-assisted therapy; craniosacral therapy; acupuncture.

Medications include: Psychostimulants; corticosteroids; megestrol acetate; testosterone.

HICCUPS

Yes, hiccups. The diaphragm is irritable, so anything pressing on it or inflaming it—whether from above in the chest or from below in the abdomen—can cause them. Pneumonia or pleurisy can do it, or liver disease, or esophageal reflux or thrush. They sound benign, but when they go on for hours or days, hiccups can interfere with any definition of quality of life. And if you're also dealing with pain or shortness of breath or other symptoms, the constant interruptions can be miserable.

Herbal and nonpharmacological options: Interrupt the respiratory cycle (try holding your breath and bearing down, tensing your abdominal muscles as though you're trying to have a bowel movement; this is called the Valsalva maneuver); sip cold water from various angles or swallow a spoonful of dry sugar; pulling your knees to your chest and leaning forward can reposition the diaphragm; acupuncture; acupressure.

Medications include: Chlorpromazine; metoclopramide; baclofen; cannabis; antiepileptics; antidepressants; psychostimulants; benzodiazepine.

ITCHINESS

Known in clinic speak as *pruritus*, itchiness can be a devilishly unnerving symptom. There are many conditions that can make a person want to scratch, including disorders of the biliary tract (liver, gallbladder); bedbugs; skin infections; psychiatric conditions (hallucination, paranoia); kidney disease; persistent skin or limb swelling; HIV; various neurological disorders (neuropathy); medication side effects (opiates); dermatological disorders (eczema); and of course good old-fashioned dry skin (xerosis).

Scratching the skin can compromise its integrity, which in turn can lead to infection, so be careful.

Herbal and nonpharmacological options: Light therapy; emollients and moisturizers; Sarna lotion; proper skin care (keeping skin clean without overwashing); avoid irritants (such as some perfumes and soaps, favor glycerin soaps); cool environment (hot showers or baths can be exacerbating); distraction; homeopathy; apply a mixture of lemon and apple cider vinegar in water; colloidal oatmeal baths (mix ½–1 cup oat flour with enough water to make a slurry, and then pour into bath water).

Medications include: Topical: antihistamines; corticosteroids; anesthetics; calcineurin inhibitors; capsaicin; cannabis. Oral: antihistamines; opiate receptor antagonists; opiate receptor agonists; antidepressants; anticonvulsants; immunosuppressants.

LOSS OF APPETITE

There are few more emotionally loaded issues than food at the end of life. Appetite varies depending on all sorts of issues, including chemotherapies and other medical treatments, mood, activity level. Loss of appetite heralds weight loss, including loss of lean muscle, leading to hollowed cheeks and skin over bone. The clinical term for this involuntary weight loss is *cachexia*. The harder word sometimes used is *wasting*. The body, now unable to handle outside nutrition, is simply using up all its inherent stores in an effort to play itself all the way out. It is the inevitable involution of a body shutting down and coming to its end, with nature's characteristic efficiency. Try the following:

- **Change position.** To optimize swallowing, let gravity help by raising the head of the bed or sitting upright. And, of course, take your time.
- **Add fat to your diet.** It's not necessary to worry about fats or cholesterol content in the context of a terminal condition. Fat in this case is more likely to help than harm, and finding ways to add calories to your food is a plus; pass the ice cream, please!
- **Chew, savor, and spit.** Some folks can't swallow and have no interest in ingesting anything, but they still love to get a hit of flavor.
- **Cook for scent or symbolism.** Just because you don't want to eat doesn't mean you can't sit at the table and participate, or that your bedside can't become the dinner table. This may be different from what you're used to, but it can give you and your family quality time. A cautionary note: often even the sight or

smell of food can be repellent, especially if anxiety has piled up around the subject. So caregivers, yield to the patient's wishes in real time.

- **Eat for pleasure rather than for sustenance.** If you find yourself wishing for cake or pizza or whatever, go for it. Once you are in the advanced stages of illness, all the broccoli in the world will not change the course of things.
- **Start with small portions.** We got this tip from the nutritionist Rebecca Katz, who reminds us that food is an emotional and complex subject. Anticipation is an important driver of appetite, so deliver the food carefully and thoughtfully and in small portions; plus, a plate left with heaps of food on it can feel like a failure. And when possible, lead with smell as a way to prime the senses. Appetite starts in the brain.
- **Try smooth textures.** Many people find that they no longer want to eat foods with challenging textures, like meats or hard vegetables, and prefer smooth or puréed foods like puddings, yogurts, or mashed potatoes.
- **Try sweetness.** Sweetness is our first taste to develop as newborns and often the last to go as death approaches. So try the sugary stuff.

Medications include: Cannabis (THC specifically); mirtazapine; corticosteroids; megestrol acetate.

Note: Medications provide limited help for the anorexia (the medical condition of loss of appetite) of terminal illness but may be worth considering for a short time in certain circumstances. Still, there are few ways to interrupt this natural cycle, and even when medications succeed at stimulating appetite, none of them has been shown to extend life.

For Caregivers

It is important to note that not eating does not represent a lack of willpower or a death wish. I have heard countless versions of the plea "We can't let Dad starve to death!" But within the context of terminal illness, loss of appetite and the commensurate weight loss are simply signs that death is coming, not the cause of it. The most you can safely do is to encourage eating and drinking, but do not force them. Optimize what you can, all the while knowing that at some point food and drink will be off the table. Though it may seem otherwise, your loved one is not going to starve to death.

NAUSEA

There are myriad causes of nausea, some inside and some outside the gut. Nausea is commonly associated with constipation, pain, headache, hunger, low appetite, anxiety, esophageal reflux, chemotherapy and other medication side effects, infection, and even grief.

Your gut is a single contiguous organ, running from your mouth all the way to your anus. Therefore, what happens in one area of it can affect other areas. What's more, because of how our nervous system is wired, sensations in any organ can "refer" to other areas of the body altogether. This means that in some occurrences, treating anxiety or constipation will end the nausea.

Herbal and nonpharmacological options: Ginger; peppermint, chamomile, or fennel tea; sparkling water and grapes; acupuncture; acupressure; Sea-Band® (or wrist band).

Medications include: Antidopaminergic; antihistamine/anticholinergic; antiserotonergic; anxiolytic; prokinetic; cannabis (THC); dexamethasone; prednisone; hydrocortisone; aprepitant; octreotide.

PAIN

Pain is a supremely compelling force of nature and can overwhelm the most hardened among us. But how any of us experiences pain will vary—it's a complex mix of stimulus, physiology, mood, and personality. The same may be said of all symptoms but seems especially true with this common beast.

From a physiological point of view, there are a few different types of pain. One important subtype is called *neuropathic pain* or *neuropathy*. Neuropathy is pain stemming from the nerve itself. In other types of pain, the nerve is dutifully transmitting a signal, telling your brain that something is amiss in some part of your body. But with neuropathy, the trouble is in the nerve itself and can stem from many causes, including diabetes. With terminal illness, it is commonly the result of damage from a tumor or chemotherapy drugs. Neuropathic pain can be particularly vexing, both in its range of sensations and for the fact that it doesn't necessarily convey any useful information to you. For example, a person with foot neuropathy may swear her foot is on fire when, upon examination, it clearly is not.

In the majority of situations, whatever the type or cause, treating serious pain toward the end of life is a matter for medication. If meds aren't working well, ask your doctor whether there are any procedures that might be helpful, such as a nerve block or pain pump.

Herbal and nonpharmacological options: Ice/heat; acupuncture; biofeedback and behavior modification; animal-assisted therapy; transcutaneous electrical nerve stimulation (TENS) unit; music therapy; meditation; psychotherapy; hugging/holding; energy healing and movement (yoga, Reiki, Healing Touch, tai chi, qigong); massage; herbs (cayenne, lavender oil, comfrey root, white willow bark, devil's claw).

Medications include: Anti-inflammatories; acetaminophen; antidepressants; anticonvulsants; muscle relaxants; lidocaine; cannabis; opiates.

SHORTNESS OF BREATH

The clinical word for this is *dyspnea*, sometimes referred to as "air hunger," and it is a common experience for people living with certain types of congestive heart failure or liver disease, lung disease, pneumonia, asthma, systemic allergic reactions, fluid buildup in the lungs or abdomen, rib fractures, anxiety, or neurological disorders. In general, it is tough for most people to tolerate a respiratory rate much greater than twenty breaths per minute for very long.

Herbal and Nonpharmacological options: Ambient airflow (a breeze from a fan across one's face can be very soothing); positioning (sitting up or lying with the head slightly elevated with pillows can be helpful); acupuncture; breathwork; guided imagery; meditation; energy healing (Reiki, Healing Touch, tai chi, qigong); ambient essential oils (eucalyptus, peppermint, frankincense, citrus); music therapy.

Medications include: Opiates; benzodiazepines; diuretics; oxygen (comes in tanks and is taken in through the nose via tubing; since it requires a prescription, we've included it under medications).

For Caregivers

A way to get a feel for what your loved one is experiencing is coupled breathing: breathe in tandem with the patient. This can sometimes calm the breathing rate and rhythm of the patient as well.

Supplemental Oxygen

It is a reflex to want to get more oxygen when you are laboring for breath. And it is often a good idea—but not always. When you are close to death, supplemental oxygen is unlikely to help you survive longer or make you more comfortable. In fact, supplemental oxygen can become a source of discomfort; oxygen is usually delivered through plastic tubing into the nose or via a face mask over the mouth and makes a high-pitched, wispy sound, all of which can complicate efforts to communicate. The dry air and hardware can chafe skin over time and be drying. That said, some people grow very attached to their oxygen and find it comforting.

Important: Oxygen is flammable, so if the person is a smoker, bad things—such as an explosive fire—can happen quickly.

SKIN BREAKDOWN

Skin is the largest organ of the human body. It protects us from infections, regulates our body temperature, and gives us the sensation of touch: a primary means of exploring our environment and feeling alive. When you are less mobile and your body is shutting down, some amount of skin irritation and breakdown is to be expected. Skin tears—lacerations, burns, and bruises—are all common in people with compromised mobility or function. They start with a little redness or tenderness. This irritation, and the poor circulation that leads to it, make the skin fragile and vulnerable. Oftentimes, sensation may be dulled, as from diabetes or neuropathy, which of course makes it easier to hurt yourself unwittingly.

Once wounds do occur in late stages of illness, healing is generally not possible. At this point, it's a matter of slowing the breakdown process and staying comfortable along the way. Why? Because the body is breaking down in totality, including the skin; also, it may not be possible to move your body to relieve the pressure without causing more discomfort and, therefore, hurting more than helping.

As ever, prevention is best when possible. And in this case "treatment" is much the same as prevention, less a matter of medications than behavior changes. Here's how to optimize your skin integrity:

- Inspect your skin daily for sore spots, blisters, and anything else that might get infected
- Stay clean and dry
- Prevent friction and injuries by using padding around any wounds and lubricants on the skin as needed
- Move your body. Even if you are unable to get out of bed, rotating from side to side every hour or so goes a long way toward relieving pressure and promoting blood flow

- If pronounced swelling is present, ask your team about options, including compression stockings, lymphedema massage, or possibly a course of diuretics
- Be extra vigilant if you are incontinent, as the added moisture can exacerbate skin breakdown. In other words, change your garments frequently
- Position a pillow between your legs to cut down on your bones rubbing together; if you are in a wheelchair, shift your weight every fifteen minutes or so

Emollients that help soften the skin, dressings, and occasionally topical antibiotics may be helpful and are worth a conversation with your care team. Home care and hospice agencies often have a nurse who is especially well versed in skin and wound care, so ask.

TASTE CHANGES

Hypogeusia is the clinical word for diminished sense of taste; *ageusia* means no taste; and *dysgeusia* means a disordered sense of taste (a persistent metallic taste, for example). Changes in taste are very common with advanced illness and treatments. It's distinct from anorexia, though the two commonly arrive together.

How we taste things is complicated, of course. It is actually a matter of both taste and smell working in concert. So anything affecting the nose or mouth or the brain can affect your experience. Infections are another cause of taste loss and can generally be treated.

Look for thrush. This is a type of yeast infection common in people with weakened immune

FAST FACT
You may be on a vitamin supplement cocktail with a very high level of zinc, which could result in a loss of taste.

systems, causing white curd-like plaques on the tongue, palate, and throat. To cut through the thick coating, try a mild astringent such as green tea, with or without lemon.

Medications can also be to blame, most notably certain chemotherapies, which often leave a metallic taste in the mouth, or liquid nutritional supplements, which can create a burning sensation. Dry mouth can also lead to diminished taste, and the wear and tear of aging can do it, too.

Medications include: Antihistamines or steroids may help if inflammation is to blame—as evidenced by mucus—as with allergies.

In general, the best approach is optimizing what taste function remains. The nutritionist Rebecca Katz likens the palate to "an electric circuit board flicking on and off." Navigating this experience once again requires agility and creativity. Here are a few tips:

- **Keep your mouth and nose clean.** Besides the obvious tooth brushing, gargling and rinsing out your nasal passages with salt water can help reduce mucus and plaque buildup. Rinsing with an astringent mouthwash, or tea, can help further.
- **Drinking or rinsing with alkaline water products**, or with a homemade solution of baking soda plus water, may help with mouth sores. Katz points us toward more yummy antidotes such as cantaloupe or watermelon granitas. Avoid acidic or spicy foods in particular.
- **Let foods surprise you.** It's happened countless times that a patient happily reports stumbling onto a food or drink she didn't like previously that now suddenly tastes good. Maybe tea wasn't your thing before but now you prefer it to coffee. Try to use fresh spices and herbs. Cinnamon, cardamom, cumin,

mint, and parsley can be very helpful in reorienting your taste buds as they wake up.

- **Change flavors.** Katz suggests a systematic way to do exactly this with what she calls FASS™ (fat, acid, salt, sweet). It's a way to rejigger ingredients to suit your changing ability to taste. Here is the gist of it:

IF FOOD TASTES:	USE THIS FIX:
Metallic	Add a little sweetener, such as maple syrup, and a squeeze of lemon. Or try adding fat, such as a nut cream or butter.
Too sweet	Start by adding six drops of lemon or lime juice. Keep adding juice in small increments until the sweet taste becomes muted.
Too salty	Add a quarter teaspoon of lemon juice. It erases the taste of salt.
Too bitter	Add a little sweetener, such as maple syrup.
Like cardboard	Add more sea salt until the flavor of the dish moves toward the front of the mouth. A spritz of fresh lemon juice also helps.

No matter how responsive you are to taste and appetite changes, there will come a time when food is no longer an option. This is not a problem to solve or force your way through but a naturally adaptive fact of living until death.

———

A Few Important Notes About Medication

AS YOU CAN SEE, THERE IS MORE TO COMFORT THAN MEDICATION. But meds are an invaluable resource and almost always a part of the mix. As with treating illness, treating symptoms takes some effort. Doing your part, which includes being open with your team about what you're experiencing and using any medications as directed, is a skill worth acquiring.

——

Managing Medications

IT'S NOT UNCOMMON FOR PEOPLE TO REQUIRE SERIOUS PRESCRIPTION medications, such as opiates, benzodiazepines, or stimulants, at the end of life. These are medications with potential for abuse; there are laws restricting access to them and pharmacies may limit their inventory. That makes it challenging to get these meds even with a perfectly legitimate prescription in hand. And we do mean "in hand." Medications "scheduled" by the Drug Enforcement Administration (DEA) require a paper prescription every time and, with some exceptions, cannot be phoned in to the pharmacy by your doctor or be automatically refilled; electronic prescriptions are increasingly allowed, with strict security protections, but it's still more complicated than phoning it in. Most hospice agencies have their own pharmacy contracts and access is not a problem. But for people not enrolled in hospice, be ready for routine clerical hurdles: multiple phone calls between your physician's office, the pharmacy, and your insurer. Jen, whom you met in chapter 10 and whose husband was in significant pain from stomach cancer, was shocked to find how much time she had to spend in this clerical loop, making a case for what seemed like basic and essential medication.

The national scourge of opiate abuse has taught everyone caution, which means that rules are more rigidly followed. Things such as early refill requests are hard for prescribers and pharmacists to accommodate, so it's important that you do everything you can to protect your medications and use them as directed; if the drug at its current dosage isn't doing the trick, call the prescribing physician right away instead of taking more drug than prescribed. Some important things to remember:

- **Keep track of your meds, including possibly keeping them locked in a drawer or cabinet to guard against theft.** When it comes to pain meds in particular, theft is a real problem. Multiple requests for early refills or replacement prescriptions are seen by providers and regulators as a red flag. If this happens more than once or twice, it can be hard to reestablish trust between patient and clinician.
- **Work with a single pharmacy.** Get to know the pharmacists. When you are within a week or so of needing a refill of your opiates, benzodiazepines, or stimulants, a call to the pharmacy (as well as to the prescribing doctor, who needs to write a fresh prescription) can get the ball rolling and help ensure that the medication you need is in stock and ready for you in time.
- **Discontinue medication carefully.** It's important to stop taking drugs that aren't helping you, but don't try stopping prescribed medications on your own; that may make you feel worse or cause withdrawal symptoms. Any discontinuation should be done in consultation with your doctor.

- **Traveling? Plan accordingly.** Think through how much medication you might need, then add some extra for situations you can't imagine. It can take a long time—weeks—for your prescriber and your pharmacy to work through the logistics of securing adequate amounts of medication in advance, so allow as much time as possible to prepare.
- **Use a pill organizer or keep a diary—preferably both.** This will help ensure that you take your meds on time and also help you not to lose them.

———

Fear of Addiction

MANY PATIENTS WISH TO AVOID CERTAIN MEDICATIONS, SUCH AS opiates—drugs generally prescribed for pain or shortness of breath—for fear of becoming addicted. But addiction, though a serious health and social problem, is *not* the same thing as tolerance or dependence. It is helpful to know the difference:

- *Tolerance* occurs when our bodies get used to a medication. This means we need to take more of something to get the benefit of it. This is a normal effect of many kinds of medication. More medication does not have to mean more harm; tolerance by itself does not pose a threat.
- *Dependency* means that your body has come to rely on the medication to function normally. In other words, it's a problem only if you stop the medication abruptly. The scary word for this phenomenon is *withdrawal*. For example, stopping some types of blood pressure medications means that your blood pressure will likely shoot up. Antidepressants can also cause withdrawal symptoms if stopped too fast. This happens with

some pain medications, too. Like tolerance, dependency is a normal phenomenon and by itself poses no risk. If you need to stop any such medication, withdrawal can generally be avoided—and dependency reversed—by tapering the dose slowly over time with your doctor.

Fears of addiction or premature death are generally unfounded at the end of life and should not interfere with opiate use, for example, for symptom control. There isn't enough time or energy left to develop an addiction. And for those of you who've struggled with addiction, actively or in the past, this should not mean that you have to do without medications at the end of your life, unless that is your wish.

TIP
Expect to be on the receiving end of a lot of judgment. From friends and family to pharmacy technicians and doctors, people are full of strong opinions about these medications.

The truth is that these drugs have been around a long time and are well understood, at least by hospice and palliative care and pain clinicians who work with them regularly. Like most medication, these drugs are inherently neither harmless nor poison; they just need to be used with care and under the direction of a skilled physician. ❖

The Bottom Line

SYMPTOMS 101

Only *you* can say whether you feel better or worse. Track, experiment, communicate; take what helps, and ditch what doesn't. Given the subjective nature of symptoms, it's impossible to know how much better you could feel without trying different things. And for every symptom, there are nonpharmacological options to try as well, many of which you can do on your own. You may not be able to banish a symptom altogether, but you're very likely to be able to feel *better*.

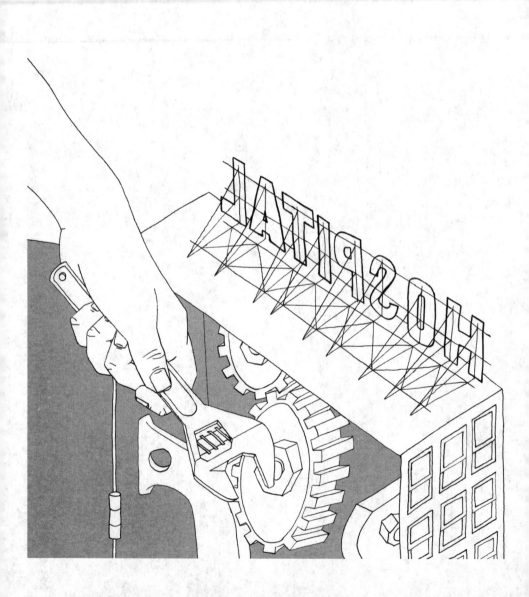

Hospital Hacks

Getting inside; what to pack; what to ask for
to get what you need; finding your person;
dealing with the intensive care unit

When you're otherwise healthy and fixable, hospitals are a godsend—twenty-four-hour drive-throughs that check your vital signs, figure out what's wrong with you, give you the prescriptions you need, and send you on your way. You might end up complaining about the wait and the food more than anything else.

But when you're further down the road with a terminal diagnosis, hospitals are not always a source of relief. Eighty percent of us say we don't want to be hospitalized at the end of life. But that's not what happens. Half of Medicare patients (those over 65) go to an emergency department in their last month of life, according to *The New England Journal of Medicine*. Of those, one-third are admitted to the intensive care unit, and one-fifth have surgery.

The mad dash for life-extending treatments is not a problem in and of itself. The problem is what gets lost in that process. In the frenzy of hospital visits, there's often an escalation of treatments to the point of futility. By then, comfort and peaceful time with loved ones are an afterthought.

Hospitals carry out aggressive treatments whether you're 20 or 90; that's their job. And hospitals can't always be avoided. But you need to take care that their effort on your behalf is aligned with what's important to you.

Here's another way to think about it: If you have advanced understanding of how the hospital works, you can learn how to hack it, and by that we mean navigate it, get the most out of it, and lose the least. We're here to help with that.

TIP

Admission is a critical time to listen, ask questions, and state your wishes so your medical team can honor them.

——

Going to the Hospital

IT OFTEN BEGINS WITH A 911 CALL. SOMETHING NEW IS GOING WRONG or something old has gotten worse. Then, an ambulance ride or a hurried trip in someone's car, bound for an emergency department waiting room where you'll meet all sorts of people who are also in rough shape, maybe even in worse shape than you.

EMTs, by rule, will take you to the nearest adequate hospital in order to get you seen as quickly as possible, depending on the nature of your particular medical emergency. You *can* request that the ambulance take you to your preferred hospital, but be prepared to sign a form stating that you went against medical advice and possibly have to conduct a heated discussion with the ambulance crew. Given the nature of an "emergency," this is not a great time for debate.

However you get there, grab a copy of your advance care directive or POLST documents (head back to chapter 3, "Yes, There's Paperwork," for more about those) and take them with you. If you forget or haven't done them yet, that's okay; the hospital doctors should address your care wishes with you directly, but having them already prepared can save time and breath.

———

Navigating the Emergency Department

TO GET FROM THE WAITING ROOM INTO THE EMERGENCY DEPARTMENT (ED) can take a *long* time; possibly many hours. You'll register with a triage nurse on arrival, and she will decide on the order in which people are seen, based on the severity of their situations.

Be sure to let her know what you're going through—fevers, pains, as well as your underlying diagnoses and whether you are receiving hospice care—but don't try too hard to game the system to get seen faster. ED staff are pretty hard-boiled and tend to know what "urgent" looks like.

Then to the ED itself. Urban hospitals and large academic or regional medical centers with specialized trauma units, in particular, can feel like asylums or crime scenes. Lots of people buzzing about. There's usually a screamer somewhere, casual bleeding, odors you never knew existed, not to mention plenty of inebriated or otherwise altered minds sleeping it off on gurneys in the hallway. You might wonder if this is the place for you.

Teams of nurses and doctors will interview you in serial, so be prepared to repeat your story. Even if you've been here before and they have your medical history on hand, each clinician is going to need to hear your story from you directly. This may be exasperating, but it also minimizes error and helps ensure that the team charged with your care gets onto the same page.

From the swinging doors to the waiting room to the ED, it's not unusual for more than a full day to pass before you're all tucked in: either patched up and good enough to go home, or admitted to the hospital for more acute care—meaning that you're assigned a bed and will move into the hospital for a stay.

FAST FACT
The ED is just the foyer, the entryway to the specialized and surreal environment that is the hospital proper.

Let's get this note up front: **if you know you're dying—meaning that you know that you are in the late stages of terminal illness or frailty from advanced age—and deeply wish to go home to do so, let the ED team know.** They may be able to figure out why you're feeling the way you are, or at least help you with acute pain or other symptoms; in addition, they can link you to hospice services that can meet with you that day or the next. Often enough they can work this all out then and there, and send you home with services lined up. Even if you need to be admitted to the hospital for a day or two, if the team knows your wishes up front, they can focus their energy on getting you home.

——

Why Death Is Not Considered an Emergency

DYING CAN'T BE "FIXED," AND HOSPITALS ARE PLACES FOR FIXING. They are also places where you might end up getting worse: you can pick up pneumonia or some new superbug, or up your risk of complications by piling on the procedures. All these risks can keep you in the hospital longer, at a cost to your health and your wallet. So it's generally a good idea to go to the hospital only when there's something it can actually help with. If you're weighing whether to go to the hospital, a call into your doctor might help answer the question. Otherwise, once you are there, the ED staff will let you know what constitutes cause for admission.

Going home from the ED is usually good news, but on occasion it comes as an unwelcome surprise. **Sometimes you might want to stay in the hospital but are denied.** That's because no matter how exhausted your family members are or how crummy you may feel, if the ED doctors deem that a hospital stay won't turn things around, your insurance will not pay for you to be there and the hospital staff will have to send you home.

If you don't meet the medical criteria for admission into the hospital but do not feel safe going home, there may be ways the hospital can help protect you. **If you, your friends, or your family is concerned for your safety at home—because you keep falling or are otherwise unsafe—let the ED team know.** If you are under the care of someone who is abusive or neglectful, or if you are having suicidal thoughts (or thoughts of hurting others), let them know. These are serious calls to action. There are legal protections and services awaiting you in the ED and ways to link you with what services exist outside the hospital, too.

You do not have to stay in the hospital if you don't want to. Maybe you start feeling better during the wait, or maybe you've changed your mind. As long as you are of sound mind and pose no threat to yourself or others, you can leave the hospital. Discuss it with the doctors and the whole team, and if they feel you should stay but you are still adamant about leaving, you can sign out against medical advice (AMA). In general, if the doctors want you to stay, that's advice to take seriously. In the end, however, it is your decision to make.

——

What to Pack

IT'S AMUSING THAT *HOSPITAL* AND *HOSPITALITY* (AND *HOSPICE*) HAVE the same Latin root: *hospes*, meaning "host." They're not exactly bed-and-breakfasts brimming with warmth. Most hospitals are fluorescent and sterile. It's up to you to bring in the feeling of home. And if you're in the hospital for anything longer than a couple of days, having your favorite pillow or sweatpants or face cream will improve your physical state *and* your mood—which in turn will affect your whole experience.

Whether you have time to pack a bag or make a list for someone who'll be coming to visit, here are some suggestions for items

what to PACK

headphones

sleepmask + earplugs

chargers

pictures from home

devices to watch movies / shows

clean underpants

comfy pants

socks

your ADVANCE CARE DIRECTIVE

slippers

books / magazines

Listening to music has been proven to reduce the stress hormone cortisol in your body, reduce pain, and relieve anxiety before surgery. No joke—music can be more effective than prescription sedatives. Don't forget headphones (not everyone will want to hear your Barry Manilow).

that may help you feel more like yourself when you're in this de-personalized zone. Don't forget to put your name on the things you bring; with so much happening in a hospital, things easily go missing.

Bring a current list of medications, including dosages and schedule. **Be ready to tell your doctors what you're taking, how often, and at what doses: don't assume it's correctly stated in your records.** If you don't have a list and are in a hurry to leave the house, just sweep all the medication bottles into a bag; they will give the doctors a clear sense of what you're taking. Once you are admitted, however, the hospital has to dispense its own medications from within, even if you brought them with you from home.

TIP
If you are taking opioids or other medications with potential for abuse, it will be helpful for the hospital to see your prescription bottles as proof of the prescription.

——

What You Can Ask For

YOUR NURSES AND AIDES WANT YOU TO BE COMFORTABLE. THEY DON'T like seeing their patients suffer and will try to accommodate you if you let them know how they can help. Here's what you can ask for (but not necessarily expect):

- **Fewer interruptions during the night.** One reason you often get a crummy night's sleep in the hospital is that nurses are charged with waking you up to take your vital signs (blood pressure and oxygen intake) every few hours. But if you're not just out of surgery or in the ICU, that might not be necessary. It's worth asking your doctors and nurses if they can hold off on checking your vital signs until morning.

- **Fewer interruptions during the day.** You can ask your nurse to put a sign on the door telling all entrants (both hospital staff and outside visitors) to check in at the nurses' station before entering. That won't always be doable, especially in places such as the ICU, but it can be a great way to make your room your own, get some peace and quiet, and protect private time with a loved one.

- **Fewer blood draws.** The analysis of your blood is critical for all sorts of reasons, including tracking your body's response to treatment. It's also true that, past a certain point, it's not necessary. Daily blood draws might be a holdover order on your chart that your care team is too busy to realize is no longer needed. This one is up to the doctor, but don't be shy about asking.

- **Quiet machines in your room.** Computers that monitor your vital signs and administer treatments are programmed to beep and set off alarms. That noise pollution is one of the most stressful things about a hospital stay. Doctors and nurses are inured to it and may not notice, but you can ask them to switch the machines to "silent."

- **A fan.** Hospitals often have fans on hand. This doesn't just improve the circulation of air in rooms that are stiflingly still with no windows to crack open; it also provides a calming white noise that can block out the hubbub. A fan blowing over the face has also been shown to help ease the work of breathing if you're feeling winded.

- **Premedication.** If you have a procedure or anything planned that day that you know will produce significant anxiety or other discomfort, talk to your nurse about premedication. It may be possible to get something for pain or anxiety *before* it starts, which is generally preferable to (and more effective than) treating discomfort once you're in the throes.

- **Help with moving.** One of the great hazards of the hospital is prolonged immobility. In the case of serious illness, what strength is lost from not moving is very hard to get back. Moving your body around also helps your immune and endocrine systems. It can help with pain, too, and it feels good. Start with a walk down the hall or just going from bed to chair and sitting upright for an hour or two or wiggling your fingers. Nurses and aides can help; physical therapists can help even more. This is possible in the ICU too. If it ain't happening, request it.

——

Hospital Dos and Don'ts

MY COLLEAGUE SRIRAM SHAMASUNDER'S FATHER WAS HOSPITALIZED for four weeks. Shamasunder, a doctor himself, as was his dad, was stunned by the lack of communication among all the specialists taking care of him. He slept at the foot of his father's hospital bed, waiting to catch them as they did their morning rounds. "The less I asked, the less doctors told me," he says.

There are ways to optimize your relationship with your care team, and they're all about knowing how to communicate effectively. By following these dos and don'ts, you're more likely to feel that you're being heard and that all members of your team are working together.

DOs

- **Find a point person.** You'll meet a dizzying number of people in a hospital. Different roles, different shifts. Work with them; they are human beings who want to help, even if they look stressed. It can be unclear who is doing what and whom to ask which question. Keep an eye out for anyone you feel particularly comfortable with, an anchor; if you get overwhelmed you can start by talking with that person. Medical students—hidden gems in hospitals—are often more open-minded, more invested in learning, and more available to chase down a question or concern for you. The same is true of a nurse, an aide, a therapist, or just about anyone involved in your care. Start with whomever you feel the closest connection to. That person is part of a team effort in a hospital whose members will communicate with each other. If you're unsure about who knows what, you can always ask your point person, "Will you please share this with my doctor?"

- **Establish a baseline.** Make sure the whole team caring for you or your loved one knows if something about your health is very different from usual. The first doctor who saw Shamasunder's father assumed that he had been confused for a long time when he'd actually been feeling fine and at the office just two weeks before. It's important to be sure you and your doctors and nurses are on the same page about what the perceived issues are.
- **Think about discharge early on.** What kind of assistance or equipment might you need at home? Or maybe it's time to consider a nursing home or assisted living; that's an important question to consider after any hospitalization. Talk with the case manager or social worker early in your stay about things like hospital beds or other equipment that could be helpful to post-hospital life. Maybe you could use outpatient physical therapy to work with you on movement or to train your family in lifting you safely. It may be the perfect time to think about hospice. Wherever you're headed next, it will likely take some

planning to get there so start that discussion with the discharge planner early.

- **Be kind.** This is true for customer service across the board, but the stakes are a lot higher when it's your life you're dealing with, not your wireless internet plan. Here's an instructive public service announcement from nurses posted on Dr. Elaine Schattner's Medical Lessons blog: "If the patient's nice, it's a lot easier to want to go back in that room with them. Their reputation travels to the nurses' station. But if they're mean, well, it's not as easy to go back in there, so I might not stop by as often."

DON'Ts

- **Don't be fooled into thinking you're an expert on disease or treatments because of what you've read online.** This is one sure way to alienate the very people who are there to help you. Ask lots of questions and be open to hearing an answer that may not jibe with your research. There's a big difference between empowerment (good) and entitlement (bad). If you or a family member starts trying to call the shots or making demands, you're more likely to offend your care team than to get what you're asking for. Just because a patient or family member says, "I want an antibiotic," doesn't mean it will be prescribed. That's still the doctor's decision, and the doctor is bound to do what she thinks is ethically and medically correct.
- **Don't worry about VIP status.** You're probably not missing anything. You might think that fancy people get better care in the hospital, but that's not necessarily so. Hospitals are pretty good meritocracies—more often than not, the sickest people

get the most attention. And some of the most spectacularly dysfunctional scenarios I've witnessed at the end of life have been with VIP patients whose clinicians are hesitant to deliver anything approaching bad news. That can make communication very difficult, leading to more desperate or futile care, not *better* care.

- **Don't complain about the food.** The food in hospitals is generally terrible. The author (and farmer) Wendell Berry put it well: "People are fed by the food industry, which pays no attention to health, and are treated by the health industry, which pays no attention to food." Ask friends to bring something in, or maybe even have food delivered. But first be sure to check with a doctor or nurse whether you're on any food restrictions so you don't inadvertently make yourself sicker.

——

Signaling Trust

FIND THE BALANCE BETWEEN BEING AN ADVOCATE FOR YOURSELF OR your loved one and signaling trust in your health care providers. You're at each other's mercy. "As my father got sicker, I blamed myself and some of his doctors. Some of this was legitimate, but some of it was colored by the challenge of starting to lose someone you hold dear," says Shamasunder.

If trust—the *therapeutic relationship*, in doctorese—is broken, it needs to get fixed. The best path is to air your concerns directly and try to work things out. Do a little soul-searching, too: *Do I not get along with this person because I don't like the news he or she is delivering? Is there something I'm not saying out of fear?* There's a subconscious power imbalance in health care, with the doctor viewed as expert on high, that can get in the way of patients advocating for themselves and that results in them asking for less or remaining silent. This puts both parties at a stalemate, so recognize that there are patterns of deference at play from which you can break free by speaking up.

We all know the long list of ways communication can break down. Remember, these are *relationships* (you and the nurse, you and the doctors, and so on), which means everyone has to own their part.

There's another important phenomenon to note here that can affect how trust flows: **Whoever is your doctor outside the hospital is not likely going to be your doctor *in* the hospital.** For the past twenty or so years, there's been a shift toward *hospitalists*. So it may happen that just as you and your hospitalist are gelling, it's time for a new one to rotate in. It can be frustrating and tedious—or a relief to have new eyes on your case. Either way, this roulette has become the norm, so prepare for it.

TIP

Hospitalists are the primary care doctors for anyone in the hospital for as long as you are there (but not longer).

——

"Hospital Time"

HOSPITALS HAVE THEIR OWN TIME ZONE. YOU SHOULD EXPECT THAT tests, doctor's visits, and delivery of medication will *not* happen on schedule. Just because you've been told that a test or procedure is scheduled for a specific time doesn't mean that's when it will happen.

There are delays and pushbacks, usually because staff are responding to five-alarm fires that take priority. Unless you are that five-alarm fire, you might need to wait.

you're on
HOSPITAL TIME

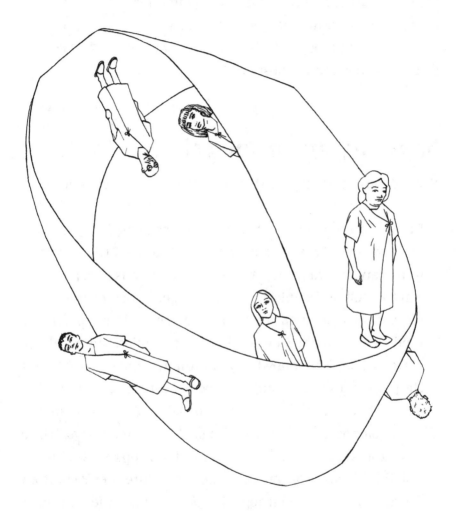

Assume that nothing will happen when you're told it will. Try not to take it personally or pick a fight with those who are doing their best to help you. Hospitals are complex systems and their staff are subject to all kinds of hidden pressures.

The hospital is a 24/7 operation, and it's important that you remain aware of night and day. When your body's rhythms are disrupted, it can affect the severity of disease symptoms, diagnostic test results, and even your body's response to drug therapy. This is one reason delirium is so common in hospitals.

–
TIP
One thing you can control to make your time spent there feel more predictable: immediately open the shades in your room. This is a small but significant intervention.

———

Speaking Up for Yourself

You are the expert on you. Make yourself known. Here's how:

- **Be your own advocate.** Be sure to tell the hospital team how you're feeling. Are you constipated, for example? Hiding symptoms happens *all the time* in a hospital because people don't want to tell and clinicians might forget to ask or miss your cues. If you're worried about something or feel that something is odd, you may not get the help you need unless you speak up.
- **Have you talked about what you want in terms of care? Now's the perfect time.** "My dad's complete clarity about not wanting to live if he wasn't able to dress himself or eat independently was a goalpost that helped guide us," Shamasunder says. "Have those tough conversations. Be as specific as possible."
- **Ask three questions, not ten, and make sure they're written down.** Questions about logistics of your stay, the treatment plan, next steps post-hospital; anything you're concerned about. Most doctors and their teams do their rounds in the mornings. Sometimes, especially in ICUs, they may come around again at the end of the day. Though morning rounds often happen at ungodly hours, such as 6:00 a.m., be sure

to use the moment well. Cap the time: three questions and a fifteen-minute meeting. The team must get on to the next patient. If you have more questions, you can always ask your nurse to page your doctor during the day (doctors are pageable overnight, too, but it's usually a covering MD who won't be as familiar with some of the details of your case). If there is anything urgent, let your nurse know and he or she can be more forceful on your behalf.

• **Call a group meeting.** It's practically impossible to follow all that's happening over the course of an average hospital stay, especially when your situation involves more than one team (cardiology and surgery, say). If it's not offered, you might ask for a group meeting once every few days or more if there's a lot going on, when your questions are piling up or the plan's unclear, or if your wishes are changing. You should have the option to sit down at the same time with everyone involved in your care, family, and clinical team. It might take a day or two to wrestle everyone into the same room, but it's often worth the trouble. Concerns get voiced, emotions get processed, people get to know one another, and you get another opportunity to state what you hope for and what you want to avoid. **This is a perfect moment to revisit your goals of care: Are you on track?**

——

Use the Hospital's Specialized Teams

THERE'S MORE SUPPORT THAN YOU MIGHT THINK TO HELP WITH THE logistical and adverse effects of hospital stays. You can ask for a consult with the **palliative care team** if you or your loved one is suffering or struggling with tough symptoms (see Chapter 11, "Dynamic Duo: Hospice and Palliative Care"). The palliative care team can also be very helpful when communication is breaking down among family members or between family and clinicians. **Geriatric services** can help make hospital stays easier for older folks. Some hospitals even have specialized areas called advanced care for the elderly (ACE) units where an interdisciplinary team will help a person stay safe and fit. There are only a few hundred ACE units among more than 4,000 hospitals in this country, so don't bank on these services, but it's worth asking.

If, after serious efforts to resolve significant differences of opinion with your primary team, you are still at odds with the course of action being taken or recommended, consider asking to speak with someone on the **ethics team.** If you experience what feels like misconduct or have concerns regarding safety, let your concerns be known by registering a formal complaint: you can talk to **Patient Relations.**

When handled proactively, hospital **billing departments** can be remarkably accommodating. Payment plans can be worked out, auxiliary funds explored, and fines avoided. And finally, most hospitals have **English as Second Language (ESL) providers** who are specially trained translators or employ a remote telephonic translation service. It's incredibly easy to miscommunicate, especially when your team is speaking doctorese in a language you don't know well, so don't hesitate to request a translator.

——

Avoiding Care You Don't Need or Want

THANKS TO A FEDERAL LAW PASSED IN 1991, HOSPITALS ARE REQUIRED to ask you at the time of admission whether you have an advance

For Caregivers

Yes, the patient is the focus of a hospital stay, but watching the monitors at the bedside or counting the hours in an overlit waiting room means that you need care, too. It doesn't do your loved one any good if you run yourself ragged. Worse: stress and exhaustion impair your ability to make decisions. Do something every day that calms your nerves so you don't burn out and lose the presence of mind to process important information when it comes your way. Some ways to take care of yourself include:

Catch a break. With your loved one safely settled in, and hospital staff around to help, get some rest, knock things off your to-do list, exercise, eat. Refill your own tank. This is an important upside of your loved one being in the hospital—use it.

Breathe. A remarkable thing happens when caretakers enter the hospital room of their beloveds: they end up mirroring their symptoms. If the patient has lung disease, say, and is breathing shallowly and at a quick pace, his loved one, when in the room, tends to start breathing that way, too. Shallow, rapid breathing heightens anxiety. And when the caregiver's blood pressure and heart rate go up, it has the effect of also revving up the patient's nervous system. Out of the depths of empathy, the caregiver can inadvertently raise the anxiety of the room.

One of the most powerful interventions, then, says clinical

For Caregivers (continued)

social worker Bridget Sumser, is for the caregiver to take a few deep breaths. Once her nervous system is calmed, the patient will respond in kind. It's important to remember that the hospital room is a closed system with its own feedback loops—that your health and well-being as a caretaker affect the health and well-being of the one you're taking care of. It's why doctors send family members and friends home to get a good night's sleep, even when they would sacrifice everything to stay at the bedside. When the caretaker takes on too much, everyone suffers.

Stay in touch. If you can't take the day off to be with your loved one and instead show up at 6:00 p.m., you may miss the doctors, who will already have done their rounds. And hospitals typically have visiting hours that may not jibe with your schedule (these vary between hospitals, and within different parts of the hospital, so ask). That can leave you in the dark as to what has transpired since your last visit. If you're working full-time or are away for whatever reason, you can request phone updates from someone on the team. Or, simpler still, start by checking in with the nurse when you do arrive.

directive and offer you one if you do not. (This is the legal paperwork that names your health care agent, who will speak for you if you can't speak for yourself, and states how much or little life-sustaining medical intervention you want). That's a good thing, but with all the frenzy of entering a hospital, it's not a great time to be pondering how you want your final moments to look. Often the "code" discussion—whether or not you want doctors to attempt to bring you back to life with CPR and other medical interventions—falls to a tired doctor to go over with you, along with a laundry list of other pressing issues. As such, this vital discussion gets short shrift.

——

Code Status

YOUR **CODE STATUS** TELLS MEDICAL PROFESSIONALS WHAT TO DO IF your heart stops or you stop breathing. In other words, when you die, or are about to. Code status is hospital jargon for the resuscitation measures enumerated in an advance directive form. You may know about this from the movies: "Code Blue!" comes over the loudspeakers, everyone jumps to attention, and hyper-controlled chaos breaks loose. Family are pushed aside; electric shocks are delivered to your heart; breathing tubes pushed down your throat; needles inserted and meds poured in.

If a doctor were to ask you, "Would you like us to do everything possible to keep you alive?" you'd likely answer that question, "Well, of course I would, fool!" A better question would be "When you are actively dying and there's little to no chance of bringing you back, do you want us to help you die comfortably and peacefully?"

FAST FACT

88.3 percent of doctors report that they would choose a Do Not Resuscitate order for themselves.

Often enough, we doctors know when there's little or no chance of bringing you back and we should spare you that question, but that's not how it usually plays out.

Every patient in a hospital has a code status. There are essentially two code statuses: Full Code and Allow Natural Death (AND, aka Do Not Resuscitate, or DNR). Unless you and your doctor state otherwise, the default status is Full Code.

Full Code means you'll get the "Code Blue" treatment we described above. This may well be worth it to you when there's a chance of success (as with trauma, such as an accident, or heart attack in a body that's otherwise healthy). The latest data tell us that about 11 percent[1] of people who receive CPR in a hospital setting are well enough to be discharged afterward. For those of you at the tail end of cancer, organ failure, or dementia, the odds of being fully revived begin to approach zero. Your body—the body of anyone living with terminal illness—is already too weak and compromised to withstand it.

To understand where you stand on this wide spectrum, you need to have a frank conversation with your medical team, over time, *whenever* your code status is being considered: from one hospital stay to the next or, sometimes, within the same stay.

We'll be very clear here with our opinion. If you know you are going to die someday from this incurable illness, are in an advanced stage, and seek a peaceful or comfortable death, we unequivocally recommend your code status be DNR. When death is imminent, DNR status means all that effort will be put into making sure you're as comfortable as can be in those final moments, which is something most people hope for at the end of their lives. If, however, you wish to remain full code, that is your prerogative and you have our support. I've met a number of people who want to "go down swinging," and there's no shame in that. We just want to make sure you have a full picture as you weigh your options.

Some people feel so strongly about not wanting life extension and the suffering it can bring that they take extreme measures. One 70-year-old man who had been living in a nursing facility was found intoxicated, unconscious, and alone on the street and rushed to Jackson Memorial Hospital in Miami. He was deteriorating fast, and, according to a story in *The New England Journal of Medicine*, as doctors ripped off his shirt to revive him, they discovered a "DO NOT RESUSCITATE" chest tattoo. The word NOT was underlined, and the tattoo included a signature. There were no family members or nursing home staff to verify his wishes, and despite the clear message, the ER doctors still felt unsure what to do. A tattoo is not a legal advance directive. (The doctors were aware of a cautionary tale published in 2012 in the *Journal of General Internal Medicine* about a 59-year-old patient who had a "DNR" tattoo across his chest but told his medical team he wanted lifesaving measures to be taken in the event that he needed them. When the patient was asked why he had the tattoo, he told them he had lost a bet while playing poker.)

The medical team bought themselves some time with medications and an IV and called a medical ethicist for advice. After reviewing the patient's case, the ethics consultants advised them to honor the patient's DNR tattoo, saying it was reasonable to assume that it expressed his wishes. It was the right decision— social workers found the patient's advance directive later. The man died peacefully in the hospital the next morning.

One last note for now: Code status applies only to resuscitation efforts—*when you are dying*—and has nothing to do with how hard you want others to work on treating you beforehand.

Code status *should not* change the amount of attention you get. It *should* affect only resuscitation and not cut you off from any other services. We suggest that you clarify this explicitly with your clinical team and keep discussing it until you feel secure in your decision.

——

The Incidentaloma

ONE OF THE PROBLEMS WITH A HOSPITAL IS THAT IT'S FILLED WITH detectives trained to find problems. Often enough, a blood test or scan will turn up new problems that are unrelated to what's ailing you. Medical slang for such a finding is *incidentaloma*, loosely translated as "a lump found by accident." Incidentalomas can be fortuitous when you're otherwise healthy, allowing for early treatment and cure before you even knew anything was wrong.

But it's more likely that problems that turn up on tests incidentally aren't problems at all, and chasing them down can do damage. This is why whole-body scans and other screens for disease aren't always a good idea. And for people with serious or terminal illness, it makes even less sense to go looking for new problems. You might get swept away treating things that are trifles compared to the one that's actually killing you. Respect the power of a hospital, but use it cautiously.

——

The Intensive Care Unit (ICU)

THE ICU IS THE HOSPITAL IN CONCENTRATE. ALL OF MEDICINE'S high-tech strengths and weaknesses are here in the extreme.

This is where the breathing machines are kept; where there are far more devices than people; where nature is kept mostly at bay and everything is as controlled as can be. Here people are specially trained for the far reaches of illness, and the limits of what's possible get pushed. That's amazing when you need it and can benefit from it but a giant, painful detour when you can't.

If you and your doctors know you're dying soon and are unlikely to benefit from that particularly intensive type of care—if this place and this mode of care are not in line with your *goals* of care—then the ICU is a place to avoid.

But if you do find yourself in an ICU by chance or by choice, apply the same rules of thumb we've discussed so far. Comfort is possible. Movement is possible. Time with your family is possible. Remember: it's still the hospital, just in the extreme.

FAST FACT
Dying in the ICU tends to be harder on you and your family; here there are more urgent things going on than your individual comfort.

——

The Cast of Characters

YOU CAN HELP THE PEOPLE WHO WORK IN HOSPITALS HELP YOU IF you know a bit about the roles they play and can ask informed questions. Here's a short list of people you'll meet in the hospital:

- **Doctor (aka physician):** The buck stops here: legally she is in charge of the care you receive, but she isn't necessarily going to be the one bandaging a wound.
- **Hospitalist:** A doctor whose practice is in the hospital.

What does an attending physician do again? If you know a bit about the roles health care workers play and what resources are available to you, you can make informed requests and ask better questions.

Hospitalists work in shifts, so you might see a few different ones over the course of your stay.

- **Fellow:** A doctor who has completed medical school and residency and has elected to get further training in a subspecialty (oncology, cardiology, nephrology, palliative medicine, and so forth).

- **Resident:** A doctor who has graduated from medical or osteopathic school. To practice medicine in the United States, these freshly minted doctors must choose a specialty and go through more on-the-job training in a clinical setting. There is a pecking order to residency:

  - **Chief residents** are either doing an extra year or in their final year of residency. Chiefs are chosen by the program brass for leadership purposes.
  - **Senior residents** are the most senior resident on any particular team.
  - **Interns** are the most junior doctor—a first-year resident.

BUT WHO'S THE EXPERT?

This is an issue only in teaching hospitals. Residents (postgraduate doctors in training) may see you several times a day, and they're generally the best ones to identify what's changing. They're at the watch post in a way that more senior physicians aren't.

Senior doctors (aka attending physicians) have experience on their side, a wonderful and useful commodity to be sure. Just don't write off residents or trainees of any stripe. When

TIP
If you're about to undertake a complicated procedure—a lumbar puncture or taking fluid out of the lung or the belly—and are at all nervous, you can request that the most experienced person be the one to carry it out, or at least be present.

its communication you're craving, for example, it may well be the medical student who is best suited to tracking down information or reminding your team on your behalf. They have the most energy, the most time, the most curiosity and eagerness to please, and the most to prove.

- **Physician assistant (PA):** PAs often take on delegated medical duties such as the coordination of care and ordering referrals to specialists. PAs can also prescribe medications but require oversight by a physician.
- **Advanced practice nurse (APN), clinical nurse specialist (CNS), nurse practitioner (NP):** Nurses who have earned extra education at a master's or doctorate level. They can assess, diagnose, treat, and manage issues related to illness. APNs can order tests and prescribe medications in most states, similar to PAs, and in many instances the skills and responsibilities of APNs are practically the same as those of doctors. You may find that the person you see for many of your medical visits is an NP.
- **Registered nurse (RN):** RNs work directly with patient, family, the rest of the clinical team, and the doctor to carry out the best care. They help manage pain and other symptoms and attend to all matters of bedside care. Most patients will remember their nurses more than anyone else; they tend to be hands-on and have an amazing array of skills.
- **Licensed vocational nurse (LVN), licensed practical nurse (LPN):** Though they can't do everything an RN can, the difference probably won't be noticeable. Their tasks range from helping a patient change position in bed or go to the bathroom to administering enemas, checking catheters, and applying wound dressings, but LVNs can't dispense medications. Once

an RN has dispensed medication, an LVN can be the one to give it to you as long as it's not intravenous.

- **Social workers (SWs):** The unsung champions of your personal care. They help complete necessary forms, advocate for the patient's mental health and well-being, find appropriate community resources to best manage illness, and help with diplomacy when difficult family dynamics arise. Licensed clinical social workers (LCSWs) are social workers who receive extra training to provide psychotherapy.
- **Chaplains:** Chaplains can lend an ear, and provide not just comfort during times of sickness but a connection to your faith or what is sacred to you. Chaplains can support in a myriad of ways: from meditation, shared prayer, and organizing faith-specific clergy to extending rites and rituals when needed, such as the Anointing of the Sick.
- **Case manager:** A case manager is automatically assigned to you and acts as the connective tissue between your medical and social services (e.g., housing, food and transportation services), and your inpatient (in the hospital) and outpatient (out of the hospital) teams. Part organizer, part advocate, a good case manager is especially adept at communication.
- **Discharge planner:** Much the same as a case manager but more specific to hospitals. When you are leaving the hospital and going to another place, the discharge planner is your go-to. They may work in tandem with a social worker in an effort to ensure continuity from one setting to the next.
- **Direct care workers (DCWs) [this workforce includes certified nursing assistant (CNA), hospice aide (HA) or home health aide (HHA), and patient care assistant (PCA)]:** These are the least heralded and most heroic helpers; the people who wipe,

clean, lift, scrub, and disinfect in the background. Many times an aide or nurse's assistant is the person who will spend the most time with you.

- **Physical therapist (PT), occupational therapist (OT), speech-language pathologist (SLP), respiratory therapist (RT):** A variety of therapists is available to help instruct you about safe body movement, eating, and easier breathing.
- **Dietitian:** A person trained in nutrition who can help you sort through which foods to eat and which to avoid, offer details about artificial nutrition, and help monitor your calories and set intake goals.
- **Psychotherapist (PhD, PsyD, LCSW, MFT, and LPCC can all act as psychotherapists; different states have different rules for credentialing):** Sometimes referred to as *counselors*, a less specific term that includes nonprofessional peer counselors. They can be very helpful with talking out your situation and processing your emotions.
- **Art Therapist:** Helps you express yourself in nonverbal ways that make sense of your situation.
- **Therapeutic Musician & Music-Thanatologist:** Musicians trained to key in to your emotional and physiological well-being in real time and guide you to a peaceful state.

——

Leaving the Hospital

IT'S SURPRISING HOW ATTACHED WE CAN GET TO A PLACE—EVEN A hospital. I wept when I left the burn unit after being a patient. Despite the pain I had experienced in there, it had become my home and its staff had seen me through incredible times. I couldn't believe how sad I was to go and how much I missed it. I've seen this

For Caregivers

Physical therapists are not just for the patient. Maneuvering more than 100 pounds from a bed to a wheelchair, or into and out of the tub, can be an Olympic sport. If you don't know how to do it properly, it's a quick way to a pulled muscle, strained back, or slipped disk. A PT, and many OTs, can teach you— while still in the hospital or later on at home or clinic—how to safely move the body of your loved one for bathing, alleviate bedsores, and prevent falls, and will recommend equipment that can help you do so.

in the eyes of my patients, too, even amid the celebration of getting out. Good questions to consider asking when preparing to leave the hospital include:

- Will you review any instructions with me and my family before I leave?
- What support should I expect to need when I get home? What support will my caregivers need?
- Do you think I would benefit from a physical therapy or occupational therapy assessment before I leave?
- Are the medications I was taking when I came to the hospital the same as what I have now? If not, what changed and why?
- Is this medication covered by my insurance? Is there someone who can help me figure that out?

- How long will these prescriptions last? Who prescribes refills?
- How will I get home?

The process can be dizzying on both the emotional and the logistical planes. There are a few reasons to take extra care here and pay close attention. Moving from one place to another is exactly when things fall through cracks or become destabilized: medication lists, care plans, personal items, your mood. Besides a change of environment, this move marks the moment where one group of people ceases to be involved in your care and another crew picks up, whether that's a different clinical team or your family or friends.

And as a rule, it will all feel rushed. One day everyone is scurrying around you, testing, prodding, contemplating, caring in all sorts of ways. And the next, it might feel like they can't wait to see you go.

The way for you to temper the momentum for discharge is to speak up about your concerns. Hospitals do have a legal and ethical responsibility to ensure that you have a viable discharge plan, but assumptions are made about what is most realistic for you. If you don't speak up with concerns and questions now, you'll be wheeled to the door before you know it, often without much warning, though there's no universal standard. It's much harder to get your questions answered once you've left the hospital. This is another moment when good communication and self-advocacy are essential.

FAST FACT
Just because you may not feel ready to leave doesn't mean the hospital can keep you. *Hospitals are only for acute medical issues,* and that's the only thing insurance will cover. Once that acute work is done, all effort must shift to the next person in line.

Switching Facilities

THROUGHOUT THE COURSE OF YOUR ILLNESS, YOU MAY SPEND TIME IN a few different facilities. It takes time and energy for you to learn the ropes of a new place and its people, and for them to learn you. Each place (even a different floor of the same hospital) will have its own rules and limitations and communication quirks. There's always too much going on, so don't assume people are talking to each other.

Every facility (hospital, rehabilitation center, nursing home) has a staff member equipped to help you make plans for your next place of care.

To find the staff member who will help you switch facilities, ask your nurse, "Who will coordinate my discharge and help me and my family plan for the next stage in my care?" It's often a social worker or case manager. Start this conversation early in your stay, well before the move happens. And once you land at the new place, it's a good idea to ask the staff whether they received the discharge summary sent from the last place and to have them review it with you to make sure they get the story straight.

Many hospices and home care agencies offer pre-hospice or "bridge" programs—hospice lite—services designed to provide support to you and your family while you undergo further treatments. These are essentially palliative care programs, whether or not they're called that. You'll still get support from the same

TIP
Cancer centers, cardiology clinics, transplant teams, and so on will have support staff who may be able to provide continuity. You can ask them to call the staff at the next site that will be receiving you to make sure they know the full story of what you'll need.

interdisciplinary players, but it'll likely be on a case-by-case basis and will probably not include after-hours help.

Some people with the means to do so end up hiring eldercare consultants or case managers (see the next chapter) who will provide guidance no matter what setting you're in and help you and your family navigate all your options. The beauty of having a neutral party to stand up for you is knowing that they are not subject to pressure from institutional forces, and are working solely for your benefit—so make sure they're actually independent and not just a representative of an assisted living facility.

———

For Caregivers

At this writing, forty-two states have passed laws requiring hospitals and clinical facilities to provide training for caregivers who will be performing medical tasks when patients are released from hospitals or nursing facilities. Make sure you don't leave the hospital without being fully briefed on what care your loved one will need and what is expected of you.

The Hospital Hangover

IF YOU HAVE A SERIOUS ILLNESS THAT LANDS YOU IN THE HOSPITAL for more than a couple of days, your physical, emotional, and mental capacity will likely take a hit.

Don't expect a quick return to your pre-hospital self. Within the context of advanced illness and prolonged physical compromise, it's more likely you'll not get back to the way you functioned before the hospital stay. The stress of the hospital and the illness that helped land you there in the first place both take their cut. So if you find yourself struggling with tasks you used to be able to pull off easily, that's normal. Basic activities such as bathing and grooming, as well as your ability to get around, your energy level, and your cognitive ability, may all suffer to some degree. Plan for it.

——

Not Leaving the Hospital

DYING IN THE HOSPITAL ISN'T A FAILURE, EVEN IF IT WAS YOUR HOPE to die at home. It can't always be avoided. Hospitals, for all their possibilities and limitations, can be fine places to die, even ideal. The staff there have seen a lot; there are many useful medications to manage pain and other symptoms, including by the fastest-acting intravenous (IV) route, which is difficult to obtain at home; there are services and layers of support that are not possible in any other place around the clock, from aides to chaplains to doctors. And for many folks, the hospital has already become a second home. Try to let go of the notion that a hospital is a lousy place to spend your final moments.

Emphasizing that hospitals are not designed for dying is simply our attempt to make sense of a disconnect you might feel. Why are these doctors buzzing about as though this weren't the most profound time in my life? Why so much fluorescent light? Why all these machines that can't help me? Fair enough, but take heart that these buildings are also filled with people who care deeply about your care and who have the skills to help you now. Here are a few things you (or family) might request:

- **"Comfort care" orders.** More and more hospitals have set protocols for doctors to prescribe medications meant to help ease the dying process.
- **Palliative care.** You might not need a whole new team involved in your care, but if you sense that more could be done to support you and your family—better symptom control, clearer communication, coordination of care—ask if there's a palliative care program at the ready.
- **A chaplain.** You don't need to be religious to benefit from the peace of mind a chaplain can bring.
- **Particular nursing.** If there's any choice, request that nurses who are well versed in end-of-life care, or with whom you or your family are most comfortable, be assigned to you.
- **A quiet room.** Some hospitals have designated rooms expressly reserved for people who are in their final days, with more space for family, better views, and less distracting equipment. Often enough, it's possible to move you to a nicer room for this important time.
- **Anything that helps you get a touch of beauty.** Music therapy, flowers, pets, just about anything that makes you feel good. ❖

The Bottom Line

HOSPITAL HACKS

Hospitals are extraordinary places in every way, including how they operate as a world unto themselves. As a patient, it can be hard to know what's going on and too easy to wind up in a situation you'd rather avoid. You or your health care agent needs to stay engaged. Listen, ask questions, and speak up.

Help! I Need Somebody

How and when to hire help; home
care and home health; friends and
family; neighborhood networks

H ow will you get to and from appointments? Who will help with shopping and cleaning and child care? Do you have family or friends nearby? Can they give you the kind of support you want or need? There's both a social and a professional circle of caregivers; often you'll be relying on a combination of both. And be open to making new friends with relative strangers who offer to bring you a meal.

———

I Don't Want to Be a Burden

THIS IS A COMMON REFRAIN, AND IT'S TRUE ENOUGH THAT BEING SICK burdens you and those around you. Illness chews through energy, takes time, steals control, irritates in all kinds of ways. And by extension, when you're sick, *you* feel like the one doing all the irritating.

For many of us, it's harder to receive care than to give it, making dependency extra challenging. But cutting off loved ones from the opportunity to demonstrate their love, and yourself from the sweet vulnerability of needing someone, is a lost opportunity. People like to be helpful. This is part of life, and it feels right to participate in the mess of it all. And don't think that just because you're sick and less independent now you've got nothing to give. People can learn from you; you can brighten days with your own kindness or humor or candor. For all that you might not be able to do now, look for what you *can* do.

Beware infantilization. It's a pernicious force that creeps in around people who are sick or disabled—whether self-inflicted or because of the projections of others. Do not let yourself be reduced. Being in need of help does not make us children; it makes us human. **Keep in mind that none of us is truly independent.**

Not ever. We need others, on some level, throughout our lives. It's only ever a matter of degree.

——

Hiring Help

IT'S ALMOST NEVER TOO SOON TO SEEK EXTRA HELP. HIRING A HOME health aide can bring immense relief, both to you and to your family. You might not want it to be your daughter who has to take you to the bathroom and hold you steady as you pee. Aides can take on some of the more intimate details of care so family members are freed up for more conventional tasks such as organizing medications and doing the shopping or vice versa. You can customize how often you want an aide present, and you can change the setup over time as your health or care plan changes.

FAST FACT
Aides can be hired for any period of time: you might only want someone to stop by for an hour or so in the mornings to help you get out of bed and ready for the day; or you can hire an aide to be there overnight.

——

Home Health Aides

There are three pathways to finding and hiring an aide, with different payment options. Here they are:

1. **Home health agencies.** (Also called in-home health care agencies.) They employ aides who are licensed. By law, these organizations must perform a criminal background check on all prospective aides. If your aide gets sick or isn't available for some reason, the agency will provide someone else to step

in. While aides get some basic training through the agency, it tends to be minimal. Agencies usually limit the scope of what their aides are allowed to offer clients; this is for the aide's protection (as well as the agency's), but it can also be a barrier.

2. **Private hire.** Private-hire aides may or may not have training or a license, but they are not necessarily limited in what services they can provide. So you can come to an agreement together on what they'll do for you. Contact a hospice agency in your area, even if you're not enrolled. Many keep a list of caregivers for hire; or, ask friends who've needed help if they have any recommendations or cautions to note. It's up to you and your family to screen the person, so ask for multiple references and take the time to interview them.

3. **Medicaid waiver.** Many states have Medicaid money set aside to help enrollees pay for aides. The word *waiver* means that dollars that would otherwise go to support institution-based services can be used instead to support you in your home. These dollars are not an entitlement per se, meaning that you often have to get on a wait list and there is no guarantee that you'll get the funds when you need them. In California, this program is called In-home Supportive Services (IHSS). Call your local Medicaid office—or whichever organization is managing your Medicaid (there should be contact info on your insurance card)—or ask a social worker or case manager about waivers in your state. These programs will either provide an aide from their own roster or pay friends or family members to act as one. How to qualify will depend on your situation and state policies.

WHEN IS IT TIME TO HIRE AN AIDE?

- If you find yourself wondering if now's the time to hire an aide
- It's getting harder for you to function around the house
- You need assistance with one or more of the six activities of daily living (ADLs):

  1. Eating on your own
  2. Getting to the bathroom, especially at night
  3. Controlling your bowel and/or bladder
  4. Bathing yourself
  5. Dressing yourself
  6. Moving without assistance, or getting into and out of a wheelchair or bed

- After a prolonged hospitalization (a few days or weeks with extra assistance will help you and your family adjust to being home again)
- If you have had a fall or two
- If you are prone to confusion in the middle of the night
- If the health of family caregivers has taken a hit (or is threatening to; prevention is best). Back injuries and other ailments are common among family members trying to do too much
- If you have gaps in care when friends or family can't be around

it's time to ASK FOR HELP when...

... dressing on your own becomes difficult

... you can't use the toilet alone

... family / friends / helpers are away at work or on vacation

... it's hard to eat

... you have trouble bathing yourself

People often wait too long to get help and end up either relying too heavily on exhausted family members or putting themselves at risk. It's never too soon to ask for help.

For Caregivers

"Failure to thrive" is a quasi-diagnosis that doesn't get as much attention as a broken hip, but it should. It's a gestalt phrase we use clinically to describe someone whose body is slowly fading but for no apparent or singular reason. "The dwindles" is another, more casual phrase. This is the path to *dying of old age* or *of natural causes*. If you're caring for an older adult, small things like dizziness and loss of vision start to pile up and can result in more serious consequences, like falls and ER visits.

GERIATRIC EVALUATION

—
TIP
If your loved one is older, which traditionally means over 65, ask the doctor or hospital for a "geriatric assessment."

This is similar to the "home safety evaluation" mentioned later in this chapter but more comprehensive and specific to the challenges of being older. When it comes to safety and quality of life, *function* is the thing that everyone—patients, caregivers, and clinicians—should be working on, and that's what these assessments identify. You will get a good idea of how things are going and of what specifically can be done to help your loved one.

HOME HEALTH

Home health care is a benefit under Medicare. It's not quite as intensive and all-encompassing as home hospice care but can be a good and useful option for those who don't yet qualify for hospice. **Confusing terminology alert:** "Home <u>health</u>" is a loose term covering aides for hire to help with basic activities at home and is *not* covered by medical insurance. "Home health care" (often shortened to "home <u>care</u>") is more medically specific and intensive and may be covered by medical insurance, depending on your policy and situation.

Details vary based on the program and your level of need, but you'll likely have a nurse assigned to you who will act as your case manager and directing services as needed. That nurse and other team members will come to your home during workday hours, on a schedule dictated by your needs and the resources available.

To qualify for a home health care program, you must be considered *homebound*, meaning that you require assistance either from another person or from medical equipment such as a walker or wheelchair. Your doctor must also declare that your health would worsen if you left home. Home health care services may include:

TIP
Your doctor will know the process to qualify for home care or at least know enough to go grab the social worker or nurse or administrator for help.

- **A nurse** who visits to help with medication and other skilled work (like wound care for bedsores)
- **A social worker** for case management and general support
- **A therapist** for physical, occupational, and speech exercises
- **A physician** who oversees your care. But once you are past the initial qualifying visit (in clinic or at home or by telephone), you probably won't see that doctor in your home

Home care teams don't make middle-of-the-night visits. Programs may have a twenty-four-hour call line, but those questions are typically kicked to the next business day; it's not an emergency service.

——

New and Alternative Sources of Help

ELDERCARE CONSULTANTS

A colleague and her family found themselves in over their heads. Whitney's father, a rugged Idaho man whose ideal dwelling place was his car, had suffered a series of setbacks, from congestive heart failure to an infection in the eyes that was causing near-blindness. The family had been trading off taking him into their homes and caring for him as he recovered from multiple surgeries, but they all had full-time jobs or families of their own, not to mention different ideas about what was best for him.

Based on the intuition that such a service should exist, Whitney searched online and found a local consultant who charges by the hour ($175) to talk to everyone in a family, assess the patient's needs, and synthesize everything into a suggested care plan. Whitney described her as part financial planner, part family therapist.

You and your caregivers are juggling so much. A deeper understanding of the eldercare landscape—what you can expect, and what you can afford—can be a godsend, so consider enlisting someone to help you navigate it. But beware of opportunists because at this time there is no such thing as getting "certified" in this area. Still, if you can find a guide near you who comes highly recommended, look into it. Even a one-time consultation may be a great help, and know, too, that some consultants will work on a sliding fee scale, so don't talk yourself into thinking this is only for rich people.

VILLAGE PEOPLE

As you think about whom you can count on, you might consider joining (or forming) a neighborhood group. There's a growing trend of grassroots networks springing up across the United States to help people age in place.

The concept is simple: as we live longer or have to live with a serious illness, often far from our families, we may need occasional help. Instead of moving into assisted living, villages rely on basic good neighborliness; people looking out for one another. Some networks are informal. More structured ones require an annual fee for membership, which will buy you access to a raft of resources from volunteers who are just a few blocks away.

Potlucks, book clubs, and other group outings help keep you connected to others. Don't underestimate the importance of being social as part of your regimen of self-care.

Beyond opportunities to gather for social occasions, many age-in-place networks offer carefully vetted service providers such as gardeners, painters, attorneys, accountants, and personal care attendants who can help with bathing and dressing. Need help with your computer? Housekeeping? Taking the dog for a walk? A ride to your doctor's appointment? Neighbors and volunteers could be there to help.

FAST FACT

According to Julianne Holt-Lunstad, PhD, a professor of psychology at Brigham Young University, greater social connections are "associated with a 50 percent reduced risk of early death."

DEATH DOULAS

Doulas are not just for birthing; there is a new subset of doulas who are trained to support patients and families at the end of life. Part coach and part assistant caregiver, doulas might help a dying person review their life and plan for their last days. Doulas work with families to create a legacy project, provide respite, and aid them with practical physical care. Involved before, during, and after death, doulas might bathe and dress the body of the deceased, and guide the family in their early experience of grief. **Unlike most hospice care, they are not part of an assigned team or reimbursable by Medicare.** Doulas are not yet available everywhere in the United States, but this unique quasi-profession is on the rise. Doulas are being trained for posts in hospices, in hospitals, and as private practitioners serving dying people directly in the home.

–
TIP
If you like to be alone, or simply are, it's only more important for you to prepare your paperwork, plan for the likely contingencies, and communicate with your doctor: what are your goals of care, your code status, who, if anyone, is around to help, whom can you afford to hire, where would you live when home is no longer possible.

UNASSISTED LIVING

Some 35 million[1] of us live alone. And there are plenty more who live with people who might not be willing or able to help. The good news is that there's still support out there; finding it just requires some creative thinking.

Dying alone is harder. There is a term for this large and growing subset of the population: elder orphans. There is so much to be done even as you grow less and less able to do it by yourself. But technology is making remote assistance more viable and effective. Telemedicine is a good start, as are social media networks and online services that deliver food or medication.

Being alone is not necessarily some second-place finish; many of us prefer solitude. For anyone who finds themselves in this scenario, much of the advice you'll get from others will be given on the assumption that you have stable friends and family at the ready to assist.

But if you don't, our advice is much the same. Think about what means you have to work with and explore the full range of what community resources exist, informal and formal alike.

OUTSOURCING RESPONSIBILITY

For some, managing the financial tasks of daily life is overwhelming. The courts have established an arrangement for this situation: if you are found to be "incapacitated" —i.e., unable to make decisions for yourself without a healthcare or financial proxy assigned—they will appoint a *conservator* to handle your financial affairs. If the need extends to your personal life and health, the courts can appoint a *guardian*. Conservators and guardians are professionals vested with the legal power to assume decision-making responsibility on behalf of another adult. This formal arrangement is generally for people who *do not* have family members at the ready to assume the role, but not necessarily; for those *who do* have family and friends available to help, conservatorship or guardianship allows for personal relationships to remain just that, while professionals handle the rest.

There is another important option for people who may be "competent" but in need of outside assistance: hiring a Private Trustee (PT) or a Professional Fiduciary (PF). The PT or PF becomes your advocate in any area that needs assistance; health and quality of life decisions, estate or finance issues, or managing multiple care providers. Their services cover the mundane, such as daily bill-paying and doctor's appointments, but can be as broad as managing your entire estate. Most PTs and PFs will provide an initial complimentary consultation with an hourly rate thereafter, based on your needs. For relatively straightforward situations, rates usually range between $75 and $150 per hour. Many practices will tailor their work according to your needs and means.

If you think any of these options would be a good route for you or someone you care about, discuss them with an estate planning lawyer or contact the Professional Fiduciary Association to get more information.

——

Safety-Proofing Your Home

MOST PEOPLE SAY THEY WANT TO STAY IN THEIR OWN HOME AND, with any luck, die in their own bed. That's beautiful and doable, and it's our bias to get you there. The virtues are obvious: your favorite blanket is where you left it; you know every nook and cranny with your eyes closed; there's no need to change out of your pajamas or smell anyone's smells but your own. Home is familiar and comforting. If you plan ahead, you'll fare better longer and make it more likely that you'll manage to stay to the end.

If you feel that you can no longer do essential tasks at home, ask your doctor about a prescription for a *home safety evaluation* from an occupational and/or physical therapist. The evaluation will tell you something about your own physical limitations and what to do about them, and teach you tricks for safeguarding your home. As with so many of these services, insurance coverage will vary, but ask. **Many people don't realize how much assistance they qualify for, leaving all sorts of services on the table.** Here are some home tips:

• **Reduce your use of stairs.** Stairs can be a tripping hazard, and you may not have the energy to get up and down them as your

Remaining at home is going to be easier if you bring in help. But there are other steps you'll need to take to make home as safe and sound as possible.

illness progresses. Think about moving your bed to the main floor, where stairs won't be a daily issue.

- **Improve the lighting.** You're more likely to trip over something left on the floor in the dark or in a shadowed hallway. Even if your vision is 20/20, a fall is more common and *more devastating* when you're frail (think: brittle bones, thinned skin). Good lighting goes a long way. And get rid of clutter; there's so much to trip over.

- **Make room around your bed.** You may need to move it to the middle of the room or to another room in order to maneuver a wheelchair around it, for example, or to make room for an easy pivot over to a commode.

- **Purchase dark-colored linens.** There will be bodily fluids, and they will ruin your crisp whites. Towels and sheets in darker shades hide stains and make for less traumatizing cleanup.

- **Add traction.** Are there rugs that have tripped you up on the way to the bathroom in the middle of the night? Time to remove those. Are your wood floors slippery? There are products such as no-slip safety strips and mats that will add traction.

- **Raise the height of your toilet.** Perhaps you need a riser—kind of like a kid's booster seat—that makes it easier to get on and off the pot. Or perhaps a portable urinal or bedside commode is in order—they're cheap, and easier than you're probably imagining.

- **Safety-proof the bathroom.** Areas with slippery surfaces can create falling hazards, and getting into a tub from a wheelchair or walker can be tricky. Install grab bars and no-slip mats, and invest in a shower chair.

- **Move your most-used kitchen items to a lower level.** If your kitchen shelves are all built for a person who is standing up, it's time to move things to the counter level and maybe buy a grabbing claw. Other issues to consider include:

- **Your household.** Are there people around who are willing and able to help you? And realistically, how available are they?
- **Your location.** If you live in a densely populated urban area, you're likely within reach of nearby medical and social services that can help with your care. If you live in a more rural setting, get ready to spend a lot of time in the car with a friend or family member, or a rideshare or taxi driver.
- **Telehealth.** Thanks to the wonders of technology, it is possible to have an official visit over video or telephone with a clinician many miles away. These services are not yet widely available, but they are spreading fast. Telehealth is covered by insurance just like a regular doctor visit. Ask your clinic whether it offers such services, or call your insurer to learn what is available through their network.

———

Can I Die at Home?

YES, YOU CAN. THERE'S A WHOLE INDUSTRY SET UP TO HELP YOU DO exactly that. We should say this right up front: if you're thinking about this, it may be time to request hospice care, which can help you through almost any distress without your having to call 911. Hospice is the way to get the most services delivered to you in your home, including someone to call in the middle of the night; enrolling may be the single most important thing you can do to live and die at home.

It can't be said often enough: electing hospice does not equate with giving up. When people tell us that they're "not ready for hospice," we have to ask, "You mean you're not ready to have more help for you and your family? You're not ready to have your pain better controlled? You're not ready to leave the hospital behind? You're not ready to have every opportunity to be comfortable at home?" As long as you qualify, as explained in chapter 11, "Dynamic Duo: Hospice and Palliative Care," it is never too soon to involve hospice. It's a singular heartache to watch people suffer more than they need to due to a misconception.

——

Helping Help Be Helpful

SOME PEOPLE HAVE TOO FEW FRIENDS TO CALL UPON, WHILE OTHERS have, in a sense, too many. Not infrequently, I see patients burning through their finite energy tending to the needs of others—not a problem itself except when it's draining you or distracting you from your own priorities when time is limited.

Of course, finding help is one thing; managing it is another. Ask a friend (preferably a type A one) to help organize all the activity: one person is in charge of grocery shopping; one stays the night with you on Wednesdays so your partner can get a break; one drives you to all your doctor appointments. Daily life is already complicated, and when you're sick, just responding to everyone's offers of help can be a full-time job.

Who's closest to you? Find a person, or two, to be your deputy. Sit down with them and figure out what you need, either week to week or day to day, so they can work on getting the assignments filled. Aging and dying are complex operations—being sick, caregiving, navigating a health care plan, just living—and it helps to handle it with well-delegated teamwork. Things to think about include:

- Recurring appointments, medical or otherwise
- Grocery needs
- Medication tracking
- Pet care
- Basic house cleaning, including garden care
- Personal hygiene
- Waking and sleeping schedule

This is an exercise in both practical and emotional delegation, and the challenge is keeping everything straight. Get basic: buy a huge wall calendar or a year planner, and start penciling things in; this will keep things clear for you and make the information easily available to any other visiting friends or family. ❖

CHAPTER FOURTEEN

The Bottom Line

HELP! I NEED SOMEBODY

We all need help. Don't wait until you're on the floor to get some. Please hear this. It may not be easy to let people see you in rough shape, but let that pride go. There's no shame in needing more support—this is where humility and grace and courage are found. People like to help people. Why would you not accept the very thing you'd give others?

Care for the Caregiver

What caregivers actually do; the gifts and
the challenges of tending to someone;
the financial toll; how to get a break

All over this country there are people like you who are driving out of their way to pick up a prescription after work, using coffee breaks to visit someone and make lunch, missing out on dates with friends in order to make sure someone is safe before they go to bed, or taking trips to the hospital. You might forget about your own backache or about how you haven't worked out or had a haircut in a year.

The joy and satisfaction that come from helping someone you love will involve real sacrifice (and probably a few escape fantasies). Your mood and energy levels will likely bounce around, and just when you think you've found a stable routine, things will change.

You are not alone. In the United States at any one time, 40 million adults are caregivers. You are more likely to be a woman—especially if you're doing the difficult work of bathing and toileting—though the percentage of male caregivers is on the rise: in 2009, 34 percent of caregivers were men; as of 2017 that number was 40 percent. It's a hard job, but when they look back on the experience, most people say they wouldn't trade it for the world.

FAST FACT
On average caregivers provide more than twenty hours per week of care for four years.

So although the rest of this book addresses "you, the patient" directly, in this chapter when we say "you," we mean family, friends, neighbors, church community, and anyone else who dares to entwine the needs of another with their own.

———

Being There

AT A CERTAIN POINT, STANLEY BERGER'S WORLD BECAME A VERY SLOW and quiet place. Just turning his head to look at me took him eons;

we were suspended in time. His doctors said he needed peace now—no drama. I am not a particularly quiet or slow person, so learning to be a good caregiver meant adjusting my dials and synchronizing to his pace. A meal consisted of holding a straw to his lips for a full minute so he could pull a few sips, then doing that again and again until an inch of the smoothie was drunk. Time spent together meant lying silently side by side on his bed with the TV on or sitting on the couch watching my children play in his living room.

That may sound easy, but it was agony for me. I had dirty laundry and grocery shopping and a sink full of dishes and hungry children holding up a sign of protest that read, *Don't just sit there, do something!* When you become a caregiver, you learn that you have to turn that phrase upside down: *Don't just do something, sit there!* When I could do that—pour all of my attention into the small corridor between my father and me—my heart was so full that it heated up my chest. There was no longer any point to livening our time with chatter; none of that nagging urgency to recite recent accomplishments, to try to impress him. He didn't need it. His internal word processor was too broken to really get what I was saying, anyway. All he needed now was someone to hold his hand and not let him slip into oblivion alone.

—

Dueling Realities

WE'RE TEMPTED TO LAY OUT A SECTION HERE ON THE "GOOD" PARTS of caregiving and then a section on the "bad." But it doesn't work that way. Caregiving is all of the above, much of the time, plus a fair amount of tedium. Love seems to be the best rudder when you find yourself exhausted and wondering what you're in for. "Learning to honor innate vulnerability, and feeling it in another person, is something I will carry with me. That ultimately made me stronger," says Tembi Locke, who cared for her husband for ten years until his death from leiomyosarcoma. "You think it's only about what goes out, but equal to that is this receiving in the form of direct love from the patient and from people who showed up in my life willing to lend a helping hand."

Caregiving can narrow your field of vision in the day-to-day, but a grander sense of perspective will also take shape. You might come to see just how long the list is of things *not* to worry about: the pettiness of office politics; the nightly news; the traffic. Now you might find yourself more moved by silence or morning birds or small signs of kindness. You care, you show up, you face reality with someone, you touch the limits, and maybe you learn something about yourself.

Meanwhile, this is your shy father whose catheter bag you're changing. Your daily work is your flesh and blood and also urine, feces, and mucus. Sometimes it's not unlike tending a newborn, just less cute. Throw years of personal relationship backstory into the mix, and it becomes even more emotionally complicated and uncomfortable than you might expect. (Or maybe just as complicated as you expect.) Jen knows this to be true. "The thing I keep running into is that I feel like I'm in my seventies, but I'm not. I'm surrounded by all these grandparents and my husband and all of them are kind of in a similar situation and then I have my children to take care of. I'll go out to dinner and go out to parties . . . we had friends over for lunch and I was like 'Oh, this is what people my age do!' So there are definitely times when I feel like I don't get that and I'll say to myself, 'This is hell.'"

Public meltdowns or spontaneous vomiting can test your endurance and pride. It's not uncommon to feel like a dramatic spectacle when you and your person leave the house together. But please do it anyway. This is what real life looks like, and there is something beautiful about revealing that real-life vulnerability to the world. More important, it's so good for your loved one to get a change of scenery along with some air, sunlight, and socializing. It's good for you, too.

——

Letting Go of Blame

WE LOVE TO HAVE SOMETHING OR SOMEONE TO BLAME—ESPECIALLY ourselves. The notion that you caused this may be more tolerable than the admission that—gulp—you have little control.

One man, who'd left a family behind in Mexico and started a new one in Texas, was convinced that he had brought on his son's cancer—that it was a punishment for his actions. Because of that, he could barely stand to be in his son's hospital room or even talk to his wife, who ended up feeling utterly alone in her suffering. Maybe you, too, believe that you could have prevented this illness by pushing your loved one to eat better or quit smoking.

TIP
Part of your own care is feeling like you're having a positive impact on your loved one; feeling that you're doing a good job. But when things are inherently a mess, what constitutes a "good job" is hard to define.

But when you personalize someone else's illness, you might accidentally diminish your ability to be there for the one who is actually ill. Your loved one needs you now, and your self-blame and guilt shift the focus back to you. If you truly are culpable, do whatever you can to make amends, and soon. But if those feelings make you swoop in and upend the carefully thought-through plans of more consistently involved family members, check yourself.

Part of being a good caregiver is accepting when the person you're caring for makes decisions you disagree with. Your loved one may be miserable no matter what you do or what anyone does. As close as you two may be, there is always an unbridgeable gap. This is his or her death, and your own confidence can't ultimately depend on how well he or she is faring or even on his or her satisfaction. Ask yourself: *Have I done my part? Have I done what I can do? Have I done what I felt was right?* If the answer is yes, try to leave it there.

——

Expect the Unexpected

PART OF PLANNING FOR THIS REALM MUST INCLUDE PLANNING FOR things you can't possibly anticipate. Flexibility will force itself on you if you don't embrace it first. There are two parts to this twister: one is to reserve some emotional and logistical space for things you can't imagine right now. A realistic caregiver to-do list might read: pick up groceries, call to refill meds, get patient to physical therapy appointment, and handle the unforeseen. That might mean being on the phone all morning with the insurance company instead of (or while) going to the grocery store.

The second part is to settle for what's possible. There's just too much beyond your control. That errand doesn't have to happen today. Or maybe it did, and oh, well, you'll try again in the morning. But your loved one's shirt definitely doesn't have to stay clean through dinner. Who cares? Your job is to get good at regrouping, not necessarily at trying harder.

——

The Task List

COOK MEALS, RUN ERRANDS, SORT MEDICATION—DOESN'T SOUND like anything too out of the ordinary, right? Yet on top of those tasks, you may find yourself doing things you never expected to do for another adult. Here are a few to add to the list:

- Changing soiled diapers, linens, and garments
- Helping someone into and out of bed or off the couch
- Giving a bath and grooming
- Dressing wounds and giving medications
- Scheduling and attending appointments; being the auxiliary note taker or set of ears
- Tracking and restocking medications and supplies
- Observing and scanning for trouble in the making
- Listening, and then listening some more, without judgment
- Holding steady when fear, sorrow, or anxiety bubbles up
- Sharing in delights and pleasant surprises or victories (even tiny ones)
- Managing other helpers

FAST FACT
People caring for loved ones with long-term dementia are at even higher risk for health problems, including heart disease, low immunity, poorer sleep, and more trouble with alcohol and cigarettes.

— —

Occupational Hazards

CAREGIVING OVER LONGER PERIODS OF TIME CAN have real effects on your health. Body aches and injuries are common from lifting someone onto and off of the toilet or into and out of bed. Caregivers often forgo their own checkups or forget to take their own meds or to exercise or to eat properly. They are at increased risk for depression, anxiety, and stress that can last well after their loved one is gone.

And with only so many hours in a day, the rest of your life can get crowded out. Caregivers are more likely to have to resign their jobs and to spend more money, all of which makes it harder to keep up the role. It's the double whammy of a life demanding more from you while simultaneously providing you less to work with. Here's the hard truth in numbers:

- The average income lost by caregivers each year is 33 percent.
- Caregivers pay for many expenses out of their own pockets, to the tune of $10,000 a year.
- Eleven percent of caregivers have to quit their job to care for someone at home around-the-clock.
- If a person has to leave her job due to caregiving needs, the lost wages, pensions, and Social Security benefits over her lifetime total more than $300,000 on average.
- The estimated value of informal, unpaid senior care provided by family members approaches $500 billion in the United States alone. That's double the amount spent on formal, paid care.

TIP

If a patient is enrolled in a Medicaid program that pays for home care, it may be possible for that person to select a friend or family member as their care provider who would be paid by Medicaid. Rules differ by state on who can act as caregiver and receive payments, so check with the Medicaid office in your area.

Vigilance is essential, and so are rest and recovery—that means scanning for trouble, and relaxing when you don't find any (or can't do anything about it). A person cannot stay in crisis mode for very long without feeling undone. Locke, the caregiver mentioned earlier in this chapter, advises caregivers to take advantage of the good days. "If the patient is feeling well

HAZARDS *of caregiving*

eating on the run

where did
all the
money go?

it's back-breaking
work.

no more days off.

Caregivers are an invisible, underserved workforce. Aside from managing the housing, insurance, physical, and emotional needs of ailing loved ones, many are holding down full-time jobs, taking care of their own families, draining their bank accounts, and in desperate need of a back rub.

313

and you're feeling well, use that time—that might just be a trip to a movie; it doesn't have to be grand." Ramp up into crisis mode when you need to, and be sure to wind down as soon as you can.

——

Caring for Yourself

AS THE AIRLINE INDUSTRY REMINDS US: IN ORDER TO HELP OTHERS we need to put on our own oxygen masks first. We'll go even further—since someone in a predicament is relying upon you: it's selfish to not take care of yourself.

Self-care is a popular phrase right now, and it doesn't mean self-indulgence. A back rub or a piece of cake or a glass of really good wine does not in itself constitute self-care. Wonderful though they are, these things are not enough. Self-care is a muscle you need to learn to flex so it becomes part of your routine, instead of a rare treat. It means paying attention to yourself, even when the only thing you want to pay attention to is your beloved. Remind yourself that tending to yourself and tending to your loved one are much the same thing. Here are some things to try:

- **Take time-outs.** Foster a contemplative practice of some sort. This means prayer, meditation, yoga, the gym, hiking, biking, dancing, gardening, writing. Find some way to connect with yourself, body as well as spirit.
- **Share.** Have a short call list of people who will listen, without judgment and talk about anything; colleague, spouse, friend, therapist. It doesn't need to be a shrink, though they can be helpful, too. Venting over coffee with someone you trust might be enough. One way or another, unbottle yourself.

- **Pace yourself.** If your loved one is already in the late stages of illness, it's likely a matter of a few weeks of serious effort. A sprint. If she seems to have months or years to live, you're in for a marathon. Don't make the mistake of trying to hold your breath until it's all over.
- **Distract yourself.** Movies, golf, books, howling at the moon— whatever transports you for a bit. A beer or two may not be a bad idea, but be careful not to slide into coping mechanisms that will hurt you over time.
- **Seek respite.** This might mean finding someone to take your place for a time, finding an adult day care program, or, if on hospice, arranging for your loved one to stay for a few nights in a hospice house or nursing home. Take small breaks as often as possible and longer breaks now and again.
- **Watch your health.** Be sure to factor in your own health and limitations. Do you need to see a doctor? Are you aching some-where? Are you keeping current with your meds? Let an hon-est answer inform how you set up living arrangements for your loved one.
- **Recruit hospice and palliative care.** It's the explicit philoso-phy of both services to support caregivers. Yes, your own well-being is reason enough to invite hospice in.
- **Find other people in a similar situation.** Just as there are support groups for patients with different illnesses, there are support groups for different types of caregivers. Are you the husband of a patient with Alzheimer's? The daughter of someone with ALS? There's a group for you. Conduct an on-line search for "caregiver support" + "(type of illness)" to find them.
- **Reach out to friends.** They probably don't know how to help

you and will be so grateful if you can simply tell them what you need. You can even prompt them: *Help me think about anything other than illness.*

- **Engage HR.** Make sure to check with your job's HR department about whether you qualify for, and how to best utilize, the Family and Medical Leave Act (FMLA). FMLA may not cover you if you work for a smaller business, but you should definitely inquire. FMLA protection or not, if you have a good and trusting relationship with your boss be sure to talk to her about your situation; often enough, there are creative ways to make it all work for everyone.

—

Share the Load

INVITING OTHERS INTO THE MIX, WHETHER FRIENDS OR PROS, MIGHT be the best thing you can do as a caregiver. Here's how to get organized:

1. **Figure out what needs to be done.** Create a numbered list of tasks: picking up medication, going grocery shopping, driving to and from doctor's appointments, ferrying the kids to and from school, scheduling the plumber, making and freezing some meals.
2. **Figure out who can help.** List friends, family, and others who may be available, capable, and willing. Make sure you have their phone numbers and email addresses, too.
3. **Notify.** Call or email everyone on the list individually. Explain what you're hoping to accomplish.
4. **Meet in person.** Meet with everyone in the group, discuss

what needs to be done, and hand out assignments based on people's expertise and available time.

Here are four things you might ask someone else to do:

1. Sit with your loved one while you go for a walk or take a break in another room.
2. Pick up something from the store or takeout for your next meal.
3. Accompany your loved one to their next medical appointment.
4. Load the dishwasher or do a load of laundry.

Not sure how to properly thank or repay someone? Never underestimate the power of pizza! ❖

The Bottom Line

CARE FOR THE CAREGIVER

Taking care of someone requires taking care of yourself; you two are directly and intimately linked. Try to remember the gifts of caregiving: purpose, perspective, love. They won't always make the toil pleasant, but they will help you keep your sanity. You are engaged in some of the most important and underappreciated work there is. For all that gets sacrificed to make room for caregiving, many come to feel that the world they entered is more true and rewarding than the one they left behind. Hard and painful though these days can be, someday you might look back and miss them.

Everyone DIES.

How to Talk to Kids

Eight common questions young ones
ask and ways to answer them

W e may think we're protecting children by not talking about death, but when death is present they will have questions, and if we don't answer them, they'll assume it's simply too dreadful to talk about. Pop positive psychology—just smile, and it will all be okay—doesn't work on kids. Little ones know more about what's going on than we think they do. If you're wondering how much to share with them, the rule of thumb is to follow their lead. They, in turn, will feel safer and be more forthcoming if they can trust you to be earnest. We don't mean to supersede what you know to be best for you and your family. These are our suggestions, not gospel. Here are a few questions that may bubble up and some guidance for how to answer:

1. "Do I have to go see Grandma at the hospital?"

You can say good-bye in any way you'd like. If you want to draw her a picture or write her a letter, I can take it to her.

There is no reason to shield kids from seeing a dying relative. Just make sure you prepare them ahead of time for what they will see. If you're planning an ICU or nursing facility visit, take a picture of the dying person on your phone ahead of time and then ask, "Do you want to see a picture of what Grandpa looks like right now?" If they do, look at the picture together and ask if they have any questions about why he looks so small and drawn, or about the life support machines, so they know that the tube coming out of his nose is *helping* him breathe and not any of the other things their imagination might spin up.

Though you don't need to run around in circles protecting them, pushing kids to visit when they don't want to isn't a good idea, either. You may think they'll regret not holding Grandma's hand one last time, but they may want to say good-bye in a

different way, by drawing a picture or writing a letter, and that's A-OK. It doesn't have to be a big moment at the bedside to count.

It's also a good idea to give kids a way to exit the scene if they need to. If a kid is visiting someone who looks scary to them, let him or her know that they can go sit in a corner of the room or hallway and draw or play quietly. Kids know when they've reached their limit, so they will step away and then come back when they're ready. Aside from being there at the bedside, there are many creative ways for kids to be engaged with a dying relative. Here are a few ideas:

- Write a note and give it to the loved one, or leave it at their bedside or under a pillow
- Record a favorite family song or make a playlist to play in the loved one's room
- Draw a picture to hang in the loved one's room
- Record a message of the child reading from a favorite book on your phone to play for the loved one
- Allow children to paint the nails or brush the hair of the dying person
- Bring in a favorite comfort item (warm socks, fuzzy blanket)

2. "What does *dead* mean?"
Dead means that the body isn't working anymore. It doesn't breathe or move or get cold or hungry or hurt. Plants and animals die, too. It's a natural part of life.

Characters in children's movies and books routinely go up in puffs of smoke and then plunk back down, apple-cheeked and full of vigor, so for young kids (under about age 6), death may

seem temporary, abstract—and something that might happen to other people, but not to them or to the people they love. Still, it's not too early to ask kids what they do and don't want to know about someone in the family who is dying. With a child as young as 2 or 3 years old, you can sit down and ask, "What do you think is going on with Daddy? Do you want to know more? Or do you *not* want to know more?" Even a three-year-old will say, "Daddy's sick; I want to go play." It's amazing how much young kids can articulate what they need.

There's nothing magical about how to talk to kids about death. It's simply a matter of putting aside your preconceptions and asking a few questions. "Regardless of what's going on in your head as a parent and the process you're going through, the most important thing you can do is to stop and ask the kids," says Cam Sutter, a child life specialist at Newton-Wellesley Hospital, near Boston, who helps kids cope with illness and death. If asked, they will tell you in a very straightforward way what they understand about the situation and what they don't. Some want to know more, and some are pretty clear that they just want to go kick a ball around.

3. "Are you going to die, too?"

I don't expect to die for a long time. I am healthy and will be here for you. And if I do die there are lots of people to take care of you, like your aunties and uncles and grandmas.

The most important thing to your children is that someone will be there to take care of them. They are tiny survivalists and may be more concerned about who's going to get them to school than anything else. Even when you're in the thick of grief and emerging from the bathroom with puffy eyes and unable to think about

anything else, your kids are likely to be completely selfish and impolitic. They will be more focused on how your grief affects your ability to care for them than on its cause.

4. "What will we do at the funeral?"

Grandpa will be in a casket, which is a container they put people's bodies in before they go into the earth. You'll be able to see his face and can touch him if you want. People will get up to talk about him and may cry because they are sad and miss him. It's okay for you to go outside and play if you want. After the funeral we are going to cremate Grandpa, and his body will turn into soft ashes. We are going to take those ashes to a place Grandpa loved and sprinkle them there.

This is a judgment call, of course, but it's fine to bring kids of any age to a funeral. Just make sure you prepare them ahead of time for what they will see.

If there's an open casket, you can let them know they'll see Grandpa's body and he'll look as if he's asleep, even though he's not going to wake up. They should also know that people may be crying or might not have much to say, and that that's a part of saying good-bye. They will likely reach their limit with all of the quiet and somberness, so enlist someone they feel close to (a babysitter or a friend of yours who's not grieving) to take them away from the church or funeral home so they can be loud and playful and cry and laugh while you stay there.

When my father died, my children, then 6 and 8 years old, wanted to write him a good-bye note. I puzzled over what kind of note they could write when he couldn't read their words. "Why can't we just put something in the ground with him so he'll have it?" my son asked. I didn't see why not. Are there rules about what

what will we do at the funeral?

you can put into a casket? I asked the funeral director, and she couldn't think of any. So my kids drew some pictures and wrote a few notes: "I love you" and "Go, Bears!" (my father's UC Berkeley team). We slid them inside the top of the coffin before lowering him into the ground. It was a small gesture, and my children seemed comforted by it. Those cards will stay with him until, together, they become dust.

5. "How come Papa has a mommy and daddy and you only have Grandpa Roger?"

My mom got sick and died before you were born. It was very sad, but I'm okay now. Can I tell you a story about her?

If your parents predeceased your children, they're likely to be curious about who their grandparents were. Telling them stories about your life with them is a beautiful way to pass down their legacy. You can also use objects you inherited—a fishing rod, a ring, a picture, or a coin collection—to teach your kids about who your parent was, what kinds of things they liked to do, and how you see certain things in them that remind you of the person who raised you.

how come Papa has a mommy and daddy and you don't?

6. "Can I catch cancer?"

You can't catch cancer or a heart attack, for that matter. You are healthy and will probably live until you're old and gray.

Kids may have all sorts of misconceptions about sickness and death—for instance, that it's contagious. It's a good idea to disabuse them of those notions now.

7. "I was mean to Grandpa when I saw him last week. Did I kill him?"

Saying something when you're angry or thinking bad thoughts doesn't make someone die. Just like being good and kind doesn't prevent someone from dying. It's not anyone's fault that Grandpa died. Death happens to all of us at different times. We're all very sad that he's gone, but it had nothing to do with anything you did.

Be direct in your language, and cast the illness as the bad guy. That will relieve your kids of any guilt they feel and make clear that the person didn't die because of anything they did. You can say things such as "Your brother's heart was tired. His heart was sick and couldn't keep beating." Kids, like adults, have a tendency to want to blame someone or something when things go wrong, and it's best to lay that blame on the illness—the kidney, the cancer, the broken hip—so that the loved one remains knowing and brave, and they don't blame themselves or others.

8. "Where do we go after we die?"

People have lots of different ideas about this. Some think you go to a place called Heaven or Nirvana or Jannah, where you'll see other people you loved who have died. Other people believe you are reborn into something else, like an animal or a person. Some think you get a special power and become an invisible spirit that can go anywhere, like a friendly ghost. Still others believe you become part of the earth and grow into trees. Where do you think we go? One thing is for sure: people live forever in your heart.

Most kids will experience the sickness or death of a grandparent (or great-grandparent) and come to understand that people don't live forever. Seven, it turns out, is when kids become logical thinkers. Even if death seems far away, they understand that it is final and irreversible. That's an important thing to come to terms with, and using euphemistic language suggesting otherwise is confusing. We know that it's hard to say point-blank, "Grandma died." But it's important to make sure they understand what has actually happened.

A first encounter with death can be a poignant time, when you impart family values and hand down spiritual and religious beliefs in a way that helps children feel they are part of the family unit and also belong to something bigger. Just make sure they are not misinterpreting your language. There are cultural influences affecting how each of us best communicates, and those norms are yours to do with as you feel right. If in doubt, avoid using abstract phrases when they have no reference or meaning for the child. For some, "passing on" might be an example; passing on to where? Saying that Grandma is "at rest" may make them afraid of going to bed. Saying that she "went to a better place" conveys

that perhaps she left for some fantastic place without taking the grandkids along—*huh, why would she do that?*

It's okay to convey to a child that death can feel random and senseless to a grown-up, too. You can say, "We don't know why this happens, it doesn't make sense to me, either."

——

How Kids Process Loss

NIGHTMARES AND OTHER BEHAVIOR BORN OUT OF LOSS TEND TO manifest in kids *after* a death, not before (when it starts for parents). Try your best to stay aware of how things are looking from your kid's point of view, even if you're knee-deep in it yourself or trying your damnedest to move on. You may see some regression (kids who recently got potty trained may start needing a diaper again). Backtracking to a safer place, somewhere familiar that's not scary, is perfectly within the realm of normal. Don't start to worry unless many months have passed and they're not pulling out of it. Kids are made of tough stuff. They will recover and grow. ❖

WHEN DEATH IS CLOSE

It may feel morbid to plan your own funeral, but if you start thinking of it as a celebration of you—who you were and what you loved—you might want to leave some pointers so your people get it right. All of the decisions involved are personal, and in the following pages we'll walk you through a range of things to consider before you make them. You'll also find chapters in this section on choosing to die (and what requirements you'll have to meet to opt for that choice), and on what active dying looks like.

It's Your Body and Your Funeral

What do you want done with your body?
Planning your funeral; what funeral homes
and mortuaries do, and alternative options

D id you hand off your wedding to someone else? Your children's births? Doubtful. They're highly personal moments where you get to be the creative director and your funeral should be no different. Not a fan of "Amazing Grace"? Would you rather that everyone sing "The Rainbow Connection"? Want to serve whiskey and Swedish meatballs? Don't want a funeral at all? Tell someone, or leave a note with instructions. It's a last gift to your friends and family, who will otherwise have to make all the decisions and plans during an already complicated time. If you know how you want your body to be dealt with and have a cemetery in mind or a favorite place where you'd like your ashes to be scattered, let your people know. Even better, buy yourself a plot.

It's becoming increasingly popular to frame funerals as "celebrations of life." One man, who drove an ice cream truck for a living, insisted that a truck be parked at the funeral home so grievers could enjoy a few scoops. If you are a person who goes to church, that's a likely place to have your funeral. If you don't, you can choose a funeral home or rented hall or even a living room in someone's home—you can be just about anywhere you would want to be.

———

How to Choose a Funeral Home

GOING TO A FUNERAL HOME AND TALKING TO THE DIRECTOR WILL tell you a lot. You may walk in and instantly feel or see or smell something that makes you want to get the hell out of there. Your gut will tell you if it's a good fit. We realize that visiting funeral homes and cemeteries can feel like a rather grim task when you're still alive. But choosing a home in advance may add to your sense of creative control.

———

For Caregivers

If that funeral home visit didn't happen before the death, that's okay; you might still have time to shop around. Ask friends for recommendations, check online for homes nearby, and take a morning off to call a few. Yelp reviews are a surprisingly reliable way to find the most sympathetic staff person at the funeral home to have a conversation with. The relationship that's built with the funeral director is a temporary but important one. They can be an "incredible guide and companion," says Bridget Sumser, a social worker in palliative care at the University of California, San Francisco. "They know everything." That might include details on getting a license to scatter ashes at sea down to how much to tip the altar boy at your service. A good director will hold your hand through the process. Though this may be the first death you've had to deal with in your immediate circle, it's most likely their hundredth or thousandth.

The Home Funeral

IN THE SAME WAY THAT PEOPLE ARE REVIVING THE HOMESTEADING arts of a time when you knew your eggs came from the neighbor's coop and preserved your own food, there is growing interest in returning to the practice of home funerals, which hold the promise of a more engaged, personalized experience. With a home funeral, loved ones prepare the body for burial or cremation by washing it and dressing it in whatever clothing or shroud you chose; hold their own rituals; allow as many guests as desired to pass through and participate and say good-bye; and there's no rush to get one family out so the next can be ushered in.

Caitlin Doughty, who worked in a crematory before opening her own undertaking practice in Los Angeles, says that sitting with the body allows you to come to terms with what has happened—to grieve not just for your loved one, but for your own future death, too, in the big-picture, cosmic sense. "[A traditional funeral can give you] a feeling of being on display and in public, and tick-tock on the funeral home's clock," she says. "It's not a comforting, held space. That's the number one design flaw, in our experience." She now teaches classes on how to have a funeral at home.

——

What's the Difference Between a Funeral Home and a Mortuary?

NOT MUCH. MORTUARIES ARE GENERALLY LESS EXPENSIVE AND focused on the basics of prepping the body for cremation or burial. Ultimately, your choice will depend on the services you're looking for and your budget. Both funeral homes and mortuaries do three main things:

1. Issue and file death certificates with the county and/or state. The funeral home or mortuary must send a death certificate worksheet to the attending or primary doctor, who will fill out the cause of death and then send it back. The funeral home will then prepare an official document for the state. That

document will ask for names of the deceased's parents and grandparents (including their maiden names, though that's not mandatory). Now a formal certificate, the document is sent back to the doctor for a signature, then faxed (yes, faxed, this is government, folks, though some states now allow doctors to phone-in their attestation) to the state to be entered into public record. The whole process can take a few days.

2. **Prepare the body for burial or cremation.** This includes cleaning, embalming if desired, and making up and dressing the body for viewing.

3. **Perform funeral services.** These can include remarks by the funeral home director or a clergyperson, a viewing of the body, and a processional to the cemetery for burial.

——

Questions to Ask

YOUR RELATIONSHIP WITH A FUNERAL HOME WILL BE BRIEF, BUT it's important to know your rights, and shop around. Here are some questions to ask:

- **How much is this going to cost?**
  The average cost of a "traditional" American funeral is $7,000 to $10,000. Here's some of what you'll be paying for: casket; burial plot; opening and closing of the grave; vault or grave liner; headstone and its installation

  FAST FACT
  The only fee you cannot refuse in the general price list is the "basic service fee."

  The funeral home will likely front-load the pricier items on its general price list (GPL). Since 1984, funeral homes have been required by law to give you quotes over the phone and an

For Caregivers

If you're having a conversation about funeral costs the day after your dad dies, you're likely to be a little out of it—an ideal condition for getting bamboozled. The Consumer Funerals Alliance tells a story of a man from Washington, DC, who called and said he had bought a $14,000 funeral for his father from a corporate mortuary. "I assumed that was a low-end funeral," he told the Alliance, "because it was the least expensive one they had." He had no idea that there were less expensive options because the mortuary's general price list had buried them behind eleven pages of package deals.

itemized GPL when you ask for it in person. They're also required to offer à la carte services, so you can pick and choose.

- **Can I make a down payment on my funeral now?**
  Sort of. Strictly speaking, funeral homes are not allowed to take money for future services. But if you have the means to pay for your funeral now, we strongly recommend that you put money aside in a separate account to cover the payments. It will ease the financial burden for your survivors.

- **What is your process for retrieving my body?**
  The way it typically works: Two or three employees will show up at the house, nursing facility, or hospital; put an ID tag on a wrist or toe; wrap the body in a sheet or place it in a zippered

For Caregivers

Some funeral directors are more like used-car salesmen than helpful advisers. When Jessica Williams and her sisters went to the graveyard with the funeral director and chose an upright marble headstone, the director responded, "No, you want a flat stone. That's what everyone's doing these days." "No, actually," they said, "we really want an upright headstone." Once again he shook his head. Williams turned to him and asked point-blank, "Are flat ones just easier to mow?" The funeral director flashed an unapologetic smile. "Yup."

bag; and transport it on a gurney to the funeral home, where it will be refrigerated until cremated or embalmed for burial. **Don't be shy about letting them know how you want your body to be transported.**

- **If my faith requires a burial within twenty-four hours of the death, can you arrange that?**
  If someone died on a Saturday night, say, the death certificate may not go out until Monday and then not be signed and returned to the state until Wednesday. The process can produce a lot of very unhappy people whose faith or tradition requires immediate burial. **This is a reason to call the funeral home ahead of time and notify them that you'll be needing an expedited process;** it may not always be possible with every funeral

home in every situation, but asking in advance can help set expectations and give time for everyone involved to prepare.

- **Can you arrange for the body to be transported long distance?**

  Yes, the funeral home will send your body on a commercial flight (you will be responsible for transport fees to the airport and for the cost of the airline ticket). When the body lands at the arrival airport, another chosen funeral home will pick it up. Your family can also cremate locally and carry ashes on the airplane, but they'll need a certification of cremation from the home to pass airport security. Make sure you understand all the fees—the entire process can cost upwards of $10,000.

- **What do you offer by way of event planning for the funeral services and reception?**

  Music? Flowers? A master of ceremonies? Food? Most funeral homes can help you book vendors for a fee.

- **Do we have to use your facility for the funeral, or can we pick another venue?**

  Most funeral homes have a room, or rooms, set up for the formal viewing and visitation portion of the funeral. They are also able to help you find another location if you wish, such as your place of worship.

- **Do you write the death notice?**

  A funeral home may be able to provide you with a template or complete the death notice on your behalf and submit it to the local newspaper for printing.

- **Will you help set up an off-site memorial?**
  Some homes will book a location and help with setup.

- **How much do you charge for duplicate death certificates?**
  A copy will be required to close each of your accounts and another one to file with the city. Determine how many to get by counting the financial accounts you have, then tack on a few more to shut down social networks and other digital accounts. The fee varies by state, but as of this writing a duplicate costs around $20.

  TIP
  We recommend getting a dozen death certificates to have on hand for various administrative tasks.

- **Can my family call you directly after I pass away?**
  In some cities, your loved ones can call the funeral home directly for the pronouncement of death and retrieval of the body, bypassing 911 and a frantic visit from emergency crews, who might try to revive you even if your death was expected and irreversible, which can be hard for loved ones to witness. Get clear on this ahead of time, as not all funeral homes offer this service.

- **Do you provide transportation for mourners?**
  If you want a ride in a limo instead of your own cars, make sure the home provides them and ask about the cost. **They can be expensive, up to $500 each, with additional costs per mile if you go outside their stated local radius.**

——

For Caregivers

No one relishes the thought of being rushed through a boilerplate service at the funeral home to clear the space for the next family.

To avoid an impersonal affair, make sure to visit the home and talk to the funeral director or clergyperson who'll be leading the service so he or she can properly eulogize your loved one.

Funeral Cooperatives

SOME NEW SERVICE MODELS ARE POPPING UP TO ADDRESS BOTH cost and environmental concerns. If you live in the state of Washington, you have the option of becoming an owner (along with 80,000 others) of Seattle's Co-op Funeral Home. The Co-op's not-for-profit model reinvests all profits to offset overhead, allowing the home to offer cremation and burial services to its members at much lower prices than normal (its caskets cost less than Walmart's or Costco's). It also offers green burial.

——

Burial or Cremation?

WHAT EACH ENTAILS

Burial: Embalming the body to preserve it for viewing, placement inside a casket that is then placed in a vault in the ground at a cemetery. **Natural (or "green") burial** places the body in the ground without any chemicals for natural decomposition.

Cremation: Burning the body using high heat to reduce it to bone ash. **Bio-cremation,** a less energy-intensive process, breaks down the body with water and chemicals instead of fire. (More on this later in this chapter.)

——

Traditional Burial

UNLESS YOU'VE OPTED FOR A NATURAL BURIAL, the first step in preparing your body is cleaning and disinfecting it before embalming, a process in which the veins are drained of blood and filled with a mix of formaldehyde and other solvents to preserve it.

TIP
Though most funeral homes will encourage embalming after eight hours, they cannot force you to choose it, and some will refrigerate the body instead for up to a week.

It can be hugely comforting to see a loved one look as though they're "at rest," especially after a long and withering illness. Just know that once the body is underground, the embalming chemicals repel insects and slow the natural process of decomposition to such a degree that a body buried in a concrete vault, which is standard practice, ends up essentially mummified. If you choose to opt out of embalming (for environmental, aesthetic, or religious reasons or to save some money), the funeral home will have your family sign a "no embalm" form. Find out how quickly your family will have to perform the funeral if the body is not preserved, especially if you want an open casket.

——

PREPARING the body

wrapping in a shroud

embalming

applying makeup

cleaning

dressing

Funeral homes typically prepare bodies for burial through an embalming process that keeps the body almost permanently preserved when buried in an impermeable vault. If you want a more natural process of decomposition and returning to earth, you can opt out.

Back to the Land (or the Backyard)

NATURAL OR "GREEN" BURIAL INVOLVES PLACING THE BODY INTO the earth in a way that allows it to decompose and become fertilizer for the soil around it—the way leaves, animals, and other organic material have been doing for eons. Many natural burial sites double as nature preserves, so visitors have the pleasure of taking a walk through a wild meadow before arriving at the grave.

If you know you want to be buried on a piece of land you own, you'll need to check with your local municipality for approval and necessary paperwork. Different counties have different rules, and you'll want to stay on the right side of the law; if somehow the body is unearthed, your heirs will want a paper trail to show you went through the proper channels. As with all government-regulated activities, this will take time for approval: start the process now so your survivors don't have to add "Wait in line at city planning department" to their to-do lists.

Cremation

NEARLY HALF OF ALL AMERICANS—48.6 PERCENT IN 2015—NOW CHOOSE cremation over burial, according to the Cremation Association of North America. The popularity of the practice is attributed to its costing less than half of burial on average and requiring no centralized location for a grave site, as well as to concerns about the environment.

How it works: The body is cleaned and disinfected and any medical devices, such as a pacemaker, are removed. The crematory operators or funeral home staff wrap the body in cloth and/or a combustible container and then place it into a crematory chamber, which looks like an industrial oven. A simple unfinished wood box or alternative combustible container is all that is needed, and you can bring your own to the funeral home.

The fire reduces the corpse to snow-white skeletal remains and bone fragments and any nonconsumed metal objects such as screws, nails, and hinges from the container. The remains also contain the parts of the body that could not be broken down by fire: dental gold, surgical screws, prostheses, or implants. These are removed with the help of strong magnets or pliers. The gases released during the process are discharged through an exhaust system and usually don't produce any smell. The remaining bone fragments are pulverized into a sandlike consistency that will weigh about five pounds and can be poured into an urn or into a plastic bag for scattering.

FAST FACT
Don't let any funeral home persuade you that a casket is required for cremation—it's not.

———

Bio-Cremation

THERE'S ALSO A HOT-WATER METHOD OF CREMATION CALLED *ALKAline hydrolysis* (also known as *bio-cremation*). Used most commonly in medical schools and for euthanized pets, the process involves placing the body into a chamber that is then filled with a mixture of water and lye and heated to 320° F at a high pressure, which prevents boiling and breaks the body down in about three hours. As of this writing, bio-cremation is legal in Colorado, Connecticut, Florida, Georgia, Illinois, Kansas, Maine, Maryland, Minnesota, Oregon, and Wyoming.

FAST FACT
Cremation is not the most environmentally friendly choice. The green prize goes to natural burial.

Getting Creative

IF AN URN OR MAUSOLEUM ISN'T WHERE YOU WANT TO END UP, YOU can now embed your ashes in a diamond, a vinyl record, a teddy bear, a portrait, pencil lead, or stained glass, or it can be used to make the ink in a tattoo. Stargazers may also choose to send a small capsule of cremated remains into low-earth orbit. The vials are supposed to circle the earth for about ten years.

——

For Caregivers

Most people don't know that they can ask to be on-site at the crematory and even push the button to begin the process, which normally lasts one to two hours. If you choose to do so, just know that crematories are not designed for mourners. They tend to be old and rely on industrial technology. "It's not pleasant for a family to come, and that's a shame because they are missing out [on an important ritual]," says Caitlin Doughty. Still, even with the industrial aesthetic, this is a profound and singular moment, and you might want to memorialize it. Give it some thought, though; it needs to feel right to you, not add to the trauma.

your ASHES can be ...

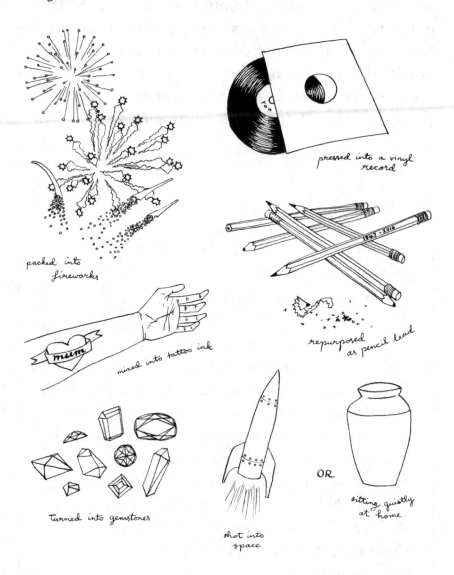

packed into fireworks

pressed into a vinyl record

mixed into tattoo ink

repurposed as pencil lead

turned into gemstones

shot into space

OR

sitting quietly at home

For those interested in one final act of the imagination, your ashes can be re-used in all kinds of creative ways these days. And if you'd rather go up in space than underground, you can send a small capsule of cremated remains into orbit.

What to Wear Forever

YOU CAN DECIDE IN ADVANCE WHAT CLOTHING YOU WISH TO BE buried in and whether or not you want to be made up. When Rebecca Soffer peered inside the casket that held her mother, who was killed in a car accident, she was horrified by what she saw. "My mother would never wear that shade of lipstick!" she thought. She was already bewildered by shock and grief, and that was a last insult. So she surreptitiously scrubbed the color off and replaced it with one that felt more like her mom's style.

The twentieth-century tradition of being buried in one's "Sunday best" is changing as a generation used to personalizing everything now wants a say in the last outfit they'll be spotted in. Search the phrase "bury me in this" online, and you'll turn up a trove of selfies taken by young people baring acres of smooth skin. The idea is that the outfit makes them look so good, they want to wear it for all eternity. As an older person, you may give up the crop top in favor of a natty jacket. But "bury me in this" isn't a bad idea for the rest of us. Why not choose for yourself? Even if your family thought you had terrible style, they are likely to grant you this last request. Maybe you're all about comfort and wish to rest in your sweats.

FAST FACT

If you're being cremated, the default will be to have you wear whatever you were wearing when you died—hospital gown, pajamas, the outfit you had on in the nursing home—unless you say otherwise.

Though it's typically the funeral home staffers who dress the body, this is another place where families and friends can reclaim a moment with their loved one and do the deed themselves. Though a lifeless body can be hard to maneuver ("dead weight" is a real thing), buttoning up a favorite shirt one last time is a powerful first step for grievers to take.

It's Your Casket

IF YOU HAVE A PARTICULAR MODEL IN MIND, IT CAN BE ORDERED through the funeral home you select or purchased online or at Costco or Walmart. No one should be judging you by the plushness of the velvet or the gauge of the steel on the casket you've chosen. Funeral home directors may try to upsell you on an extravagant product they want to move, so speak plainly and let them know what you're planning to spend. They are also likely to put the chrome up front and not display the more affordable choices at all, so ask to see the entire stock list. And again: a casket is not necessary if you would like to be cremated.

——

Casket Options

FAST FACT
By law, a funeral home may not refuse to use or charge a fee for using a casket you acquired elsewhere.

THE PRICES OF CASKETS VARY WILDLY, RANGING FROM $439 FOR A plain pine box and body bag to $18,000 for a lavish full-couch affair. The average price of a casket is $2,000 and up. You can buy a casket from the funeral home or shop around online and have it shipped to the home (just know that shipping costs will add a few hundred dollars).

MINI GLOSSARY OF CASKET TERMS

- **Half or split-couch casket:** Probably the most familiar design, where a hinged cover is in two parts, allowing only the top half of the body to be on view.
- **Full-couch casket:** In this model, the lid comprises a single piece, so you'll see the whole body.

a CASKET
for every budget

simple pine box

standard fare

deluxe

Don't be upsold on the velvet lining if you don't think your beloved would care for it.

- **Green casket:** For those who don't like to leave more environmental footprint than necessary, there are caskets made of renewable materials that biodegrade quickly underground, like bamboo, rattan, cork, and even recycled cardboard. Head to the Green Burial Council to find online vendors (and a green burial site if you're looking for that, too).

———

Choosing a Cemetery

DO A WALKING TOUR OF A COUPLE OF CEMETERIES TO SEE WHAT FEELS right—a hill with a view, under the shade of a tree, somewhere within city limits that's easy for friends to get to on the weekend? If you don't declare your preferences beforehand, the choice will belong to your survivors.

———

Choosing a Burial Plot

There are many different options for your final resting place:

TIP
The more plots you purchase at one time, the less each individual plot costs.

- **Single outdoor plot:** For one person
- **Outdoor companion plot:** For a couple (side by side or on top of each other—often called "double depth"—which can cost less)
- **Outdoor family plot:** Marked by a single large headstone engraved with the family name, and then each individual family member who is buried there—also less expensive, as you don't need an individual headstone for each family member

- Plot for cremated remains
- **Niche:** An aboveground burial space, where an urn containing cremated remains is placed inside and sealed
- **Mausoleum space:** Inside a mausoleum, a building that contains crypts for the entombment of your body or cremated remains

——

What a Burial Plot Typically Costs

BURIAL PLOTS ARE ESSENTIALLY REAL ESTATE AND THUS HAVE A corresponding variability of cost depending on where the cemetery is located and how fancy it is.

——

Prepaid Burial Plot

PURCHASING "INTERMENT RIGHTS"—A BURIAL PLOT OR CRYPT—AT A cemetery in advance will save your loved ones a crateful of money and stress. The risk of doing so is that your family may not want to be buried there. As we all know, the modern family is friable and complex. If it breaks apart and reassembles, the site of burial (or ash scattering, for that matter) can become a point of contention. If, for example, Mom bought a plot with Dad and never went back to change the arrangements when, in her sixties, she found the love of her life, you've got a situation on your hands. So what to do if you want to change arrangements for a prepaid plot? In some states, you're required to sell your interment rights back to the cemetery before selling direct, so ask first. If not, look for an online broker who will take care of all the work in exchange for a

FAST FACT
There are burial plot brokers who will sell your plot if you no longer wish to use it.

monthly advertising fee, a percentage of the final transaction, or a combo of the two. Or place your own ad in free online marketplaces such as Craigslist or eBay.

When drafting your ad, make sure to include the section, plot, and grave number and, importantly, photographs of the plot. This is a big purchase both financially and psychologically; they'll want to see the grounds and know if it's a comfortable place to visit.

SAMPLE CRAIGSLIST LISTING

This park is beautifully maintained and centrally located. The plots are located in the Garden of Reverence area. The park is open 8 a.m.–6 p.m. daily. Save thousands—call me today. $3,500 each plot. If you purchase them all I will bundle a better price.

——

When You Live in Different Places

IF YOUR PARTNER HAS A CEMETERY IN WHICH HIS OR HER FAMILY HAS been buried for generations, but it's across the country from where you've made your home as a couple for the last twenty years, it's okay to choose to be buried locally.

If your family lives in two (or more) different states and can't agree where the final resting place should be, you can buy plots in two places and bury only in one, or if cremation is acceptable, bury half the ashes in one place and half in another. Cemeteries also typically have a wall where you can buy a nameplate without interring a body or ashes (the places we called charge around $500 to $600 for one).

Of course, if you make the choice to be buried far from your children or the children of your first marriage, it may mean that they won't visit your grave. If you feel strongly about being buried in a certain place, make that known.

——

There May Be Unexpected Guests

THERE ARE FUNERAL ATTENDEES WHO CARRY SECRETS. FOR ONE widow, that came in the form of two women among the four hundred guests at the funeral whom she didn't recognize. They'd been a very social couple while her husband was alive, and she knew everyone else by name. She approached both women to introduce herself, and one admitted that she'd been seeing the widow's deceased husband romantically as recently as six months before he died. The other woman ran away. "She was, of course, stunned, not knowing what to say," says Karen Schanche, the widow's therapist, who counseled her for two years afterward. "The acute grief is already over and done, and they're tenderized; the infidelity just complicates it. Emotions like shame and guilt can arise and overwhelm the partner in grief as they attempt to make sense of what they learned—*How dare he do that!*—but, at the same time, *What did I do wrong?*"

The heightened emotion in the first days and weeks after a death will be there at the funeral, too. Be prepared to hear stories you never knew about the deceased's relationships and early life and for many feelings apart from grief to surface. Death has a way of bringing what has long been shut away, whether out of shame or guilt or fear, into the light. For the person who's been holding those secrets, that can feel like a great relief—an unburdening. But for those from whom the secret has been kept, it can feel as though someone just threw acid into a fresh wound. ❖

The Bottom Line

IT'S YOUR BODY AND YOUR FUNERAL

Your funeral is about you, so who better to say what should happen there? Making a few choices in advance will go a long way in making things easier for your friends and family, who want to think about you, not what casket they can afford. It can feel therapeutic for you to plan these final acts, but if that just doesn't happen, rest assured that there is a system in place to help your loved ones. They'll get through it; everyone does somehow.

Can I Choose to Die?

Physician-assisted death; who qualifies; where the law falls

Physician-assisted dying, or medical aid in dying, is a process by which a physician writes you a prescription for medication that is intended to end your life.

Another term you may hear is *euthanasia*, though euthanasia is considered to be when a physician knowingly *administers* a fatal dose of medication. Except within the prison system, euthanasia is illegal in the United States. With aid in dying, it is the patient's responsibility to take the medication. Death is the source of relief, not the punishment.

———

An Intensely Emotional Topic

PHYSICIAN-ASSISTED DYING HAS BEEN DEBATED IN US COURTS FOR more than a hundred years. In 1997, the Supreme Court finally kicked it back to the states, and that year Oregon passed the Death with Dignity Act. **Assisted dying is now legal in seven other jurisdictions: the District of Columbia, Vermont, Montana, California, Hawaii, Washington, and Colorado.** Similar legislation is being considered in Nevada, Tennessee, Maryland, New Jersey, New York, and Connecticut as we write. Efforts in a few other states have failed to pass, but the rising popularity and practical importance of this debate make it likely that those states will revisit the issue in the near future. We'll cite the Oregon Death with Dignity Act as an example throughout this chapter.

The idea of aid in dying arouses all sorts of strong emotions in people. Those in favor of the law believe it offers a choice to a person who otherwise feels she has none: staring down the possibility of unrelenting symptoms; being cut off from what gave her meaning or purpose; enduring a death that comes too slowly;

WHERE is it legal to request a physician-assisted death?

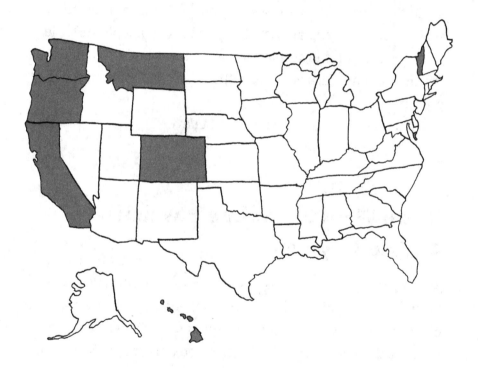

This is an evolving landscape as more and more states are considering Death with Dignity legislation.

the specter of increasing dependency. *Here's a relief from sense-less misery.*

Opponents hold that our society, and especially our health care system, needs to draw a bright line when it comes to sanctioning death; or they oppose the law for religious reasons, believing that decisions about life and death should be left up to God; or they worry that such laws pave the way to a world in which dying becomes too convenient a solution to systemic problems.

But no matter which side of the debate people fall on, most will agree that our health care system, our political system, and our society are not doing all that they can to help people suffer less. Where is the outrage at that fact? Both sides believe they're taking the high moral ground, and there isn't much room for compromise.

What do you think? What do you believe?

——

If You Want to Explore Physician-Assisted Dying

WHEN AID IN DYING IS DISCUSSED IN THE MEDIA IT'S USUALLY brought up as someone's desperate, last-ditch response to physical pain. But these requests more often stem from psychological or social distress: people feeling isolated or that they're a burden to loved ones or gripped by fear of how it will feel to die otherwise. For many, the option isn't a retreat from anguish as much as an exercise in self-determination and control. This gets at why the word *suicide* has been dropped to describe the procedure. It also helps explain why roughly one-third of people who receive the lethal prescription never use it.

My patient Thekla was among the group who never took it. "It has provided the desired effect of knowing that I have options and that I don't have to suffer more than I choose to," she said. "In a process in which we have little or no control, it allows me to still feel that I am living with intention and can manage, to some extent, the manner in which I die and not just be the victim of this damned disease." For many people, the therapeutic benefit is in knowing they have a way out in case they come to need it.

——

Talk It Out

A VERY SMALL FRACTION OF PEOPLE WHO DIE EACH YEAR IN THE United States die by choosing to take a lethal prescription. In Oregon, where the procedure has been legal for twenty years, these make up only 0.4 percent of deaths. So practically speaking, the law affects very few people—but if you're one of those few people considering it, it's important to have conversations with your family and doctors.

This is a difficult subject, so expect intense feelings to surface. A friend of mine who lives with a progressive neurological illness broached the subject with his family. It was a casual, abstract conversation at first, right after the law passed in California. He was interested in having the option sometime in the future and wanted to see how his family felt about it. They listened carefully and were supportive.

After thinking about it further, he realized that the idea did not suit him after all. When he let his family know, he was stunned to hear their shades of regret. It was subtle, but there. The idea had grown on them. They worry about money—he has full-time caregivers whom he pays out of pocket—and the idea of an end in sight provided a sense of relief. He recounted this story to me with something of a laugh, but it was easy to see that some damage had been done.

The moral of this story is that the issue is loaded and complicated; you can see why people might wish that assisted death weren't an option, so there would be no such wrenching discussions to bear. But here we are. As awkward and painful as these conversations can be, they're still important. Our decisions influence one another in ways we may not even be aware of, but we should never feel as though we can't change our mind.

At some point, you would need to discuss the idea with your doctor, too. Leave room for dialogue. After all, helping you to end your life is a lot to ask of someone. Your doctor has to make sure your decision is rational and unforced, just as you do. This big question is not easily resolved through flow charts. It deserves a real conversation. The law requires your doctor to talk to you about the following points:

- How the aid-in-dying drug will affect you and the fact that death might not come immediately
- Realistic alternatives to taking the drug, including hospice or palliative care; do you understand how they can help you?
- Whether you will notify your next of kin, have someone else present when taking the drug, or participate in a hospice program (you are not required to do so, but it is strongly encouraged)
- That you will not take the drug in a public location
- Whether you want to withdraw the request

——

Qualifying for Assisted Death

The details differ by state but share a basic framework. In Oregon, you must:

- Be at least 18 years old
- Be a resident of the state
- Have a diagnosis by your physician of an incurable and irreversible disease that will, within reasonable medical judgment, result in death within six months
- Be able to make medical decisions for yourself (as legally determined by health professionals)
- Voluntarily request a prescription for an aid-in-dying drug without coercion from others
- Be able to self-administer the aid-in-dying medication

If you are eligible, you will need to do all of the following:

- Make two oral requests, at least fifteen days apart, directly to your attending physician (known as the "prescribing physician")
- Provide one written request directly to your physician that is signed by you, in the presence of two witnesses, at least one of whom is not related to you
- Discuss the request with your attending physician; this is an effort to help ensure you are making an informed decision
- See a second physician, who will confirm your diagnosis, prognosis, and ability to make medical decisions and agree to act as "consulting physician"

CHALLENGES on your way out

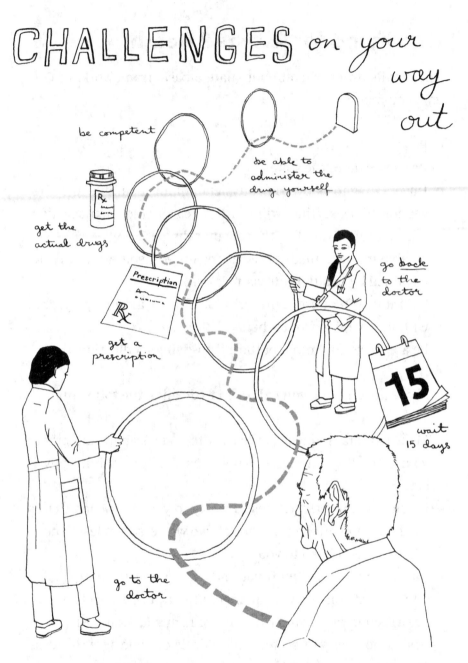

be competent

be able to administer the drug yourself

get the actual drugs

get a prescription

go back to the doctor

wait 15 days

go to the doctor

The biggest hurdle may be finding providers who agree to participate. Access is not guaranteed, and hospitals and individual doctors are not obligated to dispense medications to induce death.

Just because it's legal for any physician in your state to prescribe does not mean that it's easy to find a physician who is willing and able to do so. Physicians may have their own misgivings about hastening death and often work for larger health systems and institutions (including hospice agencies) that can opt out of the law altogether. And remember: you don't have to find just one physician, you have to find two.

——

Stopping Eating and Drinking

THERE ARE ALTERNATIVES TO MEDICAL AID IN DYING.

Voluntarily Stopping Eating and Drinking (VSED) is making the choice to no longer take in food or liquid. Without food, a person's body will die in about a month; without water, it's hard to live much longer than a week or so. So, in effect, VSED is death by dehydration.

The slower dying process of VSED can be a mixed blessing, affording more time to revisit the decision but also less certainty about the exact timing of death. You can expect to grow more and more sleepy, and owing to ketosis—the body's response to fasting—there may even be moments of dreamy euphoria. VSED is not, however, free from discomfort. In late stages of illness, when appetite is already low, the sensation of hunger is less an issue; thirst, however, can be uncomfortable, but can be soothed by keeping the mouth moist. Be prepared with medication for all the usual symptoms common to the end of life, including pain, nausea, or delirium. If the suffering is overwhelming, it is possible to be sedated with medications,

FAST FACT
Unlike aid in dying, you do not need a physician's consent to start VSED, and there are no regulatory hurdles to jump through.

helping you to sleep through the dying process. This procedure is known as terminal sedation (or palliative sedation), and, practically speaking, it is possible only with help from a hospice agency and after plenty of discussion with your clinical team; they have a duty to ensure that you are acting of your own will, free from coercion, and that no other suitable options exist.

——

Lessons from the Bedside

JACQUELINE CHOSE AID IN DYING. SOME months after she took the medication and died, her husband, Tom, told me about the experience from his point of view. They had discussed the possibility for years. It was agonizing for both of them, but she was clear that for her it was the better of two unwanted options—death by medication or death by disease—and he was clear in his enduring commitment to her. He described a sense of peace in the end—uncountable sorrows but few regrets. Upon reflection, months after Jacqueline's death, he said he'd advise others to be careful about with whom they choose to discuss this option. They were people of faith and noticed that some friends from the community were disapproving and became distant—a heartache for them both. Still, Tom gained comfort knowing that he had put

FAST FACT
Aid in dying is not considered suicide in the states where it is legal and will not affect life insurance payouts, but VSED is still considered suicide. This means that any life insurance policies may be nullified if a VSED death occurs within a two-year period of the policy purchase and survivors will not receive the full payment, but a smaller percentage. The two-year requirement is the industry standard in cases of suicide, but be sure to check your policy for details.

himself at the mercy of Jacqueline's wishes. That fact has only eased grief's sting. It was a deeply loving thing to do, and Tom knows it as no one else can.

Tom also mentioned how grateful they were to have a hospice nurse present with them throughout the process. Dr. Lonny Shavelson, a well-known Bay Area physician with a practice that focuses on medically assisted death, prefers that all his patients be on hospice care at the time of their death to help ensure that the patient and family are as well supported as possible. Shavelson advocates for the presence of a medical professional at the bedside at the time of taking the aid-in-dying medications, for both technical and emotional support. This is a stressful moment for both patient and family, and having an experienced clinician there goes a long way toward relieving some of the family's burden and ensuring that the death and subsequent mourning go as well as possible.

——

The Law Has a Long Way to Go

THESE LAWS ARE NOT PERFECT. AND THE SAFEGUARDS THAT ARE meant to help can get in the way. For example, perhaps your suffering is off the charts now and you're sure of your decision to end your life, but you have to wait fifteen days. Of course, ending your life should not be an impulsive decision, but maybe you don't want to wait fifteen days. The challenges that remain include the following:

- The most commonly prescribed drug for this purpose is secobarbital (Seconal is the brand name). It's a sedative that's been on the market for many years for use in psychosis and seizures, but at higher doses it is lethal. The process is one of drifting off to sleep, which may take thirty minutes or up to a few hours, depending on how well the body is able to absorb and metabolize the drug. To take the drug, you need to empty upward of ninety capsules and mix the powder into at least four ounces of water or other fluid and drink it. If swallowing is difficult, as it often is toward the end of life, this can be exasperating, even impossible. Aspiration can occur, as can vomiting, which means you might not get a chance to absorb the full dose. Putting it through a feeding tube is possible, but the fluid can be thick enough to clog the tube. A rectal tube is an option, but it can be uncomfortable. For all these reasons, newer combinations of medications that are more easily ingested are increasingly being used.

- **You have a disease that prevents you from physically ingesting the medication or, as with some cancers, you don't have a functioning gastrointestinal tract.** Or you're unable to physically lift the meds to your mouth and swallow them, as with ALS or quadriplegia. In their current form, these laws do not allow for intravenous administration. Though this remains a significant problem, some state medical boards are beginning to sanction looser interpretation of the law to include medicating by way of a gastrostomy tube (a type of feeding tube used by some people with head and neck or esophageal cancers) or a pump for people with neurodegenerative illnesses. For those with gastrointestinal diseases that interfere with their ability to absorb medications, newer drug combinations are also being used in nasal spray form or by rectal suppository.
- **Those in the final stages of cognitive disorders, like dementia, who are able to meet the criteria for a six-month prognosis will not be of sound enough mind to ask for aid in dying.**
- **The price is high.** As the demand has increased, so has the cost

of the drugs. The price of this once-cheap med has jumped more than 1,000 percent since 2010. Medicare does not cover the procedure. Medicaid will pay for it in California and Oregon, as will some but not all commercial insurers. One way or another, your out-of-pocket costs will range from $600 to $4,000. ❖

The Bottom Line

CAN I CHOOSE TO DIE?

This is the most personal decision you can make, and it has to come from the core of your being. At the same time, when it comes to medically sanctioned death, your doctor has the legal responsibility of deciding whether or not an early death is warranted or at least whether she can help you in good faith. If you decide to exercise the option in one of the states where it's legal, you'll need a clear mind, a few weeks, and at least two physicians to participate, and you'll need to be able to take the medication without (much) help.

Final Days

What active dying looks like; handling opiates;
sitting by the bed; stopping life support

Y ou'll hear people use the word *sacred* to describe what it's like to be at the bedside of a dying person. That feels right. All that goes into a life, into making it, comes to account now. Here you'll find yourself at the doorway to life's great mystery.

Active dying—the final hours to days of bodily life—is different from the rest of life. "Dying" is no longer abstract or rhetorical. The body is shutting down, and different rules apply now. No matter how aggressive the plan of care to date has been, the active dying phase is not a time to rush in and throw more interventions into the mix. **Hospital transfers, 911 calls, new modes of life support, other flurries of activity—such things won't help now in the way you want them to.** Getting into a frenzy will only distract you from one of the most profound experiences of life. Now is a time for staying put, for slowing down and being present.

As we have throughout this book, we're going to talk directly to you, *the patient.* But from a practical point of view, the information in this chapter will be more useful for your caregivers, since you'll likely be unconscious by this point; most of the time, people are not conscious for the active dying phase of life, at least not as far as science understands consciousness.

This section may be a little jarring to read, summoning you to imagine your own final moments of life, so read on only if it's helpful to you to consider what your body is likely to do as it finally winds down.

——

Signs That Death Is Imminent

WHEN DO YOU KNOW THAT SOMEONE IS IN THE ACTIVE DYING ZONE? There are a few ways to tell.

how to tell when someone is ACTIVELY DYING

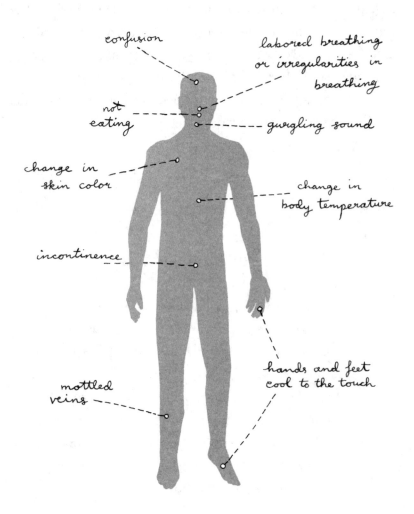

confusion

labored breathing or irregularities in breathing

not eating

gurgling sound

change in skin color

change in body temperature

incontinence

hands and feet cool to the touch

mottled veins

At this stage, the body follows a different set of rules. If you know what to look for, it will tell you what you need to know.

DELIRIUM

As your body begins to shut down, so does your nervous system, and that includes your thinking. See chapter 12, "Symptoms 101," for a more detailed explanation, but, briefly, delirium is a state of disorientation regarding time and place. Delirium typically comes and goes, so one moment you're present and thinking clearly, and the next you may think it's 1941 and you're flying through the air or on the street fighting with a cat. Onlookers might see you picking at the air, your clothes, or your sheets or gesturing to something that is not there. Physical agitation might set in, compelling you to get out of bed even when you're unable to, so falls are a common occurrence.

For Caregivers

In the throes of delirium, your loved one might say very sweet and strange things, or he might say mean and terrible things. I recently met a widow at a gathering who tearfully described how her loving husband of fifty-five years had yelled obscenities at her in the moments before he had died. It was clear from her description that he had been delirious, but that had never been explained to her and she had taken everything he said to heart, making her grief infinitely worse. Her torment was all due to a misunderstanding of delirium.

Delirium can be subtle, but hospice and palliative care nurses and doctors are particularly good at noticing and treating it, as well as instructing caregivers on how to deal with it. In my experience, especially when there is any sign of agitation, medicating delirium is a good idea. Some people might disagree with this, however, feeling that delirium is a vital part of the process not to be subverted with medication.

THE WINDOW OF LUCIDITY

It's not uncommon for there to be a short window of wakefulness and clarity at the end. Someone who's been in a coma or delirious for days might spontaneously brighten, address everyone by name, and start a coherent conversation, fully awake, aware, and engaged. It can be a remarkable sight. If it comes, this window does not stay open long.

For Caregivers

Sometimes people assume moments of lucidity to be a miraculous sign that their loved one is going to live on after all; that this was all a mistake and they aren't dying anymore. They might begin to celebrate or plan a range of activities for when the person gets their shoes on, only to be crushed yet again when the patient slips back into unconsciousness. So look for this window, but stay present, and enjoy it while it lasts.

FOOD HURTS

When approaching death, there comes a time when the body rejects food. This is the body being smart, not self-defeating. **The inability to take anything in is a *symptom* of the body shutting down, not the *cause* of it.** Forcing food or fluid—whether by mouth or tube or vein—will not help in this context and may do harm instead. (See chapter 3, "Yes, There's Paperwork," for more.)

In some cultures, it is important to send the person into the afterlife with nourishment in tow. If this is the case for you, discuss with your clinical team how you might honor tradition while also protecting comfort. If there's a feeding tube already in place, for example, you can ask the team to give just a token amount of food through the tube. Or place something with the person, in his hand or in her pocket, not to be consumed yet but to accompany.

SKIN MOTTLING

This is when the veins in the far extremities—hands and feet—become more visually pronounced and take on a lacelike pattern, often bluish or purple in color (the color change is called *cyanosis*). It's a sign that circulation is starting to falter. For those of you with varicose veins, the changes may be less obvious, but there will be a change from your baseline. With the reduced circulation, hands and feet will likely be cold to the touch.

FAST, FAINT PULSE

As your body shuts down, your cardiovascular system—made up of your heart and your blood vessels—will sputter and fade. The pulse points farthest from your heart are the first to go silent; if someone put a hand to your wrist, he wouldn't be able to find a pulse, or it would be increasingly faint. A hand to the chest or to your carotid artery (on either side of the neck) might pick up a weak, fluttering beat.

If you have a pacemaker, that thing will keep on ticking nice and even. So it is a good idea to talk with your cardiologist or hospice doctor about how to handle that when death is near. Many pacemakers are equipped with an automatic defibrillator, programmed to shock your heart when it's failing. That's great when you're otherwise living, but when your body is actively dying, those shocks are painful as well as ineffective, and they won't stop, even after you have died, until someone turns off the device. For anybody looking on, the sight of seeing their loved one defibrillated—shocked—can be tough to forget when the death was expected and otherwise peaceful. All of which makes grief harder still.

TIP
As part of preparing for death, anyone with a pacemaker and/or implanted defibrillator should discuss *in advance* with the physician *and* caregivers how, and when, to shut off the device.

CHAOTIC BREATHING
This can take many forms, including:

- **Fast or labored breathing.** Often greater than twenty breaths per minute. The muscles of the neck or chest wall may be pronounced, flexing and laboring to keep up with the work of breathing. Generally, opiates are used in order to slow and relax the effort.
- **Apnea.** "Apneic breathing" refers to long pauses between breaths. These pauses may go on for twenty seconds or more, often prompting onlookers to wonder if you have died.
- **Jaw hanging low.** Often the mandible—lower jaw—will hang low and move with inspiration and expiration.

- **The sound of retained oral secretions while breathing, also known as a "death rattle."** This is when saliva pools in the back of the throat make a gurgling sound upon respiration. In a healthy person's body, excess saliva triggers the swallowing reflex. Think about anytime something gets stuck in your throat—you instinctively snap into action to clear it without thinking. Please note that although the sound can be troubling for those around you to hear, you, the dying person, will not feel discomfort. The very existence of the rattle tells us that the conscious and unconscious reflexes are no longer functioning, which means that you won't be feeling what people around you are hearing. This is a key point for a caregiver to know: that the dying person is not struggling for breath.

For Caregivers

There are medications to help dry mouth secretions and diminish the "death rattle," but these are generally for your benefit. Try gently repositioning your loved one, if possible, elevating the head a bit and gingerly turning it to the side so that gravity helps move the saliva out of the way.

Though many people show some combination of these signs at the very end, they're not universal. **And just because you show a sign or two doesn't mean you're actively dying.** These are

For Caregivers

If you're in a facility and noticing the signs of active dying and are hoping for a quieter setting, ask the facility administrator or hospital staff if it would be possible to move to a private room.

guideposts, not rules, and every sign has to be contextualized. If there's uncertainty, an experienced nurse or hospice worker or doula can help make sense of what's occurring.

——

Will I Suffer? How Will Anyone Know?

THESE ARE IMPORTANT QUESTIONS, SINCE SUFFERING IS WHAT THE majority of us fear most. Thanks to predictable patterns of reflex and physiology, a body will generally find ways to reveal pain. So, as with recognizing when death is imminent, even when you cannot speak the words "I am suffering," there are ways for your caregivers to know, including the following:

- **Fast or labored breathing.** Slow breathing is not hard to keep up with, but fast breathing is. Watch for the respiratory rate to exceed twenty breaths per minute or for obvious straining in

For Caregivers

....

The truth is that we cannot say with absolute certainty—no one can, as far as we know—how to translate the sights and sounds coming from someone in the final moments of a life. Try your best to stay true to your gut, while taking care not to project your own thoughts and feelings onto your loved one. When it comes to walking with someone all the way to life's edge, when you have signed up to peer into the abyss, it helps to make room for mystery.

---

the muscles of the neck and chest. As we just noted in the previous section, it can be a sign of imminent death, but it's also a sign of struggle.

- **Sustained grimace and/or furrowed brow.** Pangs of expression may come and go, as though you were watching a person dream, but watch for the facial expression to persist and assume discomfort if it does.
- **Restlessness.** Watch for fidgeting. Nothing to worry about if it's transient, but if it's persistent, assume discomfort.
- **Caregiver's gut sense.** Loved ones and longtime caregivers, you know the person best and your gut will tell you when something is amiss.

Any of these signs is usually a cue for your caregiver to do something: perhaps reposition you in bed, lift or turn your head, add more blankets, take some away. Often, doctors and nurses will suggest judicious doses of a few different medications, erring on the side of comfort.

——

Opiates

OPIATES CAUSE ENORMOUS SUFFERING WHEN ABUSED. THEY ALSO bring enormous relief when used appropriately. They should be respected and administered thoughtfully and under the direction of a skilled physician. **For the treatment of pain, shortness of breath, and diarrhea, opiates are an ancient class of medications still unparalleled for their effectiveness.** Within the context of suffering toward the end of life, here's what opiates *won't* do: they will not make you an addict. And, when used appropriately, they will not hasten your death, even when treating pain or shortness of breath requires high doses. "Get the morphine" is not code for "Kill the patient."

Some people assume that if you die just after receiving a dose of morphine, it was the drug that killed you and the administering person's fault for giving it to you. Please know that this is not the case. There's always a last dose of morphine, along with a last one of everything else. Because two moments occur in sequence doesn't mean one caused the next.

——

Conscious Dying

AS WITH THE LABOR OF BIRTH, SOME PEOPLE STRIVE TO STAY AWAKE and aware throughout the dying process. This typically means limiting certain medications (pain meds, anxiety meds) in order to keep alert.

For Caregivers

When someone can't say explicitly what he or she wants
the scene around the deathbed to be, it's up to you, the
caregiver, to decide. Let the personality of the dying person
rule your thinking, including cultural preferences—whatever
rituals and styles shaped his or her life. In the hospice house
where I worked, moving from one room to the next could be
discombobulating; in one room, people would be toasting
and belly laughing over the patient, sharing stories and jokes,
the lewder, the better; in the next, you'd feel intrusive making
any sound at all. Sometimes the bedside scene can be solemn,
sometimes celebratory, and often it is a combination of the two.

If this is an important goal for you, be sure to let your family and clinicians know. Just keep in mind that staying conscious right up to the time of death usually isn't possible, no matter how determined you are. Common occurrences, such as kidney or liver failure, delirium, or infection, will alter your consciousness no matter what you do. And severe pain can be more disorienting than pain meds; in other words, withholding medications might be exactly the wrong thing to do if a conscious death is your goal. Unless you're an absolute purist, a better goal is ultimately a relative one: a *more* conscious death or *as conscious a death as possible.*

If you're wondering whether or not the dying person can hear what you're saying: he or she very well may be able to. Hospice clinicians often say that hearing is one of the last faculties to go, and we back this up with well-reasoned theory that the most primitive parts of the brain—of which the locus of hearing is one—are the last to shut down. This does not necessarily mean you should censor yourself. It has always seemed to me that dying people know they are dying and are relieved when those around them can share that truth. In other words, if they know anything in that moment, they most certainly know more about their dying than we do. Therefore it may be most respectful to speak plainly in front of the patient.

——

Stopping Life Support

WHEN TO PUSH HARDER AND WHEN TO YIELD IS A CENTRAL AND VERY difficult question. Life support takes various forms: it usually refers to a ventilator (breathing machine) but can be anything without which death will occur, such as a pacemaker, medication, kidney dialysis, or tube feeding pump. Though it can serve as a bridge back to life in some circumstances, it can also become a bridge to nowhere. It is very easy to get stuck on that bridge, and then the question becomes: When is it time to move on? Though it's possible to die on life support—in other words, without someone having to stop that support—it's also possible, thanks to advances in technology, to artificially prop up a body indefinitely, meaning that someone, sometime, has to make the decision. And stopping something, rather than never starting it in the first place, can feel like scheduling death.

There is no legal distinction between withdrawing and withholding life support. Your faith or tradition may say otherwise, which is all the more reason to think twice before starting any such treatment. But from the dominant Western legal and bio-ethical standpoint these days, it's officially okay to stop something that's already started, just as it's okay to forgo it altogether. This decision comes up in all sorts of ways: whether to turn off a pacemaker, a ventilator, or medications and tube-feeding pumps.

If you or your family is weighing whether to proceed with intubation (the placement of a plastic tube into the trachea to aid breathing), pause if possible; this is another moment for caution. Whenever you hear yourself wondering what you have to lose by trying this or that intervention, it's another reason to talk frankly with the team.

Still, whether by choice or happenstance, if at the end of your life you wind up on life support, there are ways for your family to be supported through the process of stopping it. Maybe they'd take comfort in having the hospital chaplain involved. Or if they or the team are concerned about your comfort, they might ask whether it'd be possible to speak with a palliative care team. And know that many ICUs have medications for the purpose of avoiding pain or distress throughout the process. Rest assured that protocols also call for people to gather your loved ones around you for this enormous moment. ICU staff and palliative care teams tend to be good at this kind of loving.

———

Tempering the Vigil

SOME PEOPLE ARE INTENT ON BEING PRESENT WITH THEIR LOVED ONE at the moment of death. But these can be agonizing stretches with no time out for a shower or a nap. Once death is within sight, minutes can become days and even weeks; it's common for loved ones to find themselves irked by how long the dying person lingers, how long death can take. It might feel surprising, especially after prolonged efforts to keep death away, that there comes a time when death can't come quickly enough.

Don't be ashamed—this, too, is normal and part of the paradoxical aspects of life and love and the very earthly exhaustion of tending illness. **The experience of waiting for death can become a kind of purgatory, approaching intolerable, no matter how you feel about the person in the bed.**

I've seen many intense bedside vigils where loved ones don't sleep or eat or leave the room for days, not wanting to miss the final moment for themselves or on behalf of their beloved. And just when they dare to nap or go to the bathroom or get a cup of coffee, the patient dies. Bear this in mind lest you feel guilty for leaving your loved one alone.

TIP
Experience tells us that some of the most intensely attached people need to be alone for the final moment, as though the presence of loved ones prevents them from taking that necessary step.

Our best advice here is not to attempt to time the death moment and instead to take care of yourself along the way. Eat and drink and sleep and go outside now and again; otherwise these final hours will become an unremarkable blur. When you step away, just tell your loved one you're doing so, perhaps with a kiss; tell him it's okay if he needs to go, that you will understand. Know that he may be gone when you return. It may need to happen this way, which makes leaving the bedside a loving gesture. ❖

The Bottom Line

FINAL DAYS

This is a time for peace. A dying body knows what it's doing. Neither you nor your loved ones need to do much. There is just a short list of symptoms to watch out for and a few signs that death is close. Try to settle in now. Especially when comfort is tended to, as with hospice or other skilled assistance, this final stretch can be stunningly beautiful.

how NATURE does it

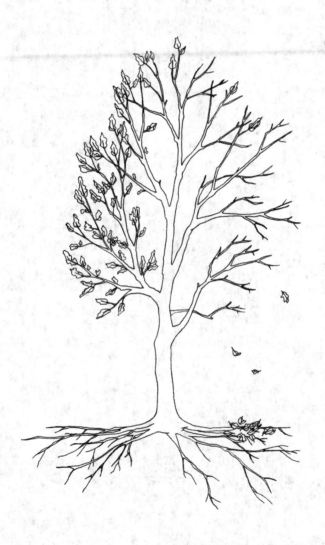

How Nature Dies

How strong, vital, enduring! how dumbly eloquent!
—Walt Whitman, "The Lesson of a Tree"

Consider the life of a tree. Its canopy and root system provide perches and habitats that host and nourish life: birds, insects, fungi, and other plants. The tree's life cycle is as much about its own health as it is about the well-being of everything around it. In the three-hundred-year life span of a big tree, for example, the first hundred years are about growing, the second hundred about living, and the final hundred about dying. The tree doesn't slow its growth as it ages; on the contrary, it actually grows fast in its dying phase. And, rather than hoarding its assets all the way to the end, it begins to give away the nutrients it has generated for the last two hundred years to nourish the ecosystem around it. It sends nutrients and energy down into its root network, connecting it to hundreds of other species. That final hundred years is actually the most productive and generous period of its life. The tree's life cycle is regenerative not because it breaks down to create something new, but because it expends a massive amount of energy to keep as many molecules viable as possible for use by the organisms that surround it. Nature has been practicing how to live and die well for a very long time.

AFTER

Despite the enormity of what has occurred, life doesn't stop after the death of a loved one. There's a lot to get done—from notifying people to having a funeral or a memorial to writing a death notice to dealing with the administrative slog of shutting down a life's worth of bank accounts and social media networks—all while you're just trying to come up for air. The world takes on an unvarnished, raw quality after the death of someone you care for, which can make you feel vulnerable, but also clear-eyed about what matters (and what doesn't). This is also the period when your relationship to what is lost takes a new form.

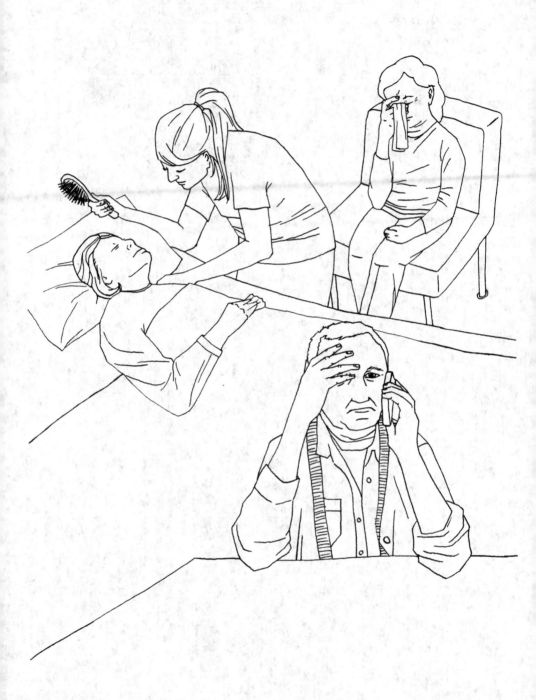

The First 24 Hours

Whom to call first; sitting with your loved one;
the all-important death certificate; telling
people; getting rid of equipment and meds

People describe the initial hours after a death as walking through fog or living in an alternate universe. Nature's anesthesia sets in, and we go through a period of numbness, or of anguish so exotic that we're not sure what the feeling is; surreal becomes real.

Moving from shock into busyness may be exactly what you need. But, do you know what steps to take? My sister and I ended up searching "What to do after someone dies" online. If you do that, checklists from *Consumer Reports*, AARP, and Everplans pop up. Helpful as those are, they can't do the moment emotional justice.

If there is someone whom you trust to take care of the practical details, by all means deputize them: that includes a relative or friend, a social worker, or someone who had been hired to help with care. One way or another, there are a few things that need to happen very soon after the death. There will be more to do later, but for now, one foot in front of the other is how you're going to get through this part. The steps to take—and feel free to change the order—are:

1. Make the death official (get a pronouncement)
2. Sit with your loved one if you'd like
3. Call the funeral home or mortuary
4. Inform family and friends
5. Take a break
6. Dispose of medications properly
7. Call the medical equipment company

——

1. Make the Death Official (Get a Pronouncement)

TECHNICALLY, YOU CAN'T PROCEED WITH INTERMENT OR CREMATION until the body has been pronounced dead by a medical official. This may feel a little ridiculous, especially if the death was expected, but it has to happen.

IF THE DEATH OCCURRED AT HOME AND THE PERSON WAS RECEIVING HOSPICE CARE

Call the hospice agency. The people there will walk you through the next steps, including sending out a nurse to pronounce the death and contacting a funeral home or mortuary to pick up the body. They should be able to assist with this whether or not one was selected before the death.

IF THE DEATH OCCURRED AT HOME AND THE PERSON WAS *NOT* RECEIVING HOSPICE CARE

Call 911. Tell the dispatcher it was an expected death, request "no sirens," and be sure to have the completed POLST or DNR form at the ready. The paramedics will come, and if a DNR or POLST form isn't readily available to prove the patient's wishes, they may try to resuscitate your loved one, which can be an excruciating thing to watch as it includes chest compressions and/or shocks. If the person is clearly dead and beyond the window for possible resuscitation—their skin is cold to the touch or rigor mortis (stiffening of the muscles) has set in—the paramedics should be able to forgo the emergency response. (This can be the case if the person passed away in the middle of the night and is not checked on until morning.) They will hook the body up to a heart monitor and confirm that there is no heartbeat before making a death pronouncement.

In some states, the paramedic may need to contact a doctor, employed by the paramedic company, to do the official pronouncement over the phone. They may also ask you for contact info for your loved one's primary doctor as well as a list of medications he or she was taking.

The body may not be moved by a funeral home or mortuary until a pronouncement has been made. If there is any suspicion whatsoever that the death wasn't from natural causes, the emergency crew must call the coroner to determine if further investigation is warranted. This is the only reason they may order an autopsy be performed; family can also request one for any reason. Otherwise, an autopsy is not required.

TIP

If you made preparations with a specific funeral home or the patient's primary doctor to pronounce the death, call them instead of 911.

IF THE DEATH OCCURRED IN THE HOSPITAL OR A FACILITY

Tell a nurse. Though in most cases the doctor has to be the one to pronounce the death, at least twenty states, including New York, California, Florida, and Ohio, have passed legislation allowing a registered nurse to pronounce the death—a huge relief to families who are more than ready to get out of the hospital. Either way, your first move is to let someone on the clinical staff know. They will have their own facility procedures to follow before the body can be removed. At a hospital this will likely involve the completion of a few forms.

———

2. Sit with Your Loved One

IF A LOVED ONE DIED AT HOME AND YOU'D LIKE to sit with the body, there's no rush to call anyone or do anything. You'll start to notice changes quickly—the mouth may hang open, the skin will cool, the muscles will stiffen—but death is not an emergency, and that body is nothing to be afraid of.

Take the time you need. "I think it's more traumatic when the funeral home comes and the family is not ready," says social worker Katie Taggart. "That's when I've seen people break down on the grass, hysterical."

If you need to buy time for relatives traveling from far away to arrive or simply aren't ready to have the body picked up, you can wait twenty-four or even seventy-two hours by keeping the body cool with dry ice.

Dry ice is widely available at Safeway, Walmart, and Costco, or look online for providers that deliver. Take a cooler to the store and ask for about thirty pounds of it. Once you get it home, pack it in ventilated bags or a pillowcase; gently shift the deceased's head to the side to prop it up on one of the bags, and surround the torso with the other bags. Ice packs can always be

Dry ice packs are available at many supermarkets and can be placed around the body to help slow decomposition, giving you time to sit with your loved one before the body is taken to the funeral home.

substituted and changed out as needed while someone is picking up dry ice.

You can take time to sit with your loved one in a nursing home, too, though it may require a bit more negotiation, as the staff has to be sensitive to other residents. Ask if you can have a private room.

At the hospital, the typical window of time between death and the time the body is sent to the morgue for refrigeration is four hours. There are times when the hospital is at capacity and the room must be vacated quickly—and we've heard some ugly stories about cleaning crews showing up to get the room prepped almost immediately after death or doctors who walk in, coolly pronounce the death, and don't say a word to the family.

FAST FACT
Dry ice has a short shelf life: every twenty-four hours, five to ten pounds of dry ice turns from a solid to a gas.

But we have also heard many people praise nurses and doctors for going to extraordinary lengths to fulfill a family's wishes. Enlist the help of anyone on the team to advocate for your getting more time; typically the best, most accessible person to start with is the nurse. If you're not getting anywhere, you might ask to speak with the nurse manager on the floor—they tend to have a lot of authority and know what the hospital's needs are one minute to the next.

A DEAD BODY IS NOTHING TO FEAR

Though we're not used to being around them and they may make us uncomfortable, **dead bodies are not dangerous.** Unless the person died of a highly contagious disease such as Ebola or was poisoned with anthrax, the body is completely safe to handle. The same simple precautions that we use when coming into contact with bodily fluids from the living apply when handling the dead.

TAKE A MOMENT FOR CLOSURE

Nora Menkin is a funeral director in Seattle who teaches people what to do after death occurs. She once got a call from a wife who said, "I'm ready for you to come pick him up," and when she asked when the husband had passed away, the response was "Oh, four o'clock on Tuesday." Two days earlier. Menkin loves getting those calls. It means the family has taken their time with the transition. When Menkin arrived at the residence, she found the man dressed to the hilt in a three-piece pinstripe suit with a pocket protector in his chest pocket full of the pens that he always used and his pocket watch with the chain laid out across his vest. The wife and her sister had washed and dressed him and sat by his side until they were ready. "He went completely dapper and looking wonderful, and the family had done what they wanted to do."

——

3. Call the Funeral Home or Mortuary

SOMEONE WILL COME OUT TO PICK UP THE BODY AND TAKE IT TO A facility for storage. Maybe you already have a funeral home in mind? If not, find out how to choose one, what they can do for you, and how to navigate the industry in chapter 17, "It's Your Body and Your Funeral."

——

4. Inform Family and Friends

IT CAN BE OVERWHELMING TO LET EVERYONE KNOW ABOUT A DEATH. You're both bearing sad news and experiencing a flood of emotions yourself. The process can also be cathartic—a way to connect and to get a hit of sympathy when you need it most.

Directly after Sarah passed away from pancreatic cancer, her daughter escaped to her childhood room, but Sarah's husband, David, picked up the phone and made a personal call to every one of her friends and family who had been part of her medical journey. He spent hours retelling the story of her last few hours each time someone picked up the phone—it was his way of coping. To be able to share and hear the condolences of those who knew her best helped him through. If that much phone time isn't for you, reach out to a trusted person who can help you tell others, or try distributing the notification load. Here's how:

1. Assign the task of gathering contacts to one or two "connectors" in every sphere of the person's life: a friend; a coworker or former coworker; a book club or sporting buddy; a former classmate; that family member who throws parties or sends holiday cards every year. (Don't forget to eventually alert friends on social networks.)
2. Have them funnel all the contact information to you in whatever way you prefer: email, phone, text, or written list.
3. Reach out directly to those closest to the deceased via phone or email. It can feel like a slight to be part of a mass update if they were someone who was part of the daily care of the patient.
4. Send out a mass email with an update to everyone else. No one will fault you for that.

My father's close friend and first graduate student took on the heroic job of reaching out to other former students and colleagues. Delegating such tasks to others is key when you just want to hide in a closet, and it meant that my sister and I got to hear from people we'd never known before.

Here's the email I sent out after my father died—short and to the point.

Hi,

I really want to talk to you all in person, but right now it's too much, so apologies for the impersonality of email.

My father, Stan, who many of you knew, died at home yesterday morning after a brief stint in hospice. I was holding his hand when he took his last breath. He went peacefully.

After a family graveside service today at 2, we'll be sitting shiva.

In Jewish tradition, the family sits at home and grieves for seven days, welcoming friends and family into the home. There will be food and wine.

We invite anyone who can to join us here at the house starting at 5:30 p.m. Tuesday night, and from 4:30–8 p.m. Wednesday night. I know it's a tough week with Thanksgiving, so please don't worry if you can't make it.

We will also have a larger memorial service at a later date and set up a fund at UC Berkeley for donations. We will let you know the details as they become available.

Here's our address and phone:

Love,
Shoshana

——

5. Take a Break

THAT MENTAL FOG WE MENTIONED EARLIER IS GOING TO HANG around; and sometimes the best medicine is to let it engulf you. You just lost someone important, someone you loved, someone you still love. It's going to take time to square the reality of a day ago with what you're living today. This period is both mundane and breathtaking all at once. Here are a few things to try:

- Take a walk; just moving can feel good. Feel your feet on the ground. If it's not too much stimulation, go outside. Air and light might help settle you
- Binge-watch your favorite TV show, maybe with a close friend
- Eat a whole batch of brownies or cookies or a pint of ice cream— your choice
- Sleep

- Have a glass of something with another human being
- Buy yourself that thing you've had your eye on
- Take a long shower or bath
- Have food from your favorite restaurant (delivered, if possible)

If staying on task helps you, that's okay, too. Otherwise, **allow others to take the reins on a few things: preparing food, letting others know that death has arrived, kid care.** With the basics tended to, you can finally start letting your guard down.

——

6. Dispose of Medications Properly

NOW THAT OPIOID ABUSE HAS BECOME A LIGHTNING-ROD ISSUE, THIS is trickier than it used to be. Your options are:

- **Take the medications to an "authorized collector" in your community.** That includes: retail and clinic pharmacies, hospitals, fire, and sheriff and police departments. It's always a good idea to call ahead to make sure they are able to accept your specific medications.
- **Use the Drug Enforcement Administration (DEA) website or the Dispose My Meds website to search for authorized collection locations in your area.**
- **If a designated safe collection site isn't within reach and there are no specific disposal instructions on the label of the medication, dispose of meds in the trash after following these steps to render them safe:**

  - With a marker or pen, obscure all personal information on the prescription label of your empty pill bottle or empty

If you do any research on drug disposal, you're likely to run into the FDA verdict that many prescription drugs can be flushed down the toilet. While this is touted as viable, we don't recommend it and suggest you take one of the other listed routes. Putting narcotics and pills into our water system just can't be a good idea.

    medicine packaging to make it unreadable, then dispose of the container.

- Mix medicines (do not crush tablets or capsules) with an unpalatable substance such as dirt, kitty litter, or used coffee grounds; place the mixture in a container such as a sealed plastic bag; throw the container into your household trash so it's not appealing to anyone on the hunt.

Long-term care facilities (LTCFs) are allowed to dispose of controlled substances for current or former residents in authorized receptacles at the facility. The facility has up to three business days to do so. Same applies to hospice employees (as of now, though the law has changed in recent years and may again); if the deceased had been receiving hospice care, the hospice staff are permitted to help with on-site medication disposal.

——

7. Call the Medical Equipment Company

NOW THAT YOUR LOVED ONE'S BODY HAS BEEN TAKEN TO A FUNERAL home, any medical equipment that was ordered needs to go back. This might include the hospital bed, wheelchairs, or tray tables. This *can* wait, but then you'll be stuck looking at a bedside commode and an oxygen tank: a stark reminder. **These items are bulky and can also get in the way of any family gathering you might be planning for later in the day. It's usually best to get rid of it all with dispatch, but know that it can take up to twenty-four hours for equipment companies to pick up their items.** ❖

The Bottom Line

THE FIRST 24 HOURS

Yes, there are tasks that need tending to. But one call to the nurse or hospice or paramedics to make the death official and one to the funeral home or mortuary are really the only tasks you *need* to get done today. This is the end of one period and the start of another, and you may not feel ready to acknowledge either just yet. So in these early hours, take whatever time you need.

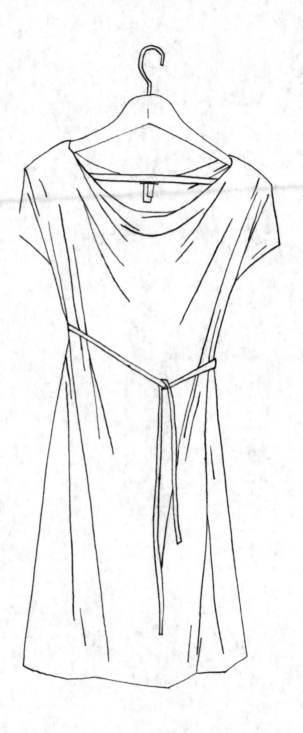

Grief

What it is, and ways to cope; how to
play a supporting role; what to give

W hen my family and I were lowering my sister, Lisa Miller's, casket into the ground, I started laughing uncontrollably. Something that sounded like a laugh anyway. It was a horrific juxtaposition, to me and no doubt to onlookers. I felt like a jackal or hyena, some sort of cackling menace. I couldn't stop. Her death felt ridiculous. Everything felt so wrong—*I* felt so wrong—and that must have been my way of being true to the moment.

Grief is a force of nature. Though it can feel problematic as hell, bereavement is an essential piece of the human picture, whichever way it surfaces. It may be asking too much for you to revel in your grief, but it's important for you to understand the relationship between grief and love. It's actually straightforward: the pain of loss stems from the power of love. If you didn't care, this would all be easier.

——

Bereavement and Mourning

LET'S TAKE A MOMENT TO DISCUSS LANGUAGE USED IN THE FIELD. *Grief* is unrestricted and occurs to some degree with any loss. *Bereavement* is specific to the death of a loved one.

Our friend Jessie compared the days after her sister died at 23 from a brain aneurysm to walking through a plate-glass window. There's the initial shock of not understanding what happened. Then days or weeks spent in bed, too injured to do much of anything, followed by the surreal experience of reentering a world that seems too loud and too bright. Getting on the bus a week after her sister's death, she was bewildered when someone yelled at the driver. *How can people be so rude to one another? Why is the world going on as though nothing happened? My sister is dead!*

Grief has a pre-loss phase, an acute phase at the time of the actual loss, and a long tail. That tail is mourning. *She's in mourning.* It's a beautiful word and connotes the process through which grief evolves from bottomless sorrow to newfound perspective. When the mourning period ends, your relationship to the lost one has not ended—it's not something you "push through"—but has been transformed. The loss is ingrained now, a part of you. Life and death reconcile, and the world is revealed as a place that can hold everything, including what's gone. If you let it, your relationship with the person who died continues and can be rich and powerful, however different.

———

Losing Support

TIP
Social visits are likely out of reach, but it may be possible to schedule a "bereavement" visit with your loved one's doctor in clinic.

OFTEN IT'S THE MEDICAL TEAM TO WHOM the family grows attached—and their attachment works in the other direction, too. Sadly for all involved, there is not much room in our health care system for ongoing contact. At the moment of death, the team must move on to the next patient. This is another way in which grief compounds.

———

Grief Is Not Always What It Seems

GRIEF IS A MASQUERADER. IT PRESENTS AS NIHILISM, BITTERNESS, jealousy, self-loathing, tears out of nowhere—and sometimes inappropriate laughter. It can be numbness or flatness or lethargy; it can be full of agitation and commotion or bursts of insight or creativity. The point is, you're *altered* by it. And unless you understand that grief presents itself in a thousand different ways, you may misjudge yourself or others.

Sometimes it's anger directed inward instead of at the deceased. People will blame themselves for not having said or done the right things before the death occurred, not saying "good-bye" or "I love you" when they had a chance. Claire Bidwell Smith, a grief therapist, sees this often: "They are so upset with themselves for not seeing it earlier, and there's so much anger, guilt, and remorse."

Bereavement is dynamic and varies in intensity as it winds its way through a person. Numbness on one side; unending tears on the other.

——

Grief Can Be Isolating

REBECCA SOFFER, A COFOUNDER OF THE MODERN LOSS WEBSITE AND community, was 30 when her mother was killed in a car accident. Soffer took two weeks off after her mother's death and had barely started to grieve before returning to her job as a television producer. Three years later, she received a call from someone asking her to arrange to get her father's body picked up; he'd had a fatal heart attack on a cruise ship while traveling abroad. Stunned by the trauma of losing both parents within a few years of each other, she again dove back into work shortly thereafter. "Honestly, after each loss I felt like I was dying inside myself, and so few people knew what to do with me," she says. "Unless you're an incredibly empathic human being, if you haven't gone through profound loss yourself, it can really be difficult to effectively connect with someone moving through it. I felt like a pariah, because this topic felt so taboo. If someone asked where my parents were, I'd say, 'In Philadelphia.' I didn't clarify that they were, in fact, underground there. It was just so much easier to be vague."

When she did come clean to people who asked about her family, it felt as though the space around her was getting sucked into a black hole. "There are few better ways to silence a conversation than to say, 'My mom just died,'" she says. "All I wanted was to feel like I could comfortably talk about my reality, not like people felt I might be contagious just because I'd used the word *dead*."

——

Complicated Grief

THERE'S TYPICALLY AN INFLECTION POINT AROUND THE SIX-MONTH mark after the death, when a sense of normalcy creeps back in. It's not a hard and fast rule, but when the clouds don't part and intense mourning persists well beyond that time, it starts to bump up against what's known as *complicated* or *prolonged* or *pathological* grief.

TIP
Complicated grief is not something to overcome alone. If you recognize this kind of grief in yourself, please see the resources list in the back of the book and reach out to a mental health professional. It needs to be taken seriously.

This grief is different. It is compounded by dips into depression, a new or exacerbated medical condition, or alcohol or drug abuse. Intrusive, even violent thoughts are not uncommon, along with profound guilt. Grief has moved from a useful, if difficult, process to a harmful one. The grief itself has become an illness.

As you'd imagine, complicated grief is more common in people predisposed to mental illness or addiction or otherwise already dealing with trauma or difficult circumstances. It is also more common in people suffering the death of a child or an unexpected death or when significant ill will between you and the deceased was left unresolved. Death by a violent act or suicide is a common cause, too.

——

Taking Care of Yourself

You never "get over" the death of a loved one—that's not the goal. Living on is. Here are a few ideas that may help:

- **Take time off work.** Sadly, businesses are not required to offer paid bereavement leave, but many do provide three to five days off for the death of an immediate family member. Talk to your HR department about what's possible for you.
- **Seek out clergy, chaplains, and faith-based services.** Faith traditions have time-tested practices around death, dying, and mourning. Chaplains and clergy are trained to counsel those in bereavement. Hospital chaplains in particular are intimately familiar with supporting people of all faiths and of none. And many churches, synagogues, mosques, and other houses of worship have free programs and groups for grief support. Services often run the gamut from practical assistance, such as transportation and meals, to counseling and prayer groups. There is very likely a warm embrace awaiting you, with centuries of collective experience and wisdom to rest upon; you just need to show up ready to receive.

  TIP
  Most congregations will welcome anyone in need, whether inside or outside their faith tradition, with no requirement that you take up their tradition as your own.

- **Contact your local hospice provider.** They are required to offer bereavement services to the community, whether or not your loved one was enrolled with their program. Despite the legal mandate, the funding for bereavement programs is paltry, so the services may not be robust, but they're a good place to start. Hospice agencies are terrific local resource centers as a rule and will often keep a list of psychotherapists and grief counselors in the community who may be further helpful to you.

- **Attend support groups or find them online.** Being with others who are working through grief can bring relief (no more pretending everything is okay). These are generally facilitated by mental health care professionals or other counselors. Less formal peer groups can be wonderfully helpful as well. The common thread is a safe place, real or virtual, where you can air your thoughts and feelings and be with others who are in a similar place. Here you are more likely to be seen and heard, not judged. Inquire with the hospice agency or your clinical team or hospital, or search for local groups online.

- **Try psychotherapy.** If you're prone to clinical depression or anxiety or are experiencing suicidal thoughts, don't mess around. It can be difficult to tease out grief from depression, so err on the safe side and get help. Therapy can work wonders, even if you're not depressed.

- **Ritualize.** American culture has largely lost touch with the grief rituals of the past and the wisdom behind them: hanging crepe in the windows, wearing black, wearing an armband, to name a few. These physical symbols buy some space for you and everyone around you. People are more forgiving and respectful; expectations of you adjust. With traditional rituals you're tapping into a time-tested collective understanding of what you're going through. With these tracks already laid, you get to step away from your swirling mind and follow an old pattern of action without the burden of thought. If, however, you don't want to follow tradition, you might gain an important but different power by creating your own ritual; a touchstone whose meaning you will always understand.

- **Journal.** Each day before you go to bed, write down one thing you've managed to do (even if it was just waking up). Or just write about your experience. There's no need to keep what you write; just get it out and throw it away if you like. Writing, much like talking with other people, is a way to understand and process what you're going through, and it can also help you not take your thoughts too literally; your mind in grief might suggest all sorts of odd things to you.

- **Get fundamental.** Since grief is discombobulating, it pays to remember the basics of life. Try taking your shoes off, and feel the ground beneath you; take slow, deep breaths; drink water; eat good food (and really taste it); sleep.

- **Make some new "family rules."** If you've lost a central part of your nuclear family, it can shake the very foundation of the unit. Writing down some family rules in a place where everyone can see them is one way to introduce much-needed stability. Things such as forgiveness, getting plenty of sleep, respecting one another's feelings, working together to get things done, and remembering to ask for help when you need it are great reminders that you are all in this together.

These ideas aside, try not to rush through this period. Grieving is a rite of passage and has immense importance in a healthy experience of full life. When my sister died, I felt I was rewarded, both by others and by myself, for moving on as quickly as possible. The pain was intolerable, and I knew I wanted to reach a sense of perspective where everything would be in its new place, so I beelined for that outcome and left too many of my feelings behind in a pile, unrecognized and unprocessed. I wanted to get on top of my grief with force. I regret this now, intensely. In my haste, all I really achieved was putting parts of our relationship behind me sooner than I had to. Now I find myself wishing I could do it again, all the gut wrenching, so that I could feel closer to her.

——

Concentric Circles of Support

EVERYONE IN YOUR CIRCLE IS ALSO DEALING WITH WHAT IS HAPPENING. And it's important for you to recognize grief in yourself as well as in others so you know how to listen with compassion. In this swirl, too many things can be taken personally, leading to hurt feelings and unnecessary isolation.

Say your best friend lost her husband, and you were also close to him. Your principal job is to be a shoulder for her to cry on—even if you miss him dearly, too. But do tell someone who was a bit more removed, such as your own partner, so he or she can support you.

The psychologist Susan Silk and mediator Barry Goldman's Ring Theory offers a helpful way to visualize this concentric network of support. Here's how it works:

1. Draw a circle, and write the name of the person who is grieving inside it.
2. Then draw a bigger circle around that one, and write the names of the people who are next most affected by the event.

3. Keep drawing larger circles and listing those who are affected: friends, colleagues, distant relatives, and so forth.

Comfort goes in, pain goes out. The idea is that wherever you are in the circle, you are getting support and giving support.

According to Silk and Goldman, this is your "kvetching order." The person in the center ring is the focal point. Your job is to listen to her and make her feel better in any way you know how. Offer her food, foot rubs, whatever she needs. She may dump her pain all over you, and your job is to take it in and hold steady, not to try to cheer her up. The concentric rings pay it forward—or outward—so when you need to cry or shake your fists at the sky, there's a ring of support out there for you, too.

——

How to Be There for Someone Who's Grieving

KNOW THAT JUST CALLING OR SHOWING UP MAKES A DIFFERENCE. WE don't call because we don't know what to say. We swear we'll visit but keep putting it off. It's almost as though we think grief is contagious.

The grieving person may not know what he or she needs. If it feels natural and right to send a text asking "What can I do for you?," go for it. But answering that question yourself and just bringing over a hot meal or leaving a card at the door may be even more helpful. The griever simply may not have the energy to respond to open questions or offers. A small gesture will be felt and appreciated, even if the grievers can't bring themselves to acknowledge it right away. Here are a few ideas for what to give:

- **Comfort food.** People often forget to eat or eat badly when they're deep in grief. Dropping off a bag of takeout or a home-cooked meal is a thoughtful and easy thing to do. There are also meal registries, such as the one you might set up for the parents of a new baby, that allow many cooks to fill in dates on the calendar, so that not everyone shows up at once.
- **Photos.** Sharing your photos of the person who died, in an on-line scrapbook or a printed one, is a beautiful way to help loved ones memorialize.
- **Time away.** For those who work full-time and get no paid bereavement leave, there is little time to yell at the universe. Offer to take the kids off your friend's hands so she can get away. Or check to see if your company will let you transfer some days off to a grieving co-worker. ❖

The Bottom Line

GRIEF

Grief is a period. A state. A place with its own weather and terrain. Even when we're feeling so many emotions we can barely stand to wake up in the morning, the sweetness of having loved—and still loving—is there, too. Look for it, because you will not feel like this forever. This can be a very tender time, raw and unprotected—more exquisitely sensitive than usual; maybe more truthful. The grieving process is an opportunity, too. Take it.

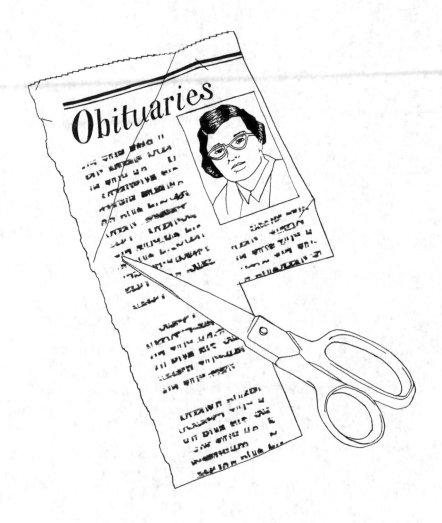

How to Write a Eulogy and an Obituary

The basics of publishing a death notice and obituary; what goes into a great eulogy; how they can go wrong

As a professional writer, I can tell you that it's absurd to expect anyone to compose a summary of their loved one's life immediately after the death. Most people get anxious about writing an important email, never mind a printed piece for all eternity. Even if you publish the death notice only online (where the majority of them go these days), it feels colossally important to get it right. The same goes for a eulogy. How do you boil the ocean of a life down to a few salty anecdotes?

There are rules and guidelines that will make the writing easier. It may even be a relief to take a few quiet hours to sit alone and write. And if you're still too raw and can't even start without soaking the paper (or keyboard) with tears, think about delegating the task to someone you trust to get it done.

———

Death Notices and Obituaries

A DEATH NOTICE IS A PRINTED ANNOUNCEMENT that a person has died. It is typically written by the family and published for a fee. It may be quite short and more of an announcement of when and where a funeral will take place.

An obituary provides more biographical information about the deceased and is written by a reporter and published for free.

The two classifications—death notices and obituaries—are used interchangeably online, but the professional obituary writers and editors we spoke to were clear about the distinction.

FAST FACT
In large-circulation, nationally syndicated papers such as the *New York Times*, you have to be a person of public interest to warrant an obituary—a celebrity, business titan, major athlete, politician, famous artist, scientist, inventor, pioneer, or other local hero. It's usually a judgment call on the part of the editors.

If the city where your loved one spent the bulk of her life still has a local paper, it may assign a reporter to interview you and publish it for free—or it may not.

———

How to Publish a Death Notice

THERE'S NO REQUIREMENT TO PUBLISH A DEATH NOTICE, BUT IF YOU want to inform the greater community and let them know when and where the funeral will occur, it has to be done quickly.

When you go to a paper's website, search for "obituaries," and you'll find an email or phone contact. You may also discover that the paper has outsourced the process of submitting paid notices to Legacy.com, a site that also posts advertising for funeral homes and news stories about death and grieving. Posting directly to the site will require that you complete an online form and upload a photo or photos.

TIP
Most funeral homes will write and publish a death notice for you. But don't assume they will get it right.

Newspapers have good archives, both online and in public libraries, where future generations will be able to learn about the deceased and how they fit into their genealogy. **A printed death notice can become a family keepsake, something to frame or put into an album. On the other hand, online death notices are cheaper and easily shared, and they run the day after you submit them.**

Follow the pointers in this chapter so the announcement is accurate and doesn't end up sounding like a Mad Lib.

———

What Makes a Good Obituary?

"GOOD" IN THIS CONTEXT MEANS THE OBITUARY REFLECTS THE person and their relationships, and helps readers imagine them. We spoke to Kay Powell, who edited the Obituaries section of the *Atlanta Journal-Constitution* for many years. Powell placed a sign on her desk that she had gotten from Richard Pearson, the obituary editor at the *Washington Post*, to remind her of the responsibility of her role. It read: "God is my Assignment Editor." Here are Powell's recommendations for writing a good death notice/obit:

- **Include the following biographical details:** Your loved one's age; the cause, date, and location of death; date and place of birth; parents' and partner's and children/grandchildren's names as well as immediate family who are deceased; where the person went to school; his or her job; hobbies; any beloved pets; location, date, and time of funeral services; where memorial donations should go or an "in lieu of" statement (see below).
- **Be honest.** Whitewashing a person's life not only misrepresents who he or she was, it makes him or her less relatable. Did your mother have bipolar disorder? When a characteristic or issue is written or spoken about in a compassionate way, people are more likely to accept the deceased for who he or she was and also to have more empathy for those left behind.
- **Use humor.** Powell edited an obit for a man who priced groceries for a living. She originally thought the obit was going to be about his job, but after a little digging with the family the obit writer found out he had collected and raised skunks for show on the side. His animals were award winners, and he'd even had a picture of his favorite skunk airbrushed onto his

motorcycle. "Everybody's got one good story in them," Powell said. "That's what I want families to capture when they're writing their own death notices; those little things that just made you laugh."

- **Include surprising details.** Readers want to feel as though they're learning who the person truly was. Bring her back to life through her charms and distinguishing quirks: "If her husband dozed off early, she handed out washable markers for her children to decorate him with."

- **Include all survivors.** It's a good idea to include all immediate family members, even if they've been disowned or come from a former marriage. "When I was at the paper," said Powell, "I would get questions like 'She's the black sheep, should we name her?' or 'He was disinherited, should we name him?' Yes, you should,'" is the answer. A few other notes: People are not "survived by" divorced spouses; and an expected child should not be named as a survivor—what if that child is never born? But there are ways of wording anything, Powell says, such as "He was looking forward to the birth of his fifth grandchild in June."

- **If you'd like to suggest something to give in lieu of flowers, say so and be specific.** For example: "In lieu of flowers, contributions may be made to X organization at X mailing address [or X website]." The best "in lieu of flowers" notes capture something quintessential about the person. Doug Kulikowski's "in lieu of flowers" was "Buy a lottery ticket. You might be lucky." Eula King's "in lieu of" asked friends to stop by her house and take hostas, daylilies, camellias, and other plants from her garden to plant in their own yards. Bud Strayer's "in lieu of": "He would want you to mix yourself a Manhattan and make a toast in celebration of his life."

- **Get feedback.** One set of siblings, a sister and brother whose father had Alzheimer's, had fought bitterly over his care. When the father died, the brother, who was a writer, took on the task of composing the notice. He quoted himself throughout, sharing whimsical comments about his father, and made only brief mention of his sister. She saw it for the first time when it was published, and it drove the wedge in further. They were orphans now and suffering separately. **Make sure to consult with family, including those with whom you don't get along or even have a relationship (such as estranged children).**

- **Use language you're comfortable with.** Though professional obituary writers avoid euphemisms such as "went home," "entered eternal rest," or "is with the angels," what you write should feel appropriate for both you and the deceased. For some, writing flat out "He died," though true, just feels wrong.

TELL IT LIKE IT IS

There are going to be situations where the cause of death may feel harder to talk about, such as suicide or a drug overdose. The family will likely have strong feelings about how they want to handle sensitive personal matters, but there are many examples of notices that are candid without diminishing the person's strengths. Here's one in which the family honored both the accomplishments of the man and also, in a straightforward way, his lifelong struggle with substance abuse:

> Marc was a kind and gentle man whom God gifted with a tremendous intellect. He was definitely a character and those who knew him liked and loved him. He will be sorely missed by his family and friends. Marc used his gift of intelligence to graduate with the highest overall average in the 140 year history of Emory University in Atlanta and then became a senior partner of the law

firm Kilpatrick & Cody (now Kilpatrick Stockton) where they put him in charge of their international legal practice. Marc was very generous, had a great sense of humor and a quick wit. He loved his dogs, reading, music and playing his guitar. He was an excellent swimmer and at age 8 won second in state for the 100 yard breaststroke in South Bend, IN. Marc won numerous swimming trophies and watching him swim the butterfly was a thing of beauty. He made it look so easy. While Marc experienced a great deal of material success at an early age, he struggled with addictions to drugs and alcohol all his life and was unable to overcome them. In March 2001, he suffered a hemorrhagic stroke and spent the last eleven years of his life in various nursing homes in Georgia. . . . In lieu of flowers we ask that you donate money to or do community service for charities that help alcoholics, drug addicts and homeless people. Marc will be cremated and a celebration of his life will be held sometime in 2013.

—*The Atlanta Journal-Constitution*
December 23, 2012

Another complicating factor is when the family doesn't approve of the sexual orientation of the person who died. For one lesbian woman the family ran two different obituaries, side by side, and you would have thought it was for two different people. Her father, who had never accepted that she was gay, ran a glamour shot of her when she was young and portrayed her as the person he wanted to remember. Her mother and her partner used a contemporary photo and included the information that she was survived by her partner—probably the same pattern of family behavior the woman had experienced all her life.

To truly honor who the person was in life, honesty is the rule. Powell once had to write the obituary for a lawyer who had made a fortune representing nude dance clubs. His wife went berserk when she read it and called the paper. Powell defended the choice to her editor. Everyone knew about it, and it would've been a glaring omission if it hadn't been included.

IS IT OKAY TO BE FUNNY?

Are you memorializing someone who loved to laugh? Funny obituaries can be great reads. Just know that it's not easy to get the tone just right, and if you don't, it could get awkward. That said, wit and humor might be the perfect reflection of the person's spirit. Take this obit for Toni Larroux:

Waffle House lost a loyal customer on April 30, 2013. Antonia W. "Toni" Larroux died after a battle with multiple illnesses: lupus, rickets, scurvy, kidney disease and feline leukemia. She had previously conquered polio as a child contributing to her unusually petite ankles and the nickname "polio legs" given to her by her ex-husband, Jean F. Larroux, Jr. It should not be difficult to imagine the multiple reasons for their divorce 35+ years ago. Two children resulted from that marriage: Hayden Hoffman and Jean F. Larroux, III. Due to multiple, anonymous Mother's Day cards which arrived each May, the children suspect there were other siblings but that has never been verified.

She is survived by the two confirmed, aforementioned children. Her favorite child, Jean III, eloped in college and married Kim Fulford who dearly loved Toni. They gave Toni three grandchildren: Jean IV, Ann Elizabeth and Hannah Grace. Toni often remarked that her son, Jean III, was "just like his father," her ex-husband, Jean Jr., a statement that haunts her son to this day. . . . Her favorite activity was sipping hot tea on her back porch with friends seated around her porch ensemble from Dollar General (again, not kidding). This will be sold to the highest bidder at her garage "estate" sale. Any gifts in her honor should be made to the Hancock County Library Foundation (to the overdue book fund).

IT'S A DEATH NOTICE, NOT A JOB APPLICATION

It's fine to include career highlights, but no one wants to read a dead person's résumé—it's not as though we're looking to hire the guy.

COST OF PUBLICATION

Publishing an obituary is not cheap. At present time, the cost runs between $200 and $5,000, depending on length, number of photos, and type of publication.

——

Eulogies

A EULOGY IS A SPEECH DELIVERED AT A MEMORIAL OR FUNERAL service by a family member, friend, or clergyperson that commemorates the life of the deceased.

WHAT MAKES A GOOD EULOGY?

When you leave a memorial or funeral having imagined the fullness of the person being memorialized, you know the speakers got it right. **The first rule for eulogists is that this is not about them. It is about paying close attention to the way a person lived and drawing out the most meaningful, memorable bits.** Most of the rules for writing a good obituary hold true here, too. You may wish to have a diverse set of speakers, as each one will add new color to the portrait that is being drawn. If you were asked to eulogize and are not a direct member of the family, know that it is a great honor. Steve Schafer, a pastor who helps people write eulogies, suggests the following guidelines:

- **Aim for 1,000 words,** or six to seven minutes' speaking time
- **Start with a story about the person.** People come alive through specific anecdotes
- **Always write down what you're going to say,** even if you plan to abandon your notes. It's a good way to gather your thoughts and make sure you're not missing any important details
- **If you aren't introduced by the emcee, do so yourself** and say what your relationship to the person was
- **Be humorous.** The best eulogies are respectful and solemn but also give mourners some comic relief. A bit of roasting is fine if it suits who the person was and the family has a sense of humor
- **Be personal and conversational.** This isn't a formal speech; it's an appreciation
- **Close with a direct address to the person who died.** Something like "Joe, thank you for teaching me how to be a good father."

Here's an example of a great eulogy, written by a woman for her grandmother. We've explained what she's done in each section:

[Starting with your memories of the person is a great way to go. Try to use descriptive details—the Almond Joy moment below—rather than abstractions such as "She was kind," or "She was a loving caretaker."]

From my earliest memories, she is right by my side, taking me on walks through the miniature golf course near our house, dutifully preparing my odd lunch requests for cheddar and mayo sandwiches, and sneaking me Almond Joy candy bars away from the dutiful gaze of my mom.

[Draw out important moments that signify lifelong connection.]

I was so close to my grandma that around the age of 23 I grew increasingly anxious that she might not live to attend my wedding unless I hurried up. Well . . . she did live to attend that wedding, and also to witness my first divorce, my second marriage, and to know and love my two children. She liked Jeff from the beginning and one day before we were engaged, she boldly told him, "Well, you better put a ring on it!" quoting Beyoncé without knowing the reference.

[Talk about advice passed down; values, sayings, and anecdotes that capture the person.]

The most remarkable quality about my grandma as she aged was her gratitude and humility. She often told me to live for myself and not worry about her—to work, focus on my family, and come visit when I had time. She loved every minute of our visits but never pushed for more. I once asked her if I should have a third child and she replied, "Why, honey? You already have the perfect family." The most important things to my grandma were family and faith; she didn't care for material possessions. In fact she was known for giving items away because "there was someone who was more in need." This selflessness and service for others leave a legacy that I will try to model for my children. Time with her family was the greatest gift and even with that, she was not greedy.

[Thank-yous to other family members who helped with caretaking.]

I am deeply thankful to our family who cared for, loved her, and relished spending time with my grammie as she aged. Knowing she had Adie to take her to church and lunch every Sunday punctuated her week with a joyful event she truly looked forward to. Dave and Aileen always arrived with a box of her favorites See's Candies, essentially confirming the Pavlovian model as she began to drool as soon as they walked in the door. And to my mom, who cared for my grandma for the last 10 years of her life with compassion and unrivaled duty. I thank her not only for giving back to her mom, but for modeling care and respect for our elders.

Close with a quote, poem, reading, or other good-bye of your choosing.

——

How a Eulogy Can Go Wrong

THERE'S NOTHING MORE CRINGEWORTHY THAN A CLERGYPERSON reciting a Hallmark eulogy full of bromides that bears no relationship to the person you knew. In some cases, the priest may know only what the family tells him, and that exchange of information often happens thirty minutes before the funeral begins.

As a pastor who wrote eulogies for funeral services well before he struck out as a professional eulogy writer, even Steve Schafer has made this mistake. "I did one for a sweet elderly man who'd been a member of my church, and afterward his wife's comment was 'Who are you talking about?'" he says. "You need to paint them as they are, not as you idolize them." If there's time, ask the officiant to share what they're going to say with you, and help them make it right. ❖

CHAPTER TWENTY-TWO

The Bottom Line

HOW TO WRITE A EULOGY AND AN OBITUARY

Summing up a life isn't easy, but it's an important exercise that serves a dual purpose. It obliges the writer to call up memories—a way to honor the person and process one's loss—and it creates an atmosphere of community with other grievers. Do your best to be honest rather than presenting some idealized portrait others won't recognize. We are drawn to true stories.

Celebrating a Life

Planning a gathering; how to scatter
remains; other ways to honor the dead

The best memorials can function as bridge builders. When the death of a patriarch or matriarch happens, there are at least two possible responses in families: allow old feuds to settle in for good, or let those tensions be eased by comforting one another through the grief. Even when it was the deceased who was the source of the tension, you might find ways to unite around what you loved about her in the first place. And don't think that your family is more screwed up than the next. As the writer Mary Karr aptly puts it, "A dysfunctional family is any family with more than one person in it."

——

What's the Difference Between a Funeral Service and a Memorial?

A FUNERAL SERVICE IS TYPICALLY A ONE-HOUR AFFAIR HELD INSIDE the funeral home or place of worship or else at graveside, often with the body present.

A memorial takes place after burial or cremation, so the body is *not* present. You can plan one anytime during the year after death and even beyond—the timing is entirely up to you.

——

Planning a Memorial

A MEMORIAL IS FOR THE LIVING, SO GIVE YOURSELF TIME TO FEEL AS though you've got the presence of mind to really plan it and take it in. You're often still in shock when the funeral happens. For that reason, you may choose to have a small, intimate gathering before burial or cremation and wait to invite a larger circle to a memorial. "So many people report that six months to a year after [the death], they felt kind of numb or in shock," says grief counselor Tom Umberger. "If the memorial takes place a little later, they feel that they were more connected to it."

WHO WILL SPEAK?

For Freewheeling Types

The open-mic style of remembrance can sometimes make the service feel warmer and more inclusive. Rabbi Ed Feinstein of Valley Beth Shalom in Encino, California, encourages everyone who comes to sit with the family to write a eulogy. "It's very cleansing to be able to put this down on paper," he says. "At some point, someone will tell a story that the family hasn't heard. There was a man who was worried it wasn't appropriate for him to speak, but I encouraged him and he told everyone, 'I worked for your dad for so many years, and there was a time my wife got sick and he paid for it, he opened his wallet and he saved my wife's life; and here are my children, who wouldn't be here if not for him.' It always happens. People tell stories, and you end up with this immortality."

A cautionary tale: At the memorial for a friend's father, a nursing home resident took to the podium and told a story about how he and the deceased had bonded in the 101st Airborne Division during World War II. In the early hours of D-Day, they'd parachuted behind enemy lines, had liberated a concentration camp, and had been the first to enter Hitler's mountain retreat in Berchtesgaden. It was a heroic tale of camaraderie. If only it had been true: turned out that the speaker, though indeed a good friend of the deceased,

TIP
Scheduling the memorial far in advance increases the odds that mourners from far away will be able to clear their schedules, plan their travel, and attend.

was a little spotty on memory and had mistakenly recounted the plot of the TV miniseries *Band of Brothers*.

For the More Formal Among Us

1. Make a list of authorized eulogists and let them know as soon as possible (even before invitations go out) that you'd like them to speak.
2. Ask for a copy of each person's speech beforehand and give each person a rough time limit of six to seven minutes. If you are concerned about what may be said, whether due to divisive family dynamics or old grudges, it's best to take this step. At one memorial I attended, the man's daughter, a product of his first marriage, got up and delivered a fifteen-minute speech full of opprobrium about how he'd been an unpredictable drunk. I knew much of what she said to be true, but it felt as though she was airing old grudges that might have been better suited to a therapist's office, and it was uncomfortable to sit there next to his grieving wife, who had lived with him for sixteen years and taken care of him as he died—with few visits from his kids. If someone you don't know well wants to speak, you can ask to see his or her remarks in writing beforehand and offer feedback (or demur and ask him or her not to speak).
3. Enlist a master of ceremonies who will orchestrate the order and limit the remarks.
4. Let speakers know that there will be a limited number of people at the podium and that you'd love to have their words in writing to include in a memorial registry.

WHERE MEMORIALS GO SIDEWAYS

If you're inviting an ex of the deceased who makes your skin crawl, prepare yourself emotionally by thinking through how you'll respond. Avoiding her altogether may not be realistic, but you can cut the confrontation short by cueing a friend to call you away for an urgent task. Try not to dwell on her presence. Hopefully you are surrounded by people who love you and are ready and willing to create something of a protective shield around you.

Something to watch out for: people who use the pulpit to force their own agenda on mourners. At one memorial we went to, for a man who'd had lung cancer, three family members gave eulogies and then two heads of charities got up, one after the other. Both went on at great length about how much the deceased had cared about these causes by way of sharing survival rates for lung cancer, how much money had been raised at the last garden party, and how we need to get the word out that you can get lung cancer without smoking. One of them closed with the fact that she was one of the few who'd made it for this long (which was a great reminder that the deceased *hadn't made it that long*). The whole thing was tone deaf. It's better to provide information on the chosen charities on a table at the memorial so friends and family have the opportunity to support them in the deceased's honor or include an "in lieu of flowers" note in the death notice, invitation, and program.

YOUR MEMORIAL CHECKLIST

Whether you're planning a small, intimate affair or an event with all the hallmarks of a wedding (including invitations, space rental, food and drink, flowers, speeches, and programs), enlist as much help as you can and give yourself plenty of time. This may not be something you want to plan while in the thick of grief, but some of the mindless preparation can be a helpful distraction. Here's a list of things to check off:

☐ **Figure out what you want to spend** and make sure it's enough to host your entire guest list. If you are short on cash, think about venues that might be less expensive, such as a park or a city-owned location.

☐ **Decide on a date and time.** The memorial service can be scheduled for any time of day. Most run around two to three hours. It's wise to check with close family and friends of the deceased before deciding on and booking a date. Not doing so may result in hurt feelings and in significant people not being able to attend.

☐ **Find a venue that feels right.** A private home or backyard, a house of worship, a favorite beach or park, a social club, or a more formal banquet hall are all good options. Also consider:

- If you're having a reception, ask if the space allows food and drink—alcohol-based or otherwise
- If you want to bring in an outside caterer, make sure it is allowed
- Ask for a price sheet for rentals (chairs, tables, tablecloths). You'll have to estimate how many people will be coming based on how many you're inviting. Your best bet is to assume that only 50 percent of out-of-towners will show up, unless they're close family. You don't want to book a hundred-seat room if only twenty people will show up or have the opposite problem, with people standing in the back
- Make sure there are plenty of places for attendees to park
- Make sure the venue you're booking has AV equipment and test it beforehand if you plan to show a video or slides

☐ **Make an invitation list.** You'll need to inform people first, which can be harder than it sounds. The deceased's personal contacts lists may be stored on password-protected phones and computers, and getting hold of all of the email addresses, postal addresses (for thank-you notes later), and phone numbers of those you want to invite often requires some sleuthing. Groups to remember include:

- **Close family**
- **Friends.** The BFFs and people who knew your loved one "way back when"; the social connections whom they only saw at holiday parties
- **Work colleagues.** They spent most of their life at work
- **Hobby connections.** The ladies Mom played mah-jongg with
- **Service providers.** Accountants and hired help may have more of a relationship with the deceased than you knew
- **Health care providers.** The doctors, pharmacists, and nurses who took care of your loved one

Assign the task of gathering invitation contacts to one or two "connectors" in every sphere of the person's life, and invite people who were close to the person, even if *you* don't like or approve of them. Magnanimity is where you want to land at this moment, so consider opening up the invitation list.

Try using an online invitation service that allows you to keep track of RSVPs in a private place. Online invitation services will also send out thank-you cards after the event.

The To-Do List

- ☐ **Decide who will emcee, who will speak, and how much control you want over their remarks.**
- ☐ **Collect photos and videos.** Having a visual breather can be a huge relief when you're listening to eulogy after eulogy. Show

slides of the person when he or she was younger, snapshots of good times, places the person traveled to. Ask the venue if you can pin things to the wall or if it can supply a freestanding board and tables for personal artwork, possessions, or memorabilia.

☐ **Create a memorial program.** Though not necessary, it will help attendees follow along during a more formal service. The program may include photos of the deceased and the order of eulogies and identify any music played or incantation or prayer with lyrics so people can follow along and join in, along with a thank-you from the family and a mention of organizations to which memorial donations can be made.

☐ **Order food and drink.** A reception can happen before or after the eulogies. Did the person love doughnuts? Was there a beloved after-work drink? Offering favorite foods and explaining as much is an excellent way to pay homage. Potluck is always an option. People like to be helpful on such occasions. If you're hiring an outside caterer, make sure it knows how many people you're expecting, how long in advance the staff can show up to set up the platters, and so on. You don't need to serve a three-course spread, but a memorial is an emotional affair, and snacks help.

☐ **Order flowers (if you want them).** If there are multiple stations where people will congregate (inside the church, in a reception hall, outside the entry doors), order multiple bouquets and tell the florist what they'll be used for. If the deceased had a favorite flower or color, this is an easy way to incorporate his or her personality into the surroundings.

☐ **Decide on music.** Do you want live or recorded music? Singers? A grand piano? Make sure the venue can accommodate your choice and that there's audio equipment to amplify if needed.

☐ **Purchase a memorial registry book and pen** for people to register their presence and leave notes for the family. It may feel like an antiquated tradition, but it's a wonderful thing to read at a later date.

———

Moments to Personalize

CREATING A MEMORABLE EXPERIENCE FOR YOUR GUESTS MAY BE WAY beyond your energy level or budget, but if you've scheduled the memorial far enough ahead of time and have a lot of help, adding personalized elements can make the difference between a boilerplate day and one that feels truly inspired. Here are a few ideas:

- Personalized seed packets, so guests can plant a favorite flower or vegetable or tree in the deceased's honor, or bird seed packets for bird lovers, available for purchase at Etsy.com or can be made yourself with small printed envelopes
- DIY memorial candles using mason jars and photos
- Instead of a literal guest book, supply a basket filled with smooth river stones for guests to sign. Later, you can place the stones into a large mason jar to put on your mantel, in a garden, or in the wild
- Bring a potted tree from the person's home or buy a small potted plant and hang photos of the deceased from the branches to create a tree of life

Jen wanted a way to collect memories of her husband to share with their young daughters. She skipped the typical guest book and instead printed a bunch of blank postcards with the prompt:

A favorite memory with Sasha was _____.

She left a pile of them in the entryway. A year later she was still receiving those postcards in the mail and now will make up a book of them for their daughters.

——

Annual Get-togethers

BILL, A "FREELANCE RUNNER AND PUNNER," AS HIS OBITUARY APTLY described him, was on the twenty-fourth of the twenty-six miles of the 2006 San Francisco Marathon when he collapsed from heart failure at 43. We'd become close friends at *Wired* magazine, where we had both gotten our start in the 1990s, and I was invited to join a memorial tradition his family has kept up for over a decade. All of us who loved Bill meet at the twenty-four-mile mark in Mission Bay on the anniversary of his death and finish his last two miles. It's a simple salute, but everyone who participates feels a little closer to him and to each other.

——

What to Do with Remains

ARE YOU FLYING YOUR GRANDPA'S ASHES TO SCATTER OFF THE COAST of Maine, where he once dropped lobster traps? Keep these things in mind:

- Luggage can get lost or damaged, so checking the urn isn't the safest bet. But carrying a container with cremated remains on board means you'll have to pass through airport security. Transportation Security Administration workers are not permitted to open nonscannable urns and check the contents,

—
TIP
If you know you'll be traveling, ask the crematorium to give you your loved one's ashes in a container made of cardboard, cloth, plastic, or wood. Transparent glass is also an option but might not be the best bet for a turbulent plane ride.

so if you're carrying a container that will set off alarms, you're likely to miss your flight.

- **Take the certificate of cremation with you to the checkpoint**—in case you need to prove that the powder in the container is in fact cremated ashes.

- **Think through how you will get the cremated remains from the cardboard container into the urn you've chosen once you arrive.** You can ask a local clergyperson or funeral home in that locale to help (most will do so for free) or just do so yourself. Just know that the ashes can be so finely pulverized that some waft away.

Scattering Ashes: What's Legal, What's Not

A FRIEND SNUCK DOWN TO THE FIELD OF THE OAKLAND-ALAMEDA County Coliseum at half-time and dumped some of his father's dust at the fifteen-yard line. His pop, a doctor, had been a hard-core Raiders fan, and though his son knew he was doing something illegal, he felt a jolt of joy, knowing that part of his father would always be in that stadium. "I felt really guilty about it and probably looked like a crazy person hiding this bag under my jacket," he said. "But I also knew he would've approved."

The funeral industry dubs such acts "wildcat scattering," and their incidence is increasing along with the number of people who choose to be cremated. Legal ways to scatter cremation ashes include the following:

- **In a park.** You can scatter ashes in public city and state parks, but it requires a permit.
- **On public land.** A "don't ask, don't tell" policy rules the day. But know that cremated remains don't look like ashes from a fireplace; they are as white as aquarium gravel, so it might be fairly conspicuous.
- **At sea.** The federal Clean Water Act requires that cremated remains be scattered at least three nautical miles from land, and you must notify the EPA within thirty days before scattering ashes at sea. If Grandma wanted to be scattered on Lake Michigan, you'll need a permit from the state agency that oversees the part you're sailing to.
- **In the air.** Dropping ashes from the sky? That's okay as long as you don't drop them in a container onto someone's property. ❖

The Bottom Line

CELEBRATING A LIFE

Whatever you do to memorialize a loved one, remember that sharing the loss with others can be an opportunity to bring people together, especially if you go out of your way to be inclusive. The memories that friends and family offer up at memorials will stay with you forever.

What's Left

Cleaning out the house; what documents
to collect to settle the estate and close
accounts; shutting down a digital identity

We began this book by telling you that even dying requires paperwork. It also leaves a paper trail for the living to follow, and the amount of time and energy required to administer it is mind-boggling. You may be faced with the task of cleaning out the house and sorting through the closets; closing accounts; and shuffling through reams of paperwork (and maybe attending a court hearing) to settle the estate. Sorrow gives way to annoyance and exasperation. Some people get so mired in the litany of clerical details that they forget to grieve.

Yes, you need to get all of this done, but despite any pressure you may be feeling from family members, an estate doesn't have to be settled immediately, or even within the first year, so take your time. There is no typical length of time, but it's usually measured in years. It took two years to close down my father's accounts and sell his house. Three years after his death, there were *still* a jointly held bank account and a safe-deposit box with his name on it that I had not dealt with.

——

The To-Do List

- ☐ **Arrange with the funeral director for a headstone or marker,** if one is desired (this can happen months and even a year down the road), if it's not already done
- ☐ **Notify the post office.** (But only to redirect the person's mail to an address where it can be received and reviewed. Don't stop mail just yet; you'll need to collect bills and magazine subscriptions and such to know what to cancel)
- ☐ **Cancel driver's license**
- ☐ **Cancel memberships in organizations and subscriptions**
- ☐ **Contact a tax preparer.** You know that old chestnut: the only

two certainties are death and taxes. You'll still have to pay Uncle Sam what was due for the year

☐ **Notify the board of elections**

☐ **Check online payment services**, such as PayPal, that may have money in them

☐ **Shut down social media accounts**

☐ **Shut down automatic payments** to any accounts you, the survivor, no longer need

——

Documents You'll Need

TO GET MUCH OF THE ABOVE DONE, YOU'LL NEED as much information about open accounts as you can collect. Check the wallet for credit cards, membership cards, and a Social Security card. You'll also want to track the mail (and email, if you have access to the account) to start collecting bills and making a list of debts owed.

Dealing with the bank alone may take multiple hours and in-person visits where you pick up a repetitive stress injury from signing so many papers. You'll end up skipping work to make business-hour appointments, spending your afternoons in institutional settings, and then going back again because you (or the person behind the desk) forgot something the first time. Even if you do manage to navigate the infuriating automated phone trees and reach the department that deals with survivor benefits or changes to an account, you will be told to fill out a form and mail it in with a certificate—only to be notified weeks later that an additional form is required. It makes the myth of Sisyphus seem like a charming fairy tale.

Then there's the issue of following up to make sure everything was closed/transferred/doled out properly, which may send you back to the starting line. Torture by a thousand administrative cuts. We don't know why companies haven't figured out a less onerous way to help grieving families through the shutting down of a life, but so it goes in a society unprepared for death. Here's a list of documents you'll need as you start to close down the person's accounts and settle his or her estate:

- ☐ **Certified death certificates.** The funeral home or mortuary will prepare and file it with the County Recorder's Office for you, but we recommend requesting a dozen from the funeral home. You must supply proof of death for everything from closing credit card and bank accounts and terminating insurance to withdrawing money, transferring accounts to your name, changing property titles (on real estate or a car), changing the name on utilities, terminating online services and social networks, and applying for VA funeral benefits.
- ☐ **Three to five copies of the will, if one exists.** You will need one to prove that you're an executor (the person who executes what the will says to do) or beneficiary (a person who benefits from what's in the will). If the estate is going into probate, the lawyer will need a copy, too.
- ☐ **Marriage certificate and birth certificates of children (if it was your partner who died).** Any organizations dispensing benefits to the widow or widower, such as a pension plan, or to the children will need to know exactly who the heirs are by the order and dates of marriages (should there be more than one)

and whether the children were born inside or outside the marriage. If those documents are missing, you can get certified copies from the state. For complicated or secretive families, says probate lawyer Laura Upchurch, family tree services such as Ancestry.com can be a great resource. They have scanned copies of all sorts of records.

☐ **Insurance policies.** Collect all insurance-related records to cancel life/home/auto policies.

☐ **Miscellaneous payouts.** Aside from any life insurance policies, **there may be other benefits, such as a bank account survivor's benefit, an employer's life insurance plan, a pension plan, and so forth.** All of these should be included in a living trust or will, making it easy for the executor of the estate to distribute the funds to heirs. But if there isn't one, check with your loved one's employer(s) and bank(s) to make sure you're not leaving money on the table. If you don't know where they banked, all you can do is wait for the mail.

—
TIP
People forget to update their wills all the time, and something might have been sold without the family being notified.

☐ **Deeds and titles to property.** In order to transfer property to the beneficiary or beneficiaries of the estate, you'll need the deed and title and to know if they still owned it upon death.

—
TIP
If the deceased is survived by children or a spouse, they may be eligible for increased Social Security benefits.

☐ **Automobile title and registration papers.** These are necessary to confirm who actually owns the vehicle. "If I buy my mom a car and it stays in my name, when she dies people may think it goes to a beneficiary," says Kay Powell. "But it's still in *my* name, it's not part of my mom's estate—it's my car."

☐ **Stock certificates or account information.** You'll need to know where the stocks are held.

☐ **Bank account statements.** Where did your loved one have a bank account, and what was the balance at the time of death? **You'll need to know when you're filing taxes for him or her.**

TIP

If you inherit an IRA, it will be subject to the same taxation rules as before death. So if your parent was over 70½ and had to take a minimum distribution, you will, too (and you'll be paying tax on that income). If you don't take the distribution, you will be charged a fine. Ask the bank to estimate what you need to withdraw every year.

☐ **Honorable discharge papers for a veteran and/or VA claim number.** There are many benefits tied to a veteran's death. Form DD-214, which is held by the United States Department of Defense, will give a full history of the deceased person's armed forces service record and awards.

☐ **Recent income tax returns and W-2 forms.** For tax-filing purposes.

☐ **Loan and installment payment books and contracts.** What did the person owe, and to whom? Did he or she still own the assets that had loans on them? If you're the executor of the estate, you'll need these to settle any debts before you distribute any assets.

☐ **Social Security card (or at least the number).** Call the agency at (800) 772-1213 to report the death so payments aren't continued.

☐ **Medicare and medical insurance company information.** Social Security should take care of notifying Medicare when it is alerted to the death, but just in case, it's good to check in with Medicare to make sure that coverage for the deceased has been ended. The same goes if the person had private insurance.

☐ **Credit card statements.** You will need to close any credit card accounts; the easiest way is to call the cards' customer service department. **Keep track of any debts on the credit cards, as they will need to be paid off.**

——

Sympathy and Responses

YOU'LL LIKELY RECEIVE CONDOLENCES IN FORMS RANGING FROM fruit baskets to ten-page tributes to standard-issue sympathy cards or emails. We're no Miss Manners, but in our view, this is the one time in life that you get a pass on acknowledging receipt at all. That said, if it's an elaborate gift or long letter or batch of photos, it's a nice gesture to affirm that you've received it and offer thanks. You can do so by mail or text, depending on your energy level. Either will be appreciated. And no one expects an immediate acknowledgment, so take your time. Some notes on how to respond:

- **Most funeral homes and mortuaries will supply you with thank-you notes.** If you don't like those, get a box of thank-you cards with envelopes that you can keep on your desk or wherever you sort mail and write a line or two acknowledging how they helped or the condolence you received. Here's an example:

  [Family Name] or [I] thank you for your thoughts and sympathy. We/I so appreciate receiving support and [prayers/good wishes/a hot meal] from friends and family as we grieve this loss.

- **Adequate is better than nothing.** If the person had a large community or was a public figure and you're dealing with a towering pile of letters and cards and flowers, try printing up an interim thank-you. Then enlist friends who've offered to help with *anything at all* to address and send them. Here's an example of a standard interim acknowledgment message:

TIP
Mark the condolence envelopes and cards with a check once you've responded, and keep any that are meaningful to you as mementos to read later.

Dear [NAME], Thank you for your kind expression of sympathy and the beautiful flowers you sent on the occasion of [person who died]'s death. [Related person] will be writing you a personal note soon. In the meantime, he/she appreciates your thoughtful gesture during this difficult time.

To keep track of the letters and notes, use a shoe box or other organizer to file them in order of receipt, and keep a stack of index cards and a bright-colored Sharpie nearby to note who sent gifts and meals.

——

Cleaning House

WHEN MY SISTER AND I FACED THE GRIM TASK OF EMPTYING OUR father's house of its contents before putting it on the market, we asked our real estate agent how we should get rid of all the stuff we didn't want. He recommended a local woman who runs estate liquidation sales. We called her, and she explained her terms: she'd do a free consultation and determine if Dad's stuff was worth a public sale; organize, advertise, and run the sale; do a run to the Salvation Army for usable stuff left over, recycle what could be recycled, then do a dump run to get rid of anything that remained; and finally cut us a check, less her fees.

We met her at the house, and she passed through like a dervish, remarking on a Danish sideboard that she thought would be a hot item, asking if the Arabia of Finland china we'd used when we had people over for dinner was a full set. She told us she had a buyer who'd take our father's entire library (he had thousands of books) and assured us that even the cans of food and boxes of tissues in the pantry would find takers. She came back the next day and slapped prices on everything in sight. Then she advertised the estate sale to take place a couple of weeks later.

FAST FACT
Expect to pay a commission of anywhere between 20 and 50 percent of the net proceeds of the sale to the company or individual you hire.

That one-day sale got rid of everything of even passing value; the pantry full of vitamins and batteries and vacuum bags and canned food were all sold.

All that was left were a few stacks of papers and family photos and the contents of his desk: pens, paper clips, little black books filled with names and addresses and numbers. Just sorting through those things for an afternoon broke our hearts, but it was a relief to have gotten rid of most of it. A few weeks later, I received in the mail the receipt book from the sale, with a check for $600, around 60 percent of the proceeds. Some liquidators will charge a smaller percentage but then a large lump sum to clean up afterward.

——

Shutting Down Social Networks

IT'S ESTIMATED THAT EIGHT THOUSAND PEOPLE WITH PROFILES ON Facebook die every day. What happens to their pages? The short answer is: not much. The dead are overtaking the living on social media, and soon there will be mass graveyards in the cloud. If no one takes the steps to delete them or turn them into legacy pages, they simply linger in the present tense: "She's a retired librarian who lives in Austin, TX." This tends to feel more creepy than comforting.

Social networks will also continue to remind you to wish your brother, who died suddenly four years ago, a happy birthday and to connect with your dead father, with whom you apparently share many contacts. There's no malice in this, of course; it's all being driven by algorithms.

For those wanting their loved ones to be remembered indefinitely by an online community, Facebook makes this possible by turning an account into a memorial. To do that, head to "Special Request for Deceased Person's Account" in the Help/Contact section. Once you've proved you're the next of kin or an executor of that person and followed the prompts, the word "Remembering" will appear next to the person's name. (For the basic instructions, go to our additional resources section at the end of the book.) Memorialized profiles don't appear in public spaces, ads, or birthday reminders, so you'll never receive suggestions for People You May Know (who are dead) again. ❖

The Bottom Line

WHAT'S LEFT

Closing down the official business of a life is not just time-consuming, it can also keep the injury fresh. But aside from doling out assets to beneficiaries of the estate, which family may be in a rush to receive, and getting taxes filed, you don't have to run yourself ragged to get these things done. Remember, there are reasons that many cultures give you a full year before they expect you to "recover" and reenter.

T he more closely you look at life, the more nature's endings and beginnings appear very much alike. All living things die and go on to become other things; our bodies host all sorts of life besides our own and will continue to do so after we're gone; our spirits live on inside the people we've known. This cycle is simple, observable, undeniable.

Still, none of that lessens our sorrow. It's also certain that *this* life ends, distinctively and decisively, and that's a hard truth to come to terms with.

With the end decided, life becomes more about how you get there. The route you take, with all its turns and vistas and crossroads—that's where richness is found. You may long for more time, you may long for less, and very likely you'll long for both. But you will find your way, with and without the help of others.

Death accepts us just as we are, and from every approach. Whether its presence helps you focus on goals or helps you let go of them, everything is welcome—every thought and every feeling, from glorious to foul and every shade between—since everything must go. No one can fail it. Total embrace is death's core dignity.

Our advice is just this: *participate*. Resist the notion that you have total control; resist the notion that you have none. However you can, with whatever you've got, participate in your care, in your dying, in life. ❖

ACKNOWLEDGMENTS

T his book would never have crossed the finish line without our rudder and researcher, Sonya Dolan, who was practically a third author and senior editor, who offered limitless reads, gut-checks, cat-herding, and an unflagging ability to crack a dirty joke or to clarify a thought when we needed it most. We also consider ourselves the luckiest strugglers to have stumbled upon Mark Lotto, whose opening gambit, "Look . . ." was a throat-clearing we came to depend on, knowing it would be followed by rapier-sharp observation.

Heaps of gratitude to our agent, Sloan Harris, and to Heather Karpas at ICM, for fiercely believing in this project from the very start, and helping us turn a rangy proposal into something much more useful. To everyone at Simon & Schuster who touched this project, including Jon Karp, Megan Hogan, Cary Goldstein, Cat Boyd, Kirstin Berndt, Richard Rhorer, and Elise Ringo, but most of all to our steadfast, compassionate, and clear-eyed editor, Priscilla Painton, who always asked for more. We are absurdly fortunate.

And to Irene Connelly, whose deft hand and aesthetic helped us immeasurably. We are also grateful to Sean Cooper, Jennifer Kahn, Allison Arieff, and others who read early chapters and offered immensely useful feedback.

Thanks to our friend, illustrator and archivist Marina Luz, who signed on to this project without a backward glance and transformed what could have been bone-dry instructional graphics into lucent visual metaphors. And to Lindsey Turner, our designer, who found a way to inject both constraint and play to the pages. Hats off to Tim Gruneisen and Alex Styck for kicking off the design of this book and inspiring a way forward. Ivor Williams and David Skulkin, you two came along at just the right moments. Addie Mullenix and Glenn Berger, we will pen another book if we can come back to your home for a writer's retreat. Thanks also to David Barrett and Peter Josson for lending your beautiful river cottage to the writer's cause; the same warning goes for you.

We owe an incalculable debt to the patients, families, and friends who opened their hearts and trusted us with their stories: Francesca, Sara and Len Pinto; Peggy Houghton; Char Barrett; Jen Panasik; Jeff Yee; Ira and Ruth Byock; Greg Segal; Fredda Wasserman; Katrina Hedberg; Rev. Denah Joseph; Chanel Reynolds; Britney Snow; Beth Earhart; Lonny Shavelson; Melissa Jones; Serene Weir; Nora Menkin; Rebecca Soffer; Shelby and Ray Rosenberg; Pam Blodgett; Siobhan Miller; Karen Schanche; Anna Else Pasternak and Alex Maasry; Jessica Tully; Jessica Zitter; Matt Lozano; Cam Sutter; Kelsey Crowe; Deborah Cohan; Marianne Matzo; Mary Melkonian; Shelley Adler; Olivia Bareham; Tim McGee; Jane Fulton Suri; Michael Simley; Susan Turnbull; Mark Rossetti; Judy Thomas; Sri and Hesaraghatta Krishna Rao Shamasunder; Barry Baines; Kathleen Kerr; Jane Marx; Ross Sussman; Joe Blumberg; Frish Brandt; Amandah Blackwell; Tom Umberger; Katie Taggart; Anne Reingold; Karen Stockmal; Kay Powell; Steve Schafer; Steve Scheier and Amy Dopelt; Rabbi Sydney Mintz; Larken Bradley; Laura Upchurch; Claire Bidwell Smith; KK Hall; Rabbi Ed Feinstein; Leethanial Blumfield; Harriet and Edith Warshaw; Margaux French; Rabbi Laura Geller; Daniel Kellman; Rebecca Katz; Virginia Palmer; Sander Florman; Caitlin Doughty; Rev. Luke Jernagan; Tembi Locke & Saro Gullo;

Marcia Sirota; Bob Hopper; Lisa Blackberry Blackstock; Tricia Webb; Nick Jehlen; Pamela Belknap and John Prichard; Andrea Schneider; Patrick Lane & Michael Reardon; Nancy and Lance Gentry; Thekla and Steve Hammond; Don Bayer and Lela Jahn; Jacqueline and Tom Gallegos; Rebecca Sudore; Whitney Mortimer; Julie Arguez; and Lisa Cole.

For their support, mentorship, inspiration, and undergirding or overarching guidance, we also shout our love to Angie Thieriot; Pico Iyer; Abraham Verghese; Steve McPhee; Vicki Jackson; Susan Barber; Susan Block; Andy Billings; Michael Kearney; Balfour Mount; Martha Twaddle; Tony Back; Diane Meier; Jennifer Mitchell; Bridget Sumser; Dianne Shumay; Camille Borgo; Molly Bourne; Delia Bales; Redwing Keyssar; Diane Mailey; Sara Matson; Jane Hawgood; Gary Heidenreich; Larry Haimovitch and Carie Harris; Alex McIntyre; Sean Lang-Brown; Ann Jurecic, Rita Charon, Kat Vlahos, Peter Schneider, Ellen and Robert MacDonald, Rachel Remen and the rest of the Kalamazoo/Fetzer learning community; Marion Weber; Bill Richards; Michael Lerner; Jeannie Sedgwick; Oren Slozberg; Loren Pogir; Catherine Dodd; Catherine Porter; Jenepher Stowell; Peter and Mimi Buckley; Anna Hawken; Fred Mitouer; Henry Fersko-Weiss; Martha Carlton-Magaña; Paul Tatum, Jillian Gustin, Bob Macauley, Holly Yang, Sarah Beth Harrington, Elizabeth Kvale, Stacie Levine, Joe Straton and the rest of the AAHPM LEAD crew; Stephanie Cheng; Kathleen Cavanaugh; Summer Segal; Greg Benson; Jessica Williams; Amanda Hughen; Kelly Duane De La Vega; Tami and Peter Linde; Alana Ofman; and Hugh Carroll.

And to everyone at IDEO who cleared a path and gave unstinting support: Whitney Mortimer, David Kelley, Tim Brown, Paul Bennett, David Webster, Dana Cho, Nadia Walker, Christine Hendrickson, Katie Clark, the superwomen of North, and especially

Debbe Stern, equal parts trusted guide and Jewish mother whose canniness was key to propelling this book into the world.

Johnny H. Burr; Sally Downey; Julia Denapoli; Nanky Cole; Mike Kelley; Justin Burke; Betsy Leslie; Dan Hollins; Franklin Coleman; Puerini's; Max Lehman; Luca Stone Ladner; Barbara and Richard Samuels; Harrison Hammig-Gerwin; and Lissa Treger.

Pete Austin, Jonathan Baker, Tammy Pinkhole, Alex Heminway, Susan Strawbridge and the rest of the Dinky Crew Unmemorial; Smellen Hudson; Mike Teti; Victor's; the Chandler, Clarke, and French families; Fruit Man; and the Peter Couture.

Staff and clinicians of the St. Barnabas Burn Unit and Rehabilitation Institute of Chicago; the Zen Hospice Project community and supporters; colleagues and patients of the Medical College of Wisconsin; Santa Barbara Cottage Hospital; Massachusetts General Hospital; Dana-Farber Cancer Institute; and UCSF; with an extra dose of love to Gayle, Sarah, Elizabeth, and Alex.

Mike Rabow; Blake Kutner and Meredith Heller; Matt Giudice; Gerry and Lynne Giudice; Enrico and Nanda Cerrato; Frank Cerrato; Jessica Safra; Luca, Ben, and Peter Reidy; Brandon Colby; Frank Ragsdale; Lulu Ezekiel; Joan Jeanrenaud; Jori Adler; Pat and Ben Heller; Patti and Peter Adler; Mill Valley Beerworks; Mary Remington; Jen Lyn, Blake, Colleen, BJ, Keri, Tim, and the lands of southern Utah.

Thank you.

Finally, to our families, for making anything possible, and for living out this book with us. We love you, Susan and Bruce Miller, Maysie, The Muffin Man, and Darkness too; Anna and Maya Berger and Danny Baldonado; and the entire Saxe family, especially Tony, Cleo, and Judah. *Love.* ❖

Chapter One: Don't Leave a Mess

Kondo, M. (2016) *Spark Joy: An Illustrated Master Class on the Art of Organizing and Tidying Up*. Emeryville, CA: Ten Speed Press.

Magnusson, M. (2018) *The Gentle Art of Swedish Death Cleaning: How to Free Yourself and Your Family from a Lifetime of Clutter*. New York: Scribner.

Stum, M. S. (2011) *Who Gets Grandma's Yellow Pie Plate? Workbook: A Guide to Passing on Personal Possessions*. University Extension Services

Chapter Two: Leave a Mark

Intelligent Change. (2016) *The Five Minute Journal: A Happier You in 5 Minutes a Day*. Toronto, Canada: Intelligent Change.

Spence, L. (1997) *Legacy: A Step-by-Step Guide to Writing Personal History* Athens, OH: Swallow Press.

CELEBRATIONS OF LIFE: ETHICAL WILLS/LEGACY LETTERS
Find resources for creating an ethical will.
https://celebrationsoflife.net/ethicalwills/

THE LEGACY CENTER
Check out sample legacies written by others to help inspire your own words.
www.thelegacycenter.net

STORYCORPS
Its mission is to preserve and share humanity's stories; the interview is forty minutes of uninterrupted time for meaningful conversation with a friend or loved one. Includes question prompts. Use the StoryCorps app to record from anywhere. www.storycorps.org

STORYWORTH
Share stories with loved ones, based on weekly emailed story prompts—questions you've never thought to ask. At the end of the year, the stories are bound in a book as a keepsake. www.storyworth.com

LIFECHRONICLES

Preserves memories of yourself, or a loved one on video. The organization takes care of filming, prompting interview questions, editing, and production. Available nationwide. www.lifechronicles.org

STANFORD MEDICINE LETTER PROJECT

Includes templates for letters to your doctor about your health and life review letters for your friends and family. Comes in eight different languages and is free to use. https://med.stanford.edu/letter.html

Chapter Three: Yes, There's Paperwork

GYST

GYST is an online service to help get your affairs into order one step at a time, starting with your will, living will/advance directive, and life insurance. Also provides links to lawyers who deal with probate, wills, and advance care planning. www.gyst.com

EVERPLANS

Store and share everything important—wills, passwords, home information, health care information, and funeral preferences—in a secure digital archive. www.everplans.com

NATIONAL POLST PARADIGM

Learn more about the POLST form and how and when it should be used; find your state's POLST program. http://polst.org

PREPARE

Free advance directives and tools to fill out and print for all states along with videos and testimonials. In English and Spanish. www.prepareforyourcare.org

AARP: ADVANCE DIRECTIVE FORMS

Select your state from a menu and download the free advance directive forms for you to use. You'll find instructions on how to fill out the forms. www.aarp.org/home-family/caregiving/free-printable-advance-directives/

MY DIRECTIVES

Create emergency and advance care plans for your family and doctors as well as share them with key caregivers. Add as much detail as you want, including

video responses, and update online if you change your mind.
www.mydirectives.com

CONVERSATIONS OF A LIFETIME

Not sure how to talk about what you want? Download the easy starter kit with basic questions to ask, tips for starting the conversation, and links to state forms for talking about and documenting your end-of-life wishes. www.conversationsofalifetime.org

FIVE WISHES

Guide on advance care planning available in twenty-six languages. Five Wishes is used in all fifty states and in countries around the world. It meets the legal requirements for an advance directive in forty-two US states and the District of Columbia. In the other eight states your completed Five Wishes form can be attached to your state's required form. https://fivewishes.org

THE CONVERSATION PROJECT

Download the free Conversation Starter Kit, available in several languages, and use it to have a conversation with your loved ones about what kind of care you do, and don't want. www.theconversationproject.org

HELLO (CARD GAME)

Not sure how to have a conversation about your end-of-life wishes? Play a game instead! This card game uses prompting questions to give players of any age insight into their choices about living and dying in a fun and engaging way. https://commonpractice.com/products/hello-game

SUPPORTIVE CARE MATTERS: ACTION PLAN

Helps you formulate priorities for all areas of your life and express them to care providers, so that you can proactively decide upon the life you want to lead. www.supportivecarematters.org/action-plan

ADVANCE DIRECTIVE FOR DEMENTIA

How much medical care would you want if you had Alzheimer's disease or another type of dementia? This downloadable form allows you to pick your level of care for the different stages of dementia. www.dementia-directive.org

CAKE

Answer questions to determine your values and preferences for end-of-life care. Includes questions such as what to do with your Facebook account after you're gone. The information is shareable, and the content is editable if you change your mind. www.joincake.com

ESTATE MAP

Prepare a comprehensive map of your most important estate information, which you can then download to your computer. Keep a copy with your most important documents, and send a copy to an adviser and your family. Or leave instructions on how to access it once you're gone. Fees apply. www.estatemap.com

DOCUBANK

Upload and store documents that you and your family need access to. Includes a card that makes all of your emergency information and critical health care documents available in two ways: online and by telephone. Fees apply. www.docubank.com

ESTATEEXEC

Generates a list of tasks that helps executors complete and document the necessary to-dos after someone dies. $99 per estate for a five-year term; can be done by yourself or with a lawyer. www.estateexec.com

NATIONAL ASSOCIATION OF ESTATE PLANNERS & COUNCILS

Need to create an estate plan? Find estate-planning professionals in a searchable database. www.naepc.org

ROCKET LAWYER

Download estate-planning and will documents and connect with lawyers on any questions or issues. Fees apply. www.rocketlawyer.com

WILLING

Designed by lawyers; makes creating a will online easy, accessible, and affordable. Includes checklists and information on estate-planning basics. Fees apply. www.willing.com

LEGALZOOM

Use online tools to create a will, health care power of attorney, and other advance care documents included in estate planning. Fees apply. www.legalzoom.com

TRUE KEY
Autosaves and enters your passwords, so you don't have to. Free for fifteen or fewer passwords. www.truekey.com

DASHLANE
Creates and saves long passwords, logs you on to sites automatically, fills in online forms with your info, and allows you to share any or all passwords and receipts of things you've paid for online with your family. www.dashlane.com

THE NATIONAL ACADEMY OF ELDER LAW ATTORNEYS
Attorneys experienced and trained in working with the legal problems of aging Americans and individuals of all ages with special needs. www.naela.org

PAD: PSYCHIATRIC ADVANCE DIRECTIVES
A legal document written by a currently competent person who lives with a mental illness. A PAD allows a person to be prepared if a mental health crisis prevents them from being able to make decisions. www.nrc-pad.org

Chapter Four: Can I Afford to Die?

Driscoll, M. (2002) *The Complete Idiot's Guide to Long Term Care Planning*. Indianapolis, IN: Alpha Books.

GENWORTH: COST OF CARE SURVEY 2018
Compare SNF and other facility long-term care costs in your area. www.genworth.com/about-us/industry-expertise/cost-of-care.html

MEDICAID: ELIGIBILITY
Medicaid information with FAQs and links to state-specific Medicaid sites. www.medicaid.gov/medicaid/eligibility/index.html

MACSTATS: MEDICAID AND CHIP DATA BOOK
Compiles a wide range of current and key statistics on Medicaid in one single place. www.macpac.gov/publication/macstats-medicaid-and-chip-data-book-2

AARP: HEALTH CARE COSTS CALCULATOR
Educational tool designed to estimate your health care costs in retirement, do not need to be an AARP member to use. www.aarp.org/retirement/the-aarp-healthcare-costs-calculator

HEALTHCARE BLUEBOOK
Search by procedure and geographic location to find range of pricing listed in your area, including a "fair" price, based on a database of rates paid by private insurers. https://healthcarebluebook.com

HEALTH INSURANCE MARKETPLACE CALCULATOR
Enter your income, age, and family size to estimate your eligibility for subsidies and how much you could spend on medical insurance.
www.kff.org/interactive/subsidy-calculator

PATIENT ADVOCATE FOUNDATION
This financially focused tool helps find resources for a broad range of needs including housing, utilities, food, transportation to medical treatment, home health care, medical devices, and pharmaceutical agents.
www.patientadvocate.org

NEEDYMEDS
A national nonprofit information resource dedicated to helping people locate assistance programs to help them afford their medications and other health care costs. www.needymeds.org

MEDICARE: HOW DO I FILE AN APPEAL?
An appeal is the action you can take if you disagree with a coverage or payment decision made by Medicare, your Medicare Health Plan, or your Medicare Prescription Drug Plan.
www.medicare.gov/claims-and-appeals/file-an-appeal/appeals.html

FAIR HEALTH CONSUMER
Information on costs for thousands of procedures.
www.fairhealthconsumer.org

Chapter Seven: Now What?
Puri, Sunita. (2019) *That Good Night: Life and Medicine in the Eleventh Hour.* New York: Penguin Random House.

Chapter Eight: Coping
Halvorson-Boyd, G., & Hunter, Lisa K. (1995) *Dancing in Limbo: Making Sense of Life After Cancer.* Hoboken, NJ: Wiley.
Keyssar, Judith R. (2010) *Last Acts of Kindness: Lessons for the Living from the Bedsides of the Dying.* CreateSpace Independent Publishing Platform.

Lief, J. L. (2001) *Making Friends with Death*. Boston and London: Shambhala.

Matousek, M. (2008) *When You're Falling, Dive: Lessons in the Art of Living*. New York: Bloomsbury.

Nuland, Sherwin B. (1995) *How We Die: Reflections of Life's Final Chapter*. New York: Vintage Books.

Ostaseki, Frank. (2017) *The Five Invitations: Discovering What Death Can Teach Us About Living Fully*. New York: Flatiron Books.

Renz, M. (2016) *Hope and Grace: Spiritual Experiences in Severe Distress, Illness and Dying*. London: Jessica Kingsley Publishers.

HEFFTER RESEARCH INSTITUTE
Promotes research into psychedelics with the goal of alleviating suffering. www.heffter.org

MULTIDISCIPLINARY ASSOCIATION FOR PSYCHEDELIC STUDIES
A nonprofit research and educational organization that develops research and protocols for people to benefit from the careful use of psychedelics and marijuana. www.maps.org

COMPASS
Developing psilocybin therapy for patients with treatment-resistant depression. www.compasspathways.com

GREATER GOOD MAGAZINE: KEYS TO WELL-BEING
Ten building blocks of individual and community well-being, the behaviors that research suggests will support your health and happiness and foster positive connections with other people. www.greatergood.berkeley.edu/key

Chapter Nine: Breaking The News

Back, A., Arnold, R., & Tulsky, J. (2009) *Mastering Communication with Seriously Ill Patients: Balancing Honesty with Empathy and Hope*. Cambridge, UK: Cambridge University Press.

Crowe, Kelsey, & McDowell, Emily. (2017) *There Is No Good Card for This: What To Say and Do When Life Is Scary, Awful, and Unfair to People You Love*. San Francisco: HarperOne.

Chapter Ten: Love, Sex, and Relationships

Guntupalli, S., & Karinch, M. (2017) *Sex and Cancer*. Lanham, MD: Rowman & Littlefield.

Chapter Eleven: Dynamic Duo: Hospice And Palliative Care

Macauley, Robert C. (2018) *Ethics in Palliative Care*. Oxford, UK: Oxford University Press.

NATIONAL HOSPICE AND PALLIATIVE CARE ORGANIZATION

Definitive source for all things hospice and palliative care, including help for patients and families along with legislation information and updates. www.nhpco.org

NATIONAL HOSPICE AND PALLIATIVE CARE ORGANIZATION: FIND A HOSPICE

Search a national directory by address, city, or zip code to locate hospice agencies and palliative care clinicians in your area. www.nhpco.org/find-hospice

GET PALLIATIVE CARE: HOW TO GET PALLIATIVE CARE?

Includes tips on how to talk to your doctor about getting palliative care, a searchable directory by zip code, city, or state, and questions to ask your palliative care team once you find a provider. www.getpalliativecare.org/howtoget

MEDICARE: HOSPICE COMPARE

Find hospices that serve your area and compare them. Includes a checklist to use when interviewing potential hospice agencies. www.medicare.gov/hospicecompare

GRACE

Nationwide hospice and assisted living directory. Find the care in your area through an easy search function. www.meetgrace.com

PALLIATIVE DOCTORS

Includes pages with patient stories, frequently asked questions, and links to important resources for both hospice and palliative care. www.palliativedoctors.org

HOSPICE ACTION NETWORK

Dedicated to preserving and expanding access to hospice care in America. www.hospiceactionnetwork.org

C-TAC: COALITION TO TRANSFORM ADVANCED CARE

Supports a national movement built on policy change, state and community organizing, and support for family caregivers. www.thectac.org

AMERICAN ACADEMY OF HOSPICE AND PALLIATIVE MEDICINE: AAHPM ADVOCACY AMPLIFIES YOUR VOICE

AAHPM brings the stories of hospice and palliative medicine directly to policy makers, promoting issues of importance to patients with serious illness and the health professionals who care for them.
www.aahpm.org/advocacy/overview

UPAYA INSTITUTE AND ZEN CENTER: BEING WITH DYING

Designed primarily for physicians and nurses, the training also includes experienced social workers, hospice workers, psychologists, administrators, chaplains, and clergy who work with end-of-life care patients.
www.upaya.org/being-with-dying

Chapter Twelve: Symptoms 101

PATIENTSLIKEME

Online community that pools patient feedback about the efficacy of therapies, side effects, and disease progression to the benefit of patients. Requires signing up and submitting personal information. www.patientslikeme.com

MEMORIAL SLOAN KETTERING CANCER CENTER'S *ABOUT HERBS* DATABASE

A tool for the public as well as healthcare professionals. Can help you figure out the value of using common herbs and other dietary supplements.
https://www.mskcc.org/cancer-care/diagnosis-treatment/symptom-management/integrative-medicine/herbs

NATIONAL CENTER FOR COMPLEMENTARY AND INTEGRATIVE HEALTH

Search for research-based info from acupuncture to zinc.
https://nccih.nih.gov/

USP QUALITY SUPPLEMENTS

Agency helping to ensure American drug supply quality. USP works to verify your dietary supplements. https://www.quality-supplements.org/

Chapter Thirteen: Hospital Hacks

MEDICARE: HOSPITAL COMPARE
Compare hospitals around the nation based on their overall rating, survey of patient experiences, and other criteria. Site summarizes up to fifty-seven measures of quality. www.medicare.gov/hospitalcompare

NATIONAL INSTITUTE ON AGING: GOING TO THE HOSPITAL– TIPS FOR DEMENTIA CAREGIVERS
What to do, what to pack, and how to prepare for a hospital stay that involves a patient with dementia.
www.nia.nih.gov/health/going-hospital-tips-dementia-caregivers

QUALITY CHECK: FIND A GOLD SEAL HEALTH CARE ORGANIZATION
Search for hospitals that have been given the Gold Seal of Approval from the Joint Commission, a nonprofit organization. The website enables the public to view their accreditation and certification status. www.qualitycheck.org

THE LEAPFROG GROUP: COMPARE HOSPITALS
Search for and compare hospitals in your area based on various criteria such as medication safety and inpatient care. Also includes links to other resources on finding care and engaging in the aspects of your hospital stay.
www.leapfroggroup.org/compare-hospitals

PLAN YOUR LIFESPAN
Plan for health events such as hospitalizations, falls, and memory loss, and learn what resources are available if you need help after a hospitalization. Follow the prompts to fill out and share your results with family after you're done. www.planyourlifespan.org

GOOD OUTCOME FOLLOWING ATTEMPTED RESUSCITATION (GO-FAR)
Based on your age and conditions, calculate the expected outcome after re-suscitation. www.gofarcalc.com

Chapter Fourteen: Help! I Need Somebody

FAMILY CAREGIVER ALLIANCE: HIRING IN-HOME HELP
Includes what to consider, pros and cons, interview questions for potential hired caregivers, and how to find professional caregiver help.
www.caregiver.org/hiring-home-help

AGING LIFE CARE ASSOCIATION

Use the searchable database to find licensed care managers and home care experts in your area. Can also search for clinicians practiced in facility referrals and placement, assessment, and guardianship. www.aginglifecare.org

ELDERCARE LOCATOR

Need assistance for yourself or your loved one? Search the site for adult day care programs, in-home help, long-term care, and other services by zip code or state or give them a call to discuss. www.eldercare.acl.gov

NATIONAL ASSOCIATION OF AREA AGENCIES ON AGING

Focuses on helping elder adults find resources for care in their community and learn tips for caregiving. Use the search function to find aging services by state and county. www.n4a.org

NEXT STEP IN CARE

Download guides and checklists such as "Hospital Admissions" for different types of patients' transitions: from hospital to home or from home to a facility. The guides come in multiple languages, and the site includes videos as well. www.nextstepincare.org

CARING VILLAGE (APP)

Shows helpers what needs doing and enables assignments and errand coordination in real time. Also acts as communication hub for patient updates, medication management, and important documents storage. www.caringvillage.com

LOTSA HELPING HANDS

Create a care calendar accessible to everyone providing, or wanting to provide, help: organize meals or caregiving schedules in one location, and assign dates and times with "help needed" or "needs met." www.lotsahelpinghands.com

CAREZONE

Document patient symptoms, create medication lists, and store important contact information such as doctor and insurance provider data. The calendar includes reminders for refills, and it's shareable with your caregiver helpers and family. www.carezone.com

CARINGBRIDGE

Create a personalized web page that has tools to keep your family and friends updated about your own or a loved one's care. Share information in one place and coordinate those who want to help with the chores that need doing. www.caringbridge.org

NEXTDOOR

Harness the power of your neighbors with this free digital social network that connects you to those living around you. Can send requests for help or general updates. www.nextdoor.com

VILLAGE TO VILLAGE NETWORK

Provides expert guidance, resources, and support to help communities establish and maintain their villages for aging in place. www.vtvnetwork.org

EYEON (APP)

Makes it easy for people living alone and their caregivers to maintain their independence by automating a call for help when needed. www.eyeonapp.com

OMEGA HOME NETWORK

National grassroots membership organization that promotes the development and expansion of community homes for dying people who cannot remain in their home during the end of their life. www.omegahomenetwork.org

MEDISAFE (APP)

Tracks medications, sends digital reminders about your next dose, and provides information on the drugs themselves and what they're used for. You can add a family member to the alerts about missed meds. www.medisafe.com

MEAL TRAIN

Organize meals for patients and their families based on a calendar system. Includes reminder emails and a way for family, friends, and neighbors to sign up for supplying meals. www.mealtrain.com

NATIONAL CARE PLANNING COUNCIL

Resource for eldercare, senior services, and care planning. Click on "Guardian / Fiduciary Services" for an interactive map of resources in your area. www.longtermcarelink.net

Chapter Fifteen: Care for the Caregiver

Capossela, C., & Warnock, S. (1995) *Share the Care: How to Organize a Group to Care for Someone Who Is Seriously Ill*. New York: Simon & Schuster.

Ellison, K.P., & Weingast, M., eds. (2016) *Awake at the Bedside: Contemplative Teachings on Palliative and End-of-Life Care*. Somerville, MA: Wisdom Publications.

Fersko-Weiss, H. (2017) *Caring for the Dying: The Doula Approach to a Meaningful Death*. Newburyport, MA: Conari Press.

NATIONAL ALLIANCE FOR CAREGIVING

A nonprofit coalition of national organizations focusing on advancing family caregiving through research, innovation, and advocacy. The site includes resources for caregivers, including sections for those dealing with dementia or cancer. www.caregiving.org

CARING.COM

Provides helpful resources on many caregiver topics such as avoiding burnout, diet and nutrition, emergency preparedness, travel tips, and dealing with conflict, as well as a comprehensive directory of eldercare services, home care agencies, and assisted living options. www.caring.com

AARP: FAMILY CAREGIVING

Download free care guides, caregiver basics, tips for safety in the home, and finance assistance, and watch online learning series. Phone support also available. www.aarp.org/home-family/caregiving

NATIONAL HOSPICE AND PALLIATIVE CARE ORGANIZATION: CARINGINFO

Helpful information on home safety, quality of life, and respite care. www.caringinfo.org

CAREGIVER ACTION NETWORK

Check out the Family Caregiver Toolbox for videos on Understanding Medicare, How to Talk to Your Doctor, and Managing the Meds. Also includes sections on being a caregiver for those with Alzheimer's and COPD. www.caregiveraction.org

ARCH NATIONAL RESPITE NETWORK AND RESOURCE CENTER

Helps families locate respite and crisis care services in their communities. Use the "Respite Locator" link at the bottom of the page to find programs and providers in your area. www.archrespite.org

FAMILY CAREGIVER ALLIANCE: FAMILY CARE NAVIGATOR

Click on your state to find public, nonprofit, and private programs and services nearest your loved one—living at home or in a residential facility. Resources include government health and disability programs, legal resources, disease-specific organizations, and more. www.caregiver.org/family-care-navigator

Chapter Sixteen: Everyone Dies: How to Talk to Kids

Erlbruch, W. (2011) *Duck, Death and the Tulip*. Wellington, New Zealand: Gecko Press.

Jeffers, O. (2010) *The Heart and the Bottle*. New York: Philomel Books.

Kilbourne, S. (1998) *Peach and Blue*. New York: Dragonfly Books.

Ringtved, G. (2016) *Cry, Heart, but Never Break*. Brooklyn, NY: Enchanted Lion Books.

Rofes, E. (1985) *The Kid's Book About Death and Dying*. Boston: Little, Brown & Co.

THE MOYER FOUNDATION

Covers information, community referrals, and age-appropriate activities to cope with loss. For children and their parents. www.moyerfoundation.org

THE MOYER FOUNDATION: CAMP ERIN

The largest national bereavement program for youths grieving the death of a significant person in their lives.
www.moyerfoundation.org/camps-programs/camp-erin

NATIONAL ALLIANCE FOR GRIEVING CHILDREN

A nonprofit organization that raises awareness about the needs of children and teens who are grieving a death and provides education and resources such as holiday tool kits and activities for kids. www.childrengrieve.org

THE DOUGY CENTER

The Dougy Center provides support for grieving children, teens, young adults, and their families in Portland, Oregon, but the website includes activities you can do with your children as well as helpful information on language to use in your own home. www.dougy.org

Chapter Seventeen: It's Your Body and Your Funeral

Bailey, S., and Flowers, C. (2009) *Grave Expectations: Planning the End like There's No Tomorrow*. Kennebunkport, ME: Cider Mill Press.

Carnell, Geoffrey C. (2005) *The Complete Guide to Funeral Planning*. Guilford, CT: Lyons Press.

Cowling, C. (2010) *The Good Funeral Guide*. London and New York: Continuum.

Doughty, C. (2017) *From Here to Eternity*. New York: W. W. Norton.

Funeral Planning Basics (2017). Long Island City, NY: Enodare Limited.

Llewellyn, J. (2004) *Saying Goodbye Your Way*. Los Angeles: Tropico Press.

PARTING

Search for and compare the pricing of funeral and cremation services in your area. www.parting.com

FUNERAL CONSUMERS ALLIANCE

Posts information about planning a funeral in an easy-to-understand format so families can make educated decisions about the funeral they want to have. www.funerals.org

THE ADVANCE DEATH CARE DIRECTIVE

Write instructions for how you want your body dealt with after death by filling out a death care directive; buy a pamphlet for $10. www.deathcaredirective.com

FUNERALS360

Everything funerals: checklists, casket information, and cremation containers, with information for planning both in advance and in the moment. Requires registration. www.funerals360.com

FUNERAL ETHICS ORGANIZATION

Links to consumer information and consumer rights in the funeral industry, as well as funding options and regulations regarding prepaying for your funeral by state. www.funeralethics.org

FEDERAL TRADE COMMISSION: FUNERAL COSTS AND PRICING CHECKLIST

Consumer information on funeral costs; includes pricing checklists to use when visiting funeral homes. www.con.sumer.ftc.gov/articles/0301-funeral-costs-and-pricing-checklist

THE NATURAL END MAP
Links, addresses, and phone numbers for burial sites around the United States that provide natural burial. www.naturalend.com

NATIONAL HOME FUNERAL ALLIANCE
Teaches families how to care for their loved ones after death. Includes resources, laws, and stories of families who have held home funerals. www.homefuneralalliance.org

SACRED CROSSINGS
Helpful advice on home funerals and death midwifery and an in-depth approach to personalizing advance directive forms. Advance directive forms sent for a fee. www.sacredcrossings.com

ELYSIUM SPACE
Send a portion of your cremated remains to space! Choose to either circle the planet and reenter the orbit as a shooting star or have your remains placed on the surface of the moon. Space is limited, and reservations are required in advance for both services. Costs run between $2,500 and $10,000. www.elysiumspace.com

CELESTIS
Have your remains launched into space and returned to Earth, launched into Earth's orbit, or launched onto the surface of the moon or the moon's orbit or into deep space. Cremated remains or DNA can be carried. Check the website for availability of each service. Prices range from $1,295 to $12,500. www.celestis.com

THE ORDER OF THE GOOD DEATH
The Order is about making death a part of your life. Staring down your death fears—whether it be fear of your own death, the death of those you love, the pain of dying, the afterlife (or lack thereof), grief, corpses, bodily decomposition, or all of the above. http://www.orderofthegooddeath.com

Chapter Eighteen: Can I Choose to Die?
United States Conference of Catholic Bishops. (June 2018) "Ethical and Religious Directives for Catholic Health Care Services," 6th ed. www.usccb.org/about/doctrine/ethical-and-religious-directives.

COMPASSION AND CHOICES: UNDERSTANDING MEDICAL AID IN DYING

The nation's oldest, largest, and most active nonprofit organization committed to improving care and expanding options for the end of life. Learn more about medical aid in dying, and get state-specific information and resources. www.compassionandchoices.org/understanding-medical-aid-in-dying

DEATH WITH DIGNITY

Promotes death with dignity laws based on the Oregon Death with Dignity Act, both to provide an option for dying individuals and to stimulate nationwide improvements in end-of-life care. Read stories of other patients and families, or check out the online resources. www.deathwithdignity.org

Chapter Nineteen: Final Days

HOSPICE PATIENTS ALLIANCE: SIGNS AND SYMPTOMS OF APPROACHING DEATH

Bullet lists of signs of the preactive phase of dying and the active phase of dying. www.hospicepatients.org/hospic60.html

Chapter Twenty: The First 24 Hours

AARP: WHAT TO DO WHEN A LOVED ONE DIES

List of tasks to deal with directly after a death and in the time following. www.aarp.org/home-family/friends-family/info-06-2012/when-loved-one -dies-checklist.html

U.S. FOOD AND DRUG ADMINISTRATION: WHERE AND HOW TO DISPOSE OF UNUSED MEDICINES

Information on where and how to dispose of unused medicines. www.fda.gov/ForConsumers/ConsumerUpdates/ucm101653.htm

ALLIANCE FOR SMILES: OTHER WAYS TO DONATE

Accepts donations of surplus medical supplies and equipment and distributes them to people who need them the most. www.allianceforsmiles.org/donate/#otherwaystodonate

AMERICAN MEDICAL RESOURCES FOUNDATION: DONATE YOUR EQUIPMENT

Distributes donated medical equipment and supplies to charitable hospitals and medical clinics in developing countries.
www.amrf.com/donate-equipment

PROJECT C.U.R.E.

Operates distribution facilities across the United States that distribute your donations to hospitals, clinics, and community health centers around the world. www.projectcure.org/procure

MUSCULAR DYSTROPHY ASSOCIATION: PRODUCT DONATIONS

MDA locations around the country accept donations of medical supplies. Product donations are also needed for MDA Summer Camp and special events. www.mda.org/get-involved/product-donations

DEA CONTROLLED SUBSTANCE PUBLIC DISPOSAL LOCATIONS

Search for locations in your area that accept unused medications for disposal.
https://apps.deadiversion.usdoj.gov/pubdispsearch

DISPOSE MY MEDS

Online resource to help you find medication disposal programs in your neighborhood. www.disposemymeds.org

Chapter Twenty-One: Grief

Dubi, M., Powell, P., & Gentry, E. (2017) *Trauma, PTSD, Grief and Loss: The 10 Core Competencies for Evidence-Based Treatment.* Eau Claire, WI: PESI Publishing & Media.

Neff, K. (2015) *Self-Compassion: The Proven Power of Being Kind to Yourself.* New York: William Morrow.

Van Der Kolk, B. (2015) *The Body Keeps the Score: Brain, Mind, and Body in the Healing of Trauma.* London, UK: Penguin Books.

Weller, F. (2015) *The Wild Edge of Sorrow: Rituals of Renewal and the Sacred Work of Grief.* Berkeley, CA: North Atlantic Books.

WHAT'S YOUR GRIEF

This organization's mission is to promote grief education, exploration, and expression in both practical and creative ways. The site authors are mental health professionals with twenty-plus years of experience. www.whatsyourgrief.com

MODERN LOSS
A platform for sharing candid conversations about grief in all its aspects. Read essays on loss, check resources, and connect with others. www.modernloss.com

PSYCHOLOGY TODAY: FIND A GRIEF THERAPIST
Search for a list of therapists in your area who specialize in bereavement and loss. www.therapists.psychologytoday.com/grief

ALLIANCE OF HOPE
Provides support for people coping with the loss of a loved one to suicide. www.allianceofhope.org

NATIONAL WIDOWERS' ORGANIZATION
A site for men and how they grieve. Includes articles, resources, and ways to connect with other widowers as a way to cope with the loss of a spouse or partner. www.nationalwidowers.org

HELLO GRIEF
Create a memorial wall for a loved one, find bereavement organizations in your area, and search for grief agencies and resources by state. www.hellogrief.org

THE DINNER PARTY
A community of 20- to 30-year-olds who connect over loss through dinner parties held in homes around the nation. Check the website to join or host a dinner. www.thedinnerparty.org

THE CENTER FOR COMPLICATED GRIEF
Offers insight and resources for finding therapists or organizations that may be helpful, as well as professional training, research findings, and a wide variety of grief support organizations for those dealing with complicated grief. www.complicatedgrief.columbia.edu

OPEN TO HOPE
Information and resources about grief, including an online forum to support those who have experienced loss. www.opentohope.com

MEALBABY
Helps friends and families arrange meals for loved ones. www.mealbaby.com

DEATH OVER DINNER

The dinner table is the most forgiving place for difficult conversation. The website walks you through planning your own dinner and gives a simple set of tools to help families and friends address issues around death and dying. www.deathoverdinner.org

Chapter Twenty-Two: How to Write a Eulogy and an Obituary

Young, K. (2013) *The Art of Losing: Poems of Grief and Healing.* New York: Bloomsbury Publishing. A great source of prose and poems to use in eulogies.

EULOGY CONSULTANTS

Go through an initial consultation and then discuss your needs with an assigned author. Receive a draft of the eulogy for editing and questions before receiving the final product. Fees apply. www.eulogy.com

GRETCHEN RUBIN: FUNERAL READINGS FROM "HAPPIER" PODCAST LISTENERS

A list of readings suitable for funerals or memorial services. https://api.gretchen rubin.com/wp-content/uploads/2017/09/FuneralReadings.pdf

PAPERLESS POST

Need to invite many people to a memorial or after-death event? Use this online service to send invitations electronically and track responses. www.paperlesspost.com

THE EULOGY WRITERS

Farm out eulogy writing to a professional. Submit information about your loved one via the website and work with a writer to perfect the final product. Fees apply. www.theeulogywriters.com

Chapter Twenty-Three: Celebrating a Life

LIFEPOSTS

Celebrate the people and moments in your life. Includes tools to help you determine the type of post and prompting questions and allows for the uploading of photos and videos. You can create over time and invite others to add info or photos. www.lifeposts.com

Chapter Twenty-Four: What's Left

AMERICAN SOCIETY OF ESTATE LIQUIDATORS
Members of this site are required to meet certain educational or experience requirements and abide by a code of ethics. Use the search function to locate an ASEL associate, professional, or accredited member within a sixty-mile radius of your location. www.aselonline.com

ESTATESALES.NET
Find an estate liquidator, or list your own sale on the site (fees apply to list). The site uses information you submit to put agencies in the requested area in touch with you via phone or email; you do not get immediate results. www.estatesales.net

VETERANS FORM DD214
Was the deceased a vet? There are benefits that you can take advantage of based on the type of discharge he or she received. Information about the form and how to obtain a certified copy of the deceased's DD214. www.dd214.us

DELETING SOCIAL MEDIA ACCOUNTS

FACEBOOK ACCOUNT:
Go to: facebook.com/help/contact/228813257197480
If the deceased set up a legacy contact ahead of time, the chosen person will be able to write a post that will remain at the top of the profile, update the previous profile photo and respond to friend requests, and download an archive of activity (posts, photos, and "likes") without being able to read your private messages.

What's Required
1. An electronic copy of the **death notice or memorial card**
2. The deceased's **email address** used for the account
3. Date the person passed away or approximation
4. **Proof you have authority:** Power of attorney document, birth certificate, will, estate letter (electronic copy)

INSTAGRAM ACCOUNT:
Go to: help.instagram.com/contact/1474899482730688

What's Required

1. Proof that you, the requestor, are an immediate family member
2. Electronic copy of the deceased person's **birth or death certificate**
3. Electronic copy of proof that you, the requestor, are the **lawful representative** of the deceased person or estate
4. The deceased's person's **Instagram username**
5. Date the person passed away or approximation

GOOGLE ACCOUNT:
Go to: https://support.google.com/accounts/troubleshooter/6357590?visit_id=1- 636553579996489811-661966917&hl=en&rd=2

What's Required

1. Date the person passed away
2. A scan of your, the requestor's, ID
3. A scan of the death certificate

TWITTER ACCOUNT:
Go to: support.twitter.com/forms/privacy and select: **"I want to request the deactivation of a deceased user's account."** An email will be sent with further instructions.

What's Required

1. The deceased person's Twitter username
2. Electronic copy of authorized requestor's ID
3. Electronic copy of the death certificate

Chapter Three: Yes, There's Paperwork

1. Sudore, Rebecca (2009). A piece of my mind. Can we agree to disagree?. *JAMA: The Journal of the American Medical Association*, 302. 1629–30. 10.1001/jama.2009.1422.

Chapter Five: I'm Sick

1. Ghandourh, W. A. (2016). Palliative care in cancer: managing patients' expectations. *Journal of Medical Radiation Sciences*, 63(4), 242–257. http://doi.org/10.1002/jmrs.188.

Chapter Seven: Now What?

1. Ryan D. Nipp, Joseph A. Greer, Areej El-Jawahri, et al. (2017). Coping and Prognostic Awareness in Patients with Advanced Cancer. *Journal of Clinical Oncology* 2017 35:22, 2551–2557.

2. Nancy L. Keating, Haiden A. Huskamp, Elena Kouri, et al. (2018). Factors Contributing to Geographic Variation In End-Of-Life Expenditures for Cancer Patients. *Health Affairs* 37:7, 1136-1143.

Chapter Eight: Coping

1. Lucius Annaeus Seneca, Translated by Richard Mott Gummere. Letter 54: "On Asthma and Death." *Moral Letters to Lucilius / Letters from a Stoic. (Epistulae morales ad Lucilium).* Loeb Classical Library Edition, 1915.

Chapter Twelve: Symptoms 101

1. Latte-Naor, Shelly, & Mao, Jun J. Putting Integrative Oncology Into Practice: Concepts and Approaches. *Journal of Oncology Practice* 2019 15:1, 7–14.

Chapter Thirteen: Hospital Hacks

1. Peberdy MA1, Kaye W, Ornato JP, Larkin GL, Nadkarni V, Mancini ME, Berg RA, Nichol G, Lane-Trultt T. Cardiopulmonary resuscitation of

adults in the hospital: a report of 14720 cardiac arrests from the National Registry of Cardiopulmonary Resuscitation. Virginia Commonwealth University's Health System, West Hospital, Richmond, VA 23298, USA; Go AS, Mozaffarian D, Roger VL, Benjamin EJ, Berry JD, Borden WB, Bravata DM, Dai S, Ford ES, Fox CS, Franco S, Fullerton HJ, Gillespie C, Hailpern SM, Heit JA, Howard VJ, Huffman MD, Kissela BM, Kittner SJ, Lackland DT, Lichtman JH, Lisabeth LD, Magid D, Marcus GM, Marelli A, Matchar DB, McGuire DK, Mohler ER, Moy CS, Mussolino ME, Nichol G, Paynter NP, Schreiner PJ, Sorlie PD, Stein J, Turan TN, Virani SS, Wong ND, Woo D, Turner, MB, on behalf of the American Heart Association Statistics Committee and Stroke Statistics Subcommittee. Heart disease and stroke statistics—2013 update: a report from the American Heart Association. Circulation. 2013;127:e6–e245.

Chapter Fourteen: Help! I Need Somebody

1. U.S. Census Bureau, Current Population Survey, Annual Social and Economic Supplements, 1960 to 2017. https://www.census.gov/content/dam/Census/library/visualizations/time-series/demo/families-and-households/hh-4.pdf

Shoshana and BJ met while working on a project for a local hospice organization. They went on to collaborate on BJ's TED talk, "What Really Matters at the End of Life," the response to which surprised them both. When Shoshana approached BJ with the idea of writing a book, he couldn't say no. In order to do the topic justice, it felt important to have one author who was inside of health care, and one who was out.

SHOSHANA

Shoshana Berger has worked in publishing for more than twenty years as a freelance writer, senior editor at *Wired*, and editor-in-chief of *ReadyMade*, the magazine she cofounded in 2001. She became editorial director of the global design firm IDEO in 2013, where she has worked on projects related to the end of life, modern Judaism, and school lunch. In 2018, she moved to Denmark for a year to work with the Copenhagen Institute of Interaction Design and to learn why everyone is so happy up in the Nordics. She has written for the *New York Times, Wired, Travel + Leisure, Sunset, Spin, Popular Science, Marie Claire,* and the *San Francisco Chronicle*. She has spoken about how to redesign our experience of death at Creative Mornings and Slush. Shoshana lives in Berkeley with her best friend Tony Saxe, and children, Cleo and Judah.

BJ

BJ Miller is a hospice and palliative care physician who has worked in many settings—inpatient, outpatient, home, and residential hospice. He sees patients and families at the UCSF Helen Diller Family Comprehensive Cancer Center as part of the Symptom Management Service, where he's worked since 2007. BJ was executive director for the Zen Hospice Project from 2011 to 2016, learning about the administration of health care and how difficult it can be for patients and families to find the care they need, and for providers to give it. He speaks around the country and beyond on the theme of living well in the face of death. He has been featured in the *New York Times* and interviewed by Oprah Winfrey, Tim Ferriss, and Krista Tippett.

BJ lives in Mill Valley with his family, Maysie, the Muffin Man, and Darkness, and loves exploring nature—including human—especially from any two-wheeled vehicle (or four).